THE TELEVISION SERIES

Troy Kennedy Martin

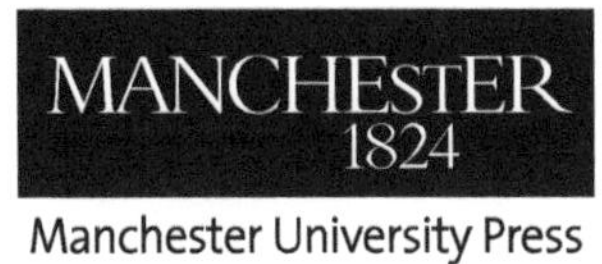

MANCHEstER
1824

Manchester University Press

THE TELEVISION SERIES

series editors

SARAH CARDWELL
JONATHAN BIGNELL

already published

Andrew Davies SARAH CARDWELL

Terry Nation JONATHAN BIGNELL AND ANDREW O'DAY

Lynda La Plante JULIA HALLAM

Jimmy Perry and David Croft SIMON MORGAN-RUSSELL

Alan Clarke DAVE ROLINSON

LEZ COOKE

Troy Kennedy Martin

Manchester University Press

MANCHESTER AND NEW YORK

distributed exclusively in the USA by Palgrave

Copyright © Lez Cooke 2007

The right of Lez Cooke to be identified as the author of this work has been asserted
by him in accordance with the Copyright, Designs and Patents Act 1988.

Published by Manchester University Press
Oxford Road, Manchester M13 9NR, UK
and Room 400, 175 Fifth Avenue, New York, NY 10010, USA
www.manchesteruniversitypress.co.uk

Distributed in the United States exclusively by
Palgrave Macmillan, 175 Fifth Avenue,
New York, NY 10010, USA

Distributed in Canada exclusively by
UBC Press, University of British Columbia, 2029 West Mall,
Vancouver, BC, Canada V6T 1Z2

British Library Cataloguing-in-Publication Data is available

Library of Congress Cataloging-in-Publication Data is available

ISBN 978 0 7190 6703 7 paperback

First published by Manchester University Press in hardback 2007

This paperback edition first published 2012

The publisher has no responsibility for the persistence or accuracy of URLs for any external or
third-party internet websites referred to in this book, and does not guarantee that any content on
such websites is, or will remain, accurate or appropriate.

Printed by Lightning Source

Contents

General editors' preface

Television is part of our everyday experience, and is one of the most significant features of our cultural lives today. Yet its practitioners and its artistic and cultural achievements remain relatively unacknowledged. The books in this series aim to remedy this by addressing the work of major television writers and creators. Each volume provides an authoritative and accessible guide to a particular practitioner's body of work, and assesses his or her contribution to television over the years. Many of the volumes draw on original sources, such as specially conducted interviews and archive material, and all of them list relevant bibliographic sources and provide full details of the programmes discussed. The author of each book makes a case for the importance of the work considered therein, and the series includes books on neglected or overlooked practitioners alongside well-known ones.

In comparison with some related disciplines, Television Studies scholarship is still relatively young, and the series aims to contribute to establishing the subject as a vigorous and evolving field. This series provides resources for critical thinking about television. Whilst maintaining a clear focus on the writers, on the creators and on the programmes themselves, the books in this series also take account of key critical concepts and theories in Television Studies. Each book is written from a particular critical or theoretical perspective, with reference to pertinent issues, and the approaches included in the series are varied and sometimes dissenting. Each author explicitly outlines the reasons for his or her particular focus, methodology or perspective. Readers are invited to think critically about the subject matter and approach covered in each book.

Although the series is addressed primarily to students and scholars of television, the books will also appeal to the many people who are interested in how television programmes have been commissioned, made and enjoyed. Since television has been so much a part of personal and public life in the twentieth and twenty-first centuries, we hope that the series will engage with, and sometimes challenge, a broad and diverse readership.

Sarah Cardwell
Jonathan Bignell

Acknowledgements

This book has a long history, dating back to 1986 when I wrote a dissertation on Troy Kennedy Martin for an MA in Film Studies at the Polytechnic of Central London. My first thanks, therefore, go to my MA tutor, Richard Collins, who planted the seed of an idea that, twenty years later, has grown into this book. Along the way many other people have contributed, in a variety of ways, to the end product. I am very grateful to Peter Duguid, Tony Garnett, Ian Kennedy Martin, the late John McGrath, David Rose, Roger Smith and Michael Wearing for giving me some of their time to talk about working with Troy. I would also like to acknowledge the help of Kathleen Dickson and Janet Moat at the British Film Institute, Trish Hayes at the BBC Written Archives Centre, Christine Slattery at the BBC TV Archive, and Veronica Taylor at the National Film Theatre.

While writing this book I was in receipt of a grant from the Arts and Humanities Research Board (now Centre), primarily to finance the completion of a Ph.D. at Manchester Metropolitan University (MMU) as part of the three-year research project, Cultures in British Television Drama, 1960–82. I am grateful to the project supervisors, Jonathan Bignell and Stephen Lacey, and to Robin Nelson at MMU, for tolerating the amount of time I spent on this book while I was also working on the Ph.D. (and writing a few other things besides!). Sincere thanks go to the series editors, Jonathan Bignell and Sarah Cardwell, and to Matthew Frost and Jonathan Bevan (and before him Kate Fox) at Manchester University Press for their patience as I tried to juggle my different research and writing commitments.

Thanks are also due to a number of other people who have contributed in ways great or small to this book: Caroline Aperguis, Nevena Dakovic, Mark Duguid, Dick Fiddy, Stephen Griffiths, Peter Hames, Elizabeth MacLennan, John Manuel, Nicky North and Jo Wright. Thanks should also go to all the students, over a period of twenty years, with whom I have shared thoughts and ideas about the work of Troy Kennedy Martin.

My most sincere thanks go to Troy Kennedy Martin himself, without whose help this book would not be as complete as it is. Over a period of some years now he has been extremely generous with his time, allowing me to quiz him for hours about his work and providing access to many scripts and notes from his personal collection. While he may not agree with everything I have written, his assistance along the way has been invaluable.

Introduction

Z Cars, Diary of a Young Man, The Italian Job, Kelly's Heroes, The Sweeney, Reilly – Ace of Spies and *Edge of Darkness* – whenever the name of Troy Kennedy Martin is mentioned it is invariably accompanied by a list of these titles, the films and television dramas with which he is most often associated as a screenwriter. These seven productions are in themselves testimony to the diversity of projects with which Kennedy Martin has been involved in a career spanning six decades. They suggest an interest in popular forms of film and television drama and an eclecticism which has tended to exclude him from the canon of television *auteurs*, a list which would no doubt include Alan Bennett, Alan Bleasdale, Trevor Griffiths, David Mercer, Alan Plater and Dennis Potter, writers whose authorial credentials have been celebrated in numerous books, articles and television programmes.

The fact that this book is the first study of any length of the work of Troy Kennedy Martin and that he has not (yet) been the subject of an *Arena* or *South Bank Show* might suggest an ambivalence towards him as a writer of popular film and television drama. The eclecticism of the above list may be one reason for Kennedy Martin's critical neglect. It is not that he is not known, but that he is known by different constituencies: by fans and critics of police drama for *Z Cars* and *The Sweeney*; by academics for his 1964 polemic against naturalism in television drama, 'Nats go home', which informed the non-naturalistic serial *Diary of a Young Man*, on which he collaborated with John McGrath, and which was an early formative directorial experience for Ken Loach; by fans of the 1960s 'cult' movie *The Italian Job*, which attracted a new audience following its re-release in the late 1990s, spawning a Hollywood remake; by movie buffs and Clint Eastwood fans alike for the popular Hollywood war film *Kelly's Heroes*, for which he was well-paid and which sparked a brief Hollywood career in the early 1970s; and by aficionados of 1980s 'quality' television serials for the historical drama *Reilly – Ace of Spies* and the award-winning nuclear thriller *Edge of Darkness*, both of which remain in the public domain with their release on DVD and repeat screenings on digital television channels.

If these seven productions appeal to different constituencies and represent the 'known' Troy Kennedy Martin there is another body of work that is equally eclectic and for which Kennedy Martin is much less well-known. There are the single plays he wrote in the late 1950s through to the mid 1960s; the adaptations of novels and short stories by writers as varied as Somerset Maugham, John Wyndham, Raymond Chandler, Frederick Pohl, C. P. Snow, Angus Wilson and Gillian Slovo; the eleven episodes he wrote for *Weavers Green* and the five episodes of *Parkin's Patch*, all written under a pseudonym; the *Armchair Thriller* serial *Fear of God*; the television films *Hostile Waters, Bravo Two Zero* and *Red Dust*; not to mention the many unproduced television dramas and screenplays Kennedy Martin has written over a period of more than forty years.

This book will explore further the 'known' Kennedy Martin while revealing the 'unknown' Kennedy Martin in a series of chapters organised according to the categories of the single play (which will also consider, in a book devoted mainly to work for television, his screenplays from the late 1960s and early 1970s), the theory and practice of experimental and non-naturalistic television drama, the creation of and contributions to popular drama series, the major drama serials of the 1980s, and the 'hostile waters' of British television since the late 1980s, as television entered a more competitive, deregulated era in which the creative role of the writer, especially the writer used to the relative freedoms of the 1960s, became increasingly circumscribed.

The eclecticism of Troy Kennedy Martin's oeuvre raises an inevitable question of authorship. How can a writer responsible for *Z Cars, Diary of a Young Man* and the situation comedy *If It Moves, File It*; for television plays and popular Hollywood movies; for episodes of drama series as diverse as *Redcap, Out of the Unknown, Weavers Green, Parkin's Patch, Colditz, Fall of Eagles* and *The Sweeney*; the creator of *Reilly – Ace of Spies* and *Edge of Darkness*; and the adapter of novels as different as *The Old Men at the Zoo* and *Red Dust*, possibly be considered an *auteur* to rank alongside the likes of David Mercer and Dennis Potter? The sheer variety of Kennedy Martin's work would seem to count against any stylistic or thematic consistency. Yet, as the following chapters will reveal, there are thematic consistencies in his work, especially in terms of an irreverent attitude towards the military and police, a scepticism about political institutions, and a consistent interest, over a period of fifty years, in social, political, moral and ecological issues.

Television, like the film industry, is a collaborative medium and, through interviews with some of the people with whom Kennedy Martin has collaborated, in addition to the analysis of individual productions, the chapters that follow will seek to reveal the ways in which the work of Troy Kennedy Martin has been the product of collaboration with other writers, producers, script editors and directors. In television, where there are so many potential checks and balances on the creative process, the question of individual authorship is problematic. Nevertheless there has, historically, been a strong case to be made for the individual input of the writer in the creation of television drama, which makes the search for signs of individual authorship legitimate. Later chapters will explore whether the writer in television drama today can be said to be the author of the work to the extent that he or she might have been in the 1950s and 1960s.

The main objective in this book has been to explore the work of one writer in relation to historical developments in British television drama. The book therefore adopts a largely chronological structure, starting with Kennedy Martin's early television scripts, which were broadcast live, and tracing his involvement in the aesthetic debates that accompanied technological and institutional changes in British television in the 1960s, which led to his 'Nats go home' polemic, as well as exploring the impact of social and political change on his work from the early 1960s through to the 2000s. In many respects not only was Kennedy Martin central to some of the important developments in British television drama, he also anticipated the ways in which television might develop. Witness his 1986 MacTaggart Lecture in which he predicted the advent of mini-dramas on small portable television screens, a prediction which has come to pass twenty years later with the ability of mobile telephones and iPods to receive television images.

Researching and writing this book has been a voyage of discovery, an adventure in television historiography involving the examination of a wide range of original material, drawn from a variety of sources. One source has been the television programmes themselves, where they exist and are available for viewing. Much of the early history of British television, extending in some cases right up to the 1970s, has disappeared as a result of the junking of films and videotapes, or the wiping of tapes for re-use. This is the case with much of the drama Kennedy Martin wrote in the late 1950s and early 1960s and also includes his six-part situation comedy, *If It Moves, File It*, transmitted in 1970. All of these programmes are now part of the 'lost' history of British television. In their absence, and in addition to the programmes that are still available, scripts constitute an invaluable resource, in their various forms of original manuscripts, typescripts, rehearsal scripts, camera scripts and screenplays. Many of Troy Kennedy Martin's scripts are held as a Special Collection in the British Film Institute Library, along with other documentation. Some scripts are also held at the BBC Written Archives Centre in Caversham, which is also an extremely valuable repository of other forms of documentation including official BBC correspondence, audience research reports on individual programmes, and press cuttings. Additionally, the research for this book has been considerably enhanced by the assistance of Troy Kennedy Martin in making available a number of scripts, including several unproduced scripts, from his own personal collection.

The other main source of information on which this book has drawn has been original interviews, with Troy Kennedy Martin and with producers, directors and script editors with whom he has worked since the late 1950s. Interview material has always to be treated with care – memories can be inaccurate and misleading, especially when the interviewee is trying to recollect events from thirty or forty years before – but oral history can be a valuable source of information, especially in the absence of other material or where a different perspective or insight is needed on a particular production or event. Interviewing writers, producers and directors about projects with which they, especially the writer, may have been involved for months or even years can bring a project to life – especially if it is a 'lost' programme or unproduced project – in a way that reading scripts and other written documentation cannot. Spending many hours talking to Troy Kennedy Martin, and several of his collaborators, about his extensive and varied output has been one of the many pleasures in researching and writing this book. It has not, I trust, resulted in a hagiography but an informed, critical interpretation of the work of one of Britain's leading screenwriters.

Biographical sketch 1

Francis Troy Kennedy Martin was born on Bute, an island on the Clyde, on the west coast of Scotland, on 15 February 1932. His father named him Troy after a Glasgow priest, Father Troy, who had helped the young Frank Martin to rehabilitate following his return from the First World War, where he had been wounded. Kennedy was added to the name by Frank Martin in memory of his commanding officer in the war, Colonel Kennedy. They went through the Battle of the Somme together and later the Battle of Cambrae where Kennedy was killed at Bourlon Wood and Frank was wounded. Kennedy, in peacetime a Professor of History at University College London, had been a father-figure to the working-class teenager and wanted him to go to university after the war. He was also childless and expressed a wish that any children Frank might one day have would bear his name. So when, fifteen years later, Troy was born, Frank dutifully did this. The names Troy and Kennedy were also given to the other children born to Frank and his wife Kathleen (including the girls), but only Troy was actually called by that name, no doubt to distinguish him from his father – Frank and Francis being too confusing.

The route by which Troy Kennedy Martin arrived at his name could have come from one of his own scripts. Indeed the military experience and strong character of his Glaswegian father, together with the nurturing influence of his mother, a Montessori teacher who encouraged her children to read from an early age, were clearly formative influences, not only on Troy but also on his younger brother Ian, both of whom went on to pursue successful careers as screenwriters, with a tendency to specialise in genres featuring the police and armed forces.

They grew up in a lower-middle-class Catholic family, in London, where Frank and Kathleen Martin went to live in the mid 1930s. During the 1920s Frank Martin worked for the Anglo-Persian Oil Company in the Middle East and on returning to London got a job as the manager of a laundry in Streatham, so Troy's very early years were spent in South

London, until the outbreak of the Second World War when the children were evacuated to Bute and to Aran, enabling the family to reconnect with relatives in Glasgow: 'Those were quite formative years I spent up there, in Scotland, but not in Glasgow, on the islands.'[1]

Having spent his early years in London, experiencing some of the Blitz before being evacuated to Scotland, Troy Kennedy Martin had acquired an English accent, which led to him getting into some scraps with the local Scottish kids:

> Certainly the first occasion I was at school up there – I guess I must have been ten – at the local Catholic school at Bute, I used to have to fight my way home every night because they absolutely loathed the English. Looking back it was really odd because they were more angry with the English than they were with the Germans. A lot of their fathers were in the 51st Highland Division and had to surrender at Saint Valéry so they were all in POW camps, but still it was the English who were the real enemy.

Despite his London accent Troy grew up feeling half Scottish, but with a sense also of Irish identity, for his family was descended from Irish immigrants who left Ireland for Scotland in the nineteenth century: 'I guess it was like John McGrath's generation, they were Irish and they went to Liverpool, and mine were Irish and they went to Glasgow. So when we met, John and I, years later, there was this natural affinity, which was never discussed, it was just there.'

It was this, no doubt, which influenced his decision to go to Trinity College, Dublin, in 1949, to reconnect with his Irish ancestry. After Streatham the Martin family moved to North London, living first in Finchley and then Muswell Hill. Troy attended Finchley Catholic Grammar School, 'but I wasn't a real academic high flyer. I had loads of ambitions and certainly none of them was to do with writing. So the writing thing came when I went to Trinity.'

Although he grew up in a Catholic family and went to a Catholic school, Catholicism did not have a lasting influence on him. It may be that the death of his mother, a practising Catholic, when he was young caused Troy to lose interest in the Catholic faith, for his father was not a devout Catholic: 'My mother was very practising, but my father just went along with it. My mother died of cancer just after the war, when I was about sixteen, in London, and I think that had an immense effect on all of us.' According to Troy, the death of his mother was a severe blow to his father and the family's troubles were compounded when Frank Martin lost his job after the war:

> He was devastated by my mother's death ... he never really recovered from that and he never really worked again. Once he lost his job we

became really poor, I mean but really poor. There was some money that was going to come on stream from my mother's father, which had been left in some kind of trust for her children, and that helped us through university, particularly in Trinity where the rest of the family didn't have grants. I got a full grant, from Middlesex, and went over, but from about 1946 to 1951 or '52 we were really poor ...

Frank Martin was very keen for his children to go to university and was excited when Troy got a place at Trinity to read history. Troy was there for four years and stayed on after graduating, by which time the whole family had relocated to Dublin, his brother and sisters also going to Trinity, although Ian and his younger sister, Maureen, dropped out. The years at Trinity were liberating for Troy and he began to think of himself as a writer during this period, coming into contact with other writers and immersing himself in Dublin literary life:

Brendan Behan lived just next door and one day he just chucked this copy of a book, which turned out to be *The Borstal Boy*, over. He said 'You're a writer, what do you make of this?' and of course I didn't really like it. I thought 'Who wants to read something about a borstal boy?', so I'd say, 'Oh it's very good Brendan ... ' By the end of that time, before I went into the army, I knew all those sort of people and was working with grown-ups and thinking like a grown-up, rather than like a student.

At a loose end after university, Troy decided to volunteer for the army, knowing that if he went back to England he would get called up for National Service anyway. In Northern Ireland, he discovered, it was possible to get a better deal than if he signed up for the regular army in England:

They didn't have conscription because of the political situation, but ever since the war they'd accepted people from the north and the south to do what would be the equivalent of National Service, but for regular pay and with regular holidays, so you could go to the north and actually get out quicker than you would if you did your two years here, because I think you could end up with about twenty one months or something, plus getting about six weeks/two months leave, plus quite decent pay. So I went up there and volunteered. I didn't know what regiment to go in for and then I remembered 'A Gordon for me', so I put down the Gordon Highlanders!

The choice of the famous Scottish regiment was significant given his upbringing on the islands. After basic training Kennedy Martin did officer training and before long was on his way to Cyprus as a Second Lieutenant in an infantry battalion. Cyprus was still a British colony but there was a guerrilla movement of Greek-Cypriots seeking *enosis* (integration with Greece) and also a large Turkish minority, so it was a volatile situation. Kennedy Martin's battalion was based in the mountains, where there was guerrilla activity, and as a Second Lieutenant he had a platoon which he would take out on patrol: 'Our job was to hunt down these *enosis* people who were conducting a kind of guerrilla campaign, very much like the ones that happened in Greece during World War Two, and we were up in the mountains, in Troodos. It was really exciting in a way.'

Although Kennedy Martin was in Cyprus for less than a year, being stationed there when the Suez Crisis happened in 1956, the experience was to be a lasting one, providing material for some of his early television scripts. But his first attempt to prove himself as a writer was as a novelist. Three months after returning to England from Cyprus Kennedy Martin left the army, returned to Dublin and decided he was going to write a novel:

> So I wrote this novel, or at least a draft of it, and then went to London with it. I wrote it on Achill Island, on the west coast of Ireland ... I went down there with some friends and I think Ian and Mo [Maureen, his sister] came a bit later. You know, it was peat fires, or turf fires, and gathering mushrooms in the morning, and still having no money and I wrote the draft of this novel down there.

The novel was *Beat on a Damask Drum*, set in Indo-China in 1954. Its subject was an elite unit of soldiers, a multinational group comprising an Englishman, American, Irishman, French and German, operating as a sort of trouble-shooting unit, often behind enemy lines, at a time when communist aggression against the French colonial troops was escalating into what would eventually become the Vietnam War. Into this situation enters a beautiful woman, Joey Castle, a friend of the Englishman, Adam Canning, who she has known since childhood and who she tries to persuade to return with her to England.

The novel enabled Kennedy Martin to draw on his military experience, but given that his experience of active service had been in Cyprus it seems curious that he chose to set the novel in South East Asia. It does, however, demonstrate his interest in world politics at the time, as well as giving an indication of his literary influences: 'One was showing interest in that [the situation in Indo-China] and what was happening in Russia and so on. I was reading everything and having ideas I guess. Also I think I was very influenced by Graham Greene and Hemingway.' According to Kennedy Martin, Graham Greene gave *Beat on a Damask Drum* a very good review and indeed the novel bears some similarity to Greene's own South East Asia war novel, *A Quiet American*, published in 1955, although Kennedy Martin says he had not read Greene's novel when he wrote *Beat on a Damask Drum*. The novel was published by John Murray in 1959, but by then Kennedy Martin had embarked on a career as a television scriptwriter and, apart from a 1962 novelisation of *Z Cars*, was not to return to novel writing:

> That was my first and only novel but I did think of myself as a novelist ... I guess for the first two years I was involved in television, or even a little longer, I felt 'I'm only doing this in a temporary kind of way and I'm really a *real* writer and these people who work in television aren't as real as I am!', so I had that rather cocky attitude.

Kennedy Martin spent two years working on *Beat on a Damask Drum* but for his first television play, *Incident at Echo Six* (BBC, 9 December 1958), he drew directly from his National Service experience in Cyprus. The play is about an attack on a police station in the mountains in northern Cyprus and follows the unfolding of the event over the course of one night. Transmitted as a live studio drama the play, like most studio dramas of the time, was dialogue-led and played out on a limited number of studio sets, although it did include some short film sequences for exterior scenes. As with *Beat on a Damask Drum* Kennedy Martin was concerned to explore the tensions and the relationships between the men (the play featured an all-male cast, including Barry Foster in a leading role and a young Tony Garnett in one of his early acting roles) as they tried to deal with the aftermath of the attack, as well as seeking to describe the reality of the political situation in which these British soldiers were involved.

Incident at Echo Six resulted in Kennedy Martin being taken on by the BBC as a scriptwriter/adapter and he worked on a number of adaptations over the next three years plus a second original play set in Cyprus which was eventually screened as *The Interrogator* (BBC, 22 December 1961). Between *Incident at Echo Six* and *The Interrogator* there were adaptations of stories by Somerset Maugham (*The Traitor*) and Bernard Newman (*Element of Doubt*) and also an adaptation of a play by John Heron and Maureen Quiney called *The Price of Freedom*, set in a refugee camp and screened as part of the BBC's contribution to World Refugee Year in 1960.

In 1961, while working as a scriptwriter/adapter, Kennedy Martin worked on six half-hour plays for a series called *Storyboard*, one of which was an original script while the others were adaptations. *Storyboard* was an attempt to explore the potential for experimentation in live television drama and it was the first series that the innovative director James MacTaggart worked on after being brought down from Glasgow by Elwyn Jones to work in the Drama Department at the BBC. None of these experimental dramas survive, but they mark the beginnings of a tradition of innovation in television drama that eventually led to *The Wednesday Play*, the first series of which was produced by MacTaggart in 1965.

Also in 1961, apart from completing *The Interrogator* and working on at least two other television plays, Kennedy Martin began work on *Z Cars*, the groundbreaking police series which was to become one of the BBC's popular successes in the early 1960s. There is some dispute about the origins of *Z Cars*, Elwyn Jones sometimes being credited for coming up with the idea, but it was Kennedy Martin who developed the format for the series and who did most of the initial research, in addition to writing the majority of the early episodes. The impact of *Z Cars* was enormous and the series transformed the representation of the police on British television, introducing a new benchmark for realism in television drama. Although *Z Cars* was largely studio-based there was an increased use of film which helped to give the series added realism and a much faster pace than in most drama series of the time. In addition, some of the episodes written by Kennedy Martin incorporated several different storylines, with narratives interwoven through the episode in a manner unprecedented in the early 1960s.

Kennedy Martin and John McGrath wanted to place the focus of the series on the people in the fictional towns of Newtown and Seaport, as much as the police, and to explore the social problems which such new towns were encountering at the time. As McGrath put it: 'The series was going to be a kind of documentary about people's lives in these areas, and the cops were incidental – they were the means of finding out about people's lives' (Laing, 1986: 170). The series was an immediate success, attracting audiences of fourteen million within a matter of weeks and the initial run of thirteen episodes was extended to thirty-one. However, contrary to the original intentions of Kennedy Martin and McGrath, it was the police who became the focus as the series became established. Having launched it as a groundbreaking social–realist drama they decided to leave.

John McGrath joined the BBC as a scriptwriter/adapter in 1960, the year after Kennedy Martin, and they were like-minded in their ambition to develop a new kind of television drama. Their relationship was cemented while working on *Z Cars* and, following their departure from the series, they decided to work together to develop new forms of television drama. The major outcome of their collaboration was *Diary of a Young Man*, a six-part experimental serial produced by James MacTaggart and directed by Peter Duguid and Ken Loach. *Diary of a Young Man* was transmitted in August–September 1964 but an extract from one of the scripts was included in an article which Kennedy Martin wrote for the theatre magazine *Encore* in April 1964. Entitled 'Nats Go Home: First Statement of a New Drama for Television', the article was a manifesto for a new kind of television drama, opening with a critique of the dominant tradition of naturalism in television drama before proceeding to outline a model for a new form of non-naturalistic drama. The script extract from *Diary of a Young Man* was used to illustrate the narrative possibilities of this new drama, the essential aims of which were 'to free the camera from photographing dialogue, to free the structure from natural time, and to exploit the total and absolute objectivity of the television camera' (Kennedy Martin, 1964: 25).

Roger Smith, who was to become the first story editor on *The Wednesday Play*, was also someone Kennedy Martin worked closely with in this period. Having worked together on the *Storyboard* series, in which Smith also appeared as an actor, they collaborated on an adaptation of Muriel Spark's novel, *Memento Mori*, which was never produced, and also co-adapted a novel by James Jones, *The Pistol* (BBC 1, 16 June 1965), as a *Wednesday Play*. Smith was also the story editor on *Diary of a Young Man* and *The Man Without Papers* (BBC 1, 9 June 1965), a *Wednesday Play* written by Kennedy Martin in 1965.

The Chase (BBC 2, 19 December 1964), co-written with the director Michael Elster, was another BBC script Kennedy Martin worked on at this time for a series called *Six*, which John McGrath produced. McGrath also directed *Mo* (BBC 2, 25 July 1966), featuring Maureen Kennedy Martin, Troy's sister, for a follow-up series to *Six* called *Five More* (although the films were not transmitted under this series title). *Mo* was a cinema verite-style documentary in which Maureen Kennedy Martin featured as a mother and folk-singer, along with friends and relatives including Troy, her husband Ken Wlaschen, the poets Michael Horovitz and Adrian Mitchell, folk-singer John Renbourne, and Diane Aubrey, an actress who Troy married in 1967.

In 1964 Kennedy Martin wrote his first scripts for an ITV company with the first of six episodes for *Redcap*, an ABC Television series about the military police starring John Thaw, on which his brother, Ian Kennedy Martin, was working as the story editor. Troy wrote three episodes for the first series and another three for the second series in 1966. In between he adapted *The Successor* (Anglia, 13 September 1965), a play about the election of a pope, for Anglia Television, for whom he also wrote *The New Men* (Anglia, 8 November 1966), an adaptation of a novel by C. P. Snow, about the development of the atomic bomb. Meanwhile his last script for the BBC in the 1960s was an adaptation of a Frederick Pohl story called *The Midas Plague* (BBC 2, 20 December 1965), for the science fiction series *Out of the Unknown*.

Attracted by the lifestyle he saw his brother leading, Ian Kennedy Martin followed Troy to the BBC in the early 1960s, working in the script department for a while before leaving to work for ITV companies such as ABC (later Thames), Anglia and Yorkshire as a story editor and scriptwriter. Having recruited Troy to write episodes for *Redcap*, Ian Kennedy Martin persuaded Troy to write episodes for a rural drama serial called *Weavers Green* (Anglia, April–September 1966), on which Ian had been brought in as story editor. Troy wrote eleven episodes for *Weavers Green*, under the *nom de plume* of Tony Marsh, a pseudonym he was to use on several other occasions, including the five episodes he wrote for the Yorkshire TV police series *Parkin's Patch* (Yorkshire, September 1969–March 1970).

In between *Weavers Green* and *Parkin's Patch* Kennedy Martin wrote an episode for an untransmitted London Weekend Television (LWT) series called *The Inquisitors* when LWT started up in 1968 and, following *Parkin's Patch*, he also wrote a six-part situation comedy for LWT called *If It Moves, File It* (LWT, August–October 1970). It is one of the intriguing anomalies of Troy Kennedy Martin's career that, while he was writing episodes for these largely unknown television series he was also pursuing a career as a Hollywood screenwriter. His first taste of screenwriting came in the mid 1960s when he did some work on *Darling* (UK, 1965), the classic 'swinging sixties' movie directed by John Schlesinger and starring Julie Christie, but his first full screenplay was another classic 1960s film which has since become a cult movie, *The Italian Job* (UK, 1969), directed by Peter Collinson and starring Michael Caine. Kennedy Martin got the original idea for *The Italian Job* from his brother, who had submitted a similar idea to the BBC for a television play about a bank robbery. Troy bought the idea from Ian and developed it, transposing the heist to Italy and persuading Michael Caine, who he had worked with on the BBC *Storyboard* series in 1961, to take the leading role. Not a great success on its original release, the film has acquired cult status over the years and was re-released on its twentieth anniversary in 1999 and remade in Hollywood in 2003.

Following *The Italian Job* Kennedy Martin received a lucrative contract from Metro-Goldwyn-Mayer to write *Kelly's Heroes* (USA/Yugoslavia, 1970), a Second World War movie starring Clint Eastwood, Telly Savalas and Donald Sutherland. It was *Kelly's Heroes* which really established Kennedy Martin as a Hollywood screenwriter and he followed it with *The Jerusalem File* (USA/Israel, 1971), also for MGM, plus a screenplay about the Black Panthers, *One More Time*, which was not produced. After writing another two unproduced screenplays Kennedy Martin's brief Hollywood career came to an end when film production in Hollywood slumped in the early 1970s and he returned to Britain to resume writing for television.

The situation in British television, however, was also changing and Kennedy Martin found a less hospitable broadcasting environment than the one he had experienced in the early–mid 1960s. After writing episodes for *Colditz* (BBC 1, 1972–4) and *Fall of Eagles* (BBC 1, March-June 1974) he found himself once again indebted to his brother Ian, whose script for *Regan* (Thames, 4 June 1974), an *Armchair Cinema* drama for Thames Television, became the pilot for a new police series, *The Sweeney* (Thames, 1975–8). Troy wrote six episodes for the series (including one under the pseudonym of Tony Marsh when he had a dispute with the producer and director), plus the second *Sweeney* feature film, *Sweeney 2* (UK, 1978). Produced by Euston Films, a separate company set up by Thames to make filmed drama for television, *The Sweeney* set a new benchmark for representations of the police in the 1970s, trans-forming the genre just as *Z Cars* had in the early 1960s. Around the time of his last *Sweeney* episode Kennedy Martin was reunited with John McGrath when they collaborated on the final episode of *Z Cars* (BBC 1, 20 September 1978), a series which *The Sweeney* had, ironically, made redundant.

The 1970s saw television series eclipsing the single play as 'cost-effectiveness' became the main criterion in television drama produc-tion. While progressive television drama was still being produced Kennedy Martin felt there was less scope for doing progressive work within popular series drama, which is where he wanted to work:

> You find out that the more popular the corridor, or the avenue, down which you're going, then the more it is controlled. One of the great disap-pointments of the sixties and seventies I think was that all these guys began addressing much smaller audiences and left the series depart-ment – which is now [1986] becoming one of the strongest forms of television – entirely to right-wing writers. When Gordon Newman did *Law and Order* it was the first series that Tony Garnett really saw the strength of series and how you could reinforce things every week, but he did it from within the Plays Department, so every time he went and asked for four 90 minute plays he was in fact denying three playwrights of a chance at a crack of the whip. Whereas in the Series Department there was loads of room for that sort of thing but none of them wanted to make the crossover into series and be up there under the control of the Head of Series, who was basically either apolitical or hostile to any progressive ideas.[2]

As the single play declined, virtually disappearing in the 1980s, writers seeking an outlet for original, innovative drama turned to the multi-part serial which, though expensive, was more cost-effective for the television companies than the single play. This development enabled Kennedy Martin to revitalise his career in the 1980s after a relatively lean period in the 1970s when he had difficulty getting projects off the ground. In trying to develop drama serials he was supported by the patronage of Verity Lambert at Thames Television and Jonathan Powell at the BBC and it is significant that the four serials he wrote in the late 1970s and early 1980s were for those two companies. The four-part *Fear of God* (Thames, February–March 1980), adapted from a novel by Derry Quinn and shown in ITV's *Armchair Thriller* series, was a routine exercise in serial dramatisation, while the twelve-part *Reilly – Ace of Spies* (Thames, September–November 1983) was a much more ambitious project and one which Kennedy Martin had been trying to get commissioned since his return from Hollywood in the early 1970s. Loosely based on Robin Bruce Lockhart's book about the British spy Sidney Reilly, the serial dramatised Reilly's involvement in some of the major international events of the early twentieth century, most notably his attempts to undermine the Bolshevik-led Russian Revolution. The research that Kennedy Martin did for his *Fall of Eagles* episode, on the background to the Russian Revolution, sparked his interest in the subject and he began to develop the idea for a serial on Sidney Reilly around this time, in the early 1970s. Ten years later the project finally came to fruition, as a twelve-part serial written entirely by Kennedy Martin.

Reilly was broadcast at the same time as another Kennedy Martin serial, a five-part adaptation of Angus Wilson's novel, *The Old Men at the Zoo* (BBC 2, September–October 1983). Jonathan Powell commissioned this during a very productive period for drama serials at the BBC which extended from *Pennies From Heaven* and *Tinker, Tailor, Soldier, Spy* in 1978/79 to *The Monocled Mutineer*, *The Singing Detective* and *Fortunes of War* in 1986/87. *The Old Men at the Zoo* was a satirical novel written at the end of the 1950s and set in the 1970s which Kennedy Martin updated for the early 1980s, inviting parallels to be drawn with Margaret Thatcher's Conservative government, especially its support for nuclear weapons.

This theme was further developed in *Edge of Darkness* (BBC 2, November–December 1985), a six-part nuclear thriller which ranks as one of the highpoints of Kennedy Martin's career. *Edge of Darkness* was the product of a unique cross-fertilisation of talents. Commissioned for the BBC by Jonathan Powell, the serial had Michael Wearing as producer, Martin Campbell as director, a soundtrack by Eric Clapton, and featured Bob Peck, Joe Don Baker and Joanne Whalley among an impressive cast. Where *Reilly – Ace of Spies* was a work of historical fiction, based on the real-life exploits of Sidney Reilly, *Edge of Darkness* was a work of contemporary fiction which resonated with contemporary political events and concerns. Extending its complex narrative over five hours of screen time the drama exemplified Kennedy Martin's *penchant* for long-form drama:

> I've come out of a literary rather than a theatre tradition and my bent is towards the long form. Long-form drama is really what I do best and I do think the writer still has a major role to play in it. I think it's one of the few areas where naturalism or realism still has a role to play. It links up with the nineteenth-century novel, it's a development of that. That's its heritage, not Terence Rattigan or the 1930s stage and not really cinema. So it's a kind of literary form, long convoluted stories and lots of characters.[3]

Edge of Darkness was a popular and critical success and was repeated on BBC 1 within days of the final episode being screened on BBC 2, a rare event at the time. The serial received six BAFTA awards and is now regarded as one of the best television dramas ever made in Britain.

This makes it all the more surprising that Troy Kennedy Martin has had relatively little work produced in the twenty years since *Edge of Darkness*. Not that he has been idle. In the late 1980s he spent some time in Australia and America, writing screenplays and developing ideas for television serials. His only screen credit from this period however was a shared screenwriting credit on Walter Hill's *Red Heat* (USA, 1988), a post-Cold War thriller starring Arnold Schwarzenegger. Although Kennedy Martin worked on several television projects in the late 1980s and 1990s his next television credit did not come until 1997 when *Hostile Waters* (BBC 1, 26 July 1997) was screened in the BBC *Screen One* series. Based on a real-life incident that had been kept quiet at the time, *Hostile Waters* dramatised the events following a collision between Russian and American submarines off the east coast of America in 1986 which nearly caused a major nuclear incident at a time when Presidents Reagan and Gorbachev were about to meet in a historic summit between the world's two superpowers.

Two years later Kennedy Martin was involved with another BBC drama documentary when he assisted Andy McNab with the dramatisation of his book, *Bravo Two Zero*, about McNab's SAS mission in Iraq during the first Gulf War. *Bravo Two Zero* (BBC 1, 3–4 January 1999) was initially shown on BBC 1 in two parts, a scheduling decision which effectively turned this BBC film into a two-part television drama, eliding the distinction between the two forms. Following several more unrealised projects (see the list of unproduced work in the Appendix) another six years elapsed before *Red Dust* (BBC 2, 9 July 2005) was screened on

BBC 2. Another BBC Films production, *Red Dust* was adapted from Gillian Slovo's novel about the Truth and Reconciliation Commission in post-apartheid South Africa and featured Hilary Swank and Chiwetel Ejiofor in the two main roles. Kennedy Martin's screenplay was complimented by Slovo: 'It honours the spirit of the novel, even though it is different, which it has to be as it is a different medium' (Eeden, 2005: 36) but it was Slovo's name that featured in the publicity for the film, while Kennedy Martin's role in adapting the novel for the screen was largely overlooked.

In August 2005 Troy and Ian Kennedy Martin were ranked twenty-seventh in a poll of the fifty most influential figures in British television conducted by the industry magazine *Broadcast*, two among only eight writers in the list, coming behind Tony Warren (ranked at number five for creating *Coronation Street*), Dennis Potter (9) and Alan Bleasdale (17), and ahead of Andrew Davies (46) and the comedy writing partnership of Galton and Simpson (43). Apart from a few producers and directors, including Tony Garnett (8), Ken Loach (12), Michael Wearing (38) and Verity Lambert (42), the *Broadcast* list was dominated by television executives, from the media mogul Rupert Murdoch at number one to Charles Allen, head of the new consolidated ITV, at number fifty. The poll illustrated the extent to which, according to the 400 or so industry representatives who voted, 'creative' personnel form a minority of 'the 50 most influential people in TV history' (Anon, 2005: 24). That Troy and Ian Kennedy Martin featured at all was, evidently, based largely on Troy's track record as the creator of *Z Cars* and *Edge of Darkness* and his contributions to the series created by his brother, *The Sweeney*. As the following chapters will show, Troy Kennedy Martin's contribution to British television extends far beyond these three programmes.

Notes

1 Troy Kennedy Martin, interviewed by the author, 4 April 2003. Unless otherwise indicated, all quotes in this biographical sketch are from this interview.
2 Troy Kennedy Martin, interviewed by the author, 27 March 1986.
3 Ibid.

Single plays

In the 1950s and 1960s the single play was the most prestigious form of drama on British television. Throughout the 1950s *Sunday Night Theatre* provided the dramatic highpoint of the week on the BBC and from 1957–9 *BBC Television World Theatre* offered an additional showcase for classic literary adaptations, traditional BBC territory onto which ITV had begun to encroach, for despite ITV's commitment to more populist programming the single play was also an important part of the commercial network's schedules. The three ITV anthology play series: *Television Playhouse* (1956–64), *Play of the Week* (1956–67) and *Armchair Theatre* (1956–74), leant prestige to the ITV schedules and provided stiff opposition for the BBC. ABC's *Armchair Theatre* in particular, under the guidance of the flamboyant Canadian Sydney Newman, provided British television with some ground-breaking plays in the late 1950s and early 1960s with original work by writers such as Clive Exton, Alun Owen, Harold Pinter and Ted Willis.

Newman's appointment at ABC Television in April 1958 was not, however, the only significant event in British television that year. A few months later a BBC Press Release announced that:

> A new and highly topical play by a new and talented young author will be seen on BBC Television on Tuesday, December 9.
>
> The play is *Incident at Echo Six*, subtitled 'a story of National Servicemen in Cyprus'. The action is spread over the twelve hours of a winter night. A police station high in the Troodos Mountains is shot up by terrorists, and two crash action patrols are sent to investigate. The programme focuses on the two National Service officers in charge, and shows the tensions and the dangers under which they have to carry out their work.
>
> The author, Troy Kennedy Martin is a twenty-six year-old Scotsman with a University training in history and political science who went into the British Army on a short-service commission from Ireland. He spent nine months in Cyprus as an Infantry Officer in the Troodos Mountains, holding a short-service commission in the Gordon Highlanders.[1]

Incident at Echo Six (1958)

Troy Kennedy Martin's first television play, *Incident at Echo Six* (BBC, 9 December 1958), marked the beginning of what was to be a long and illustrious screenwriting career embracing original television plays, adaptations, episodes for popular drama series, experimental dramas, drama serials, a situation comedy, television films and Hollywood movies. Yet the starting point was a single play, in the late 1950s still the most celebrated form of television drama. Not all BBC plays were shown as *Sunday Night Theatre* or *Television World Theatre* plays, some were screened at other times and *Incident at Echo Six* was one of these, transmitted live on Tuesday 9 December at 8.00 pm.

As the BBC Press Release proclaimed, the play came out of Kennedy Martin's own military experience as an infantry officer in Cyprus, where he was stationed for several months in 1956. As he stated in the press release '*Incident at Echo Six* was written to show what responsibility the National Serviceman carried in a situation which is short of war but is magnified many times over by the interest of world press and politics.'

Cyprus had been a British colony since 1878, when Turkey agreed to sign the island over to the British in return for support against Russian encroachment. Situated at the eastern end of the Mediterranean the island occupied a strategic position in the Middle East and it was because of its usefulness as a military base in the region that Britain retained sovereign control of the island until the late 1950s, resisting demands by Greek Cypriots, the majority population on the island, for *enosis*, or union with Greece. After the Second World War the Greek Cypriot struggle for *enosis* was stepped up following the election of Archbishop Makarios and began to take the form of active resistance to British rule with the founding of an underground guerilla movement called EOKA (*Ethniki Organosis Kypriou Agonista*), under the leadership of Colonel Grivas, an ex-Greek army officer. Meanwhile the minority population of Turkish Cypriots, who were even less happy with the Greek Cypriot struggle for *enosis* than were the British, established their own underground organisation, called VOLKAN, adding to the volatility of the situation in the 1950s. The number of British troops on Cyprus was increased to deal with the growing number of terrorist attacks, which were at their peak at the time of the Suez Crisis, in October–November 1956, when the British were using Cyprus as a base for the ill-fated Suez operation.[2]

It was at this time that Troy Kennedy Martin was stationed in Cyprus, serving as a Second Lieutenant in a battalion of the Gordon High-landers, based up in the Troodos mountains where EOKA was most active, and it was this explosive situation that he used as the basis for his first television play. Forty years later Kennedy Martin reflected on the origins of *Incident at Echo Six*:

> I'd been in Cyprus on a National Service gig and I'd come back and I was absolutely sure that there was going to be big trouble between the Turks and the Greeks. I tried to write a piece for the New Statesman but they didn't take it. I think they said it was nonsense, more trouble than there was at the time. Subsequently it's proven true. So I decided to write a screenplay about my time there. It was just a play about an evening, or a night, when a patrol was ambushed and the kind of problems that were related to it. I sent it off to the BBC and I was very surprised when they said come in and talk about it.[3]

In the period between his national service 'gig' and the writing of *Incident at Echo Six* Kennedy Martin had written a novel, *Beat on a Damask Drum*, which, although it was set in South East Asia rather than Cyprus, also dealt with a group of men in a war situation, an elite multinational unit carrying out undercover operations. Ostensibly a war novel, *Beat on a Damask Drum* is surprisingly lacking in action scenes, until the end of the book when the reality of war is vividly described as the group go on a suicidal mission behind enemy lines. The first three-quarters of the novel is more psychological, concerned with the effect which a beautiful woman, film star Joey Castle, has on the men into whose lives she enters when she arrives in Vietnam to try to persuade one of the group, the Englishman Adam Canning, to return with her to England. Much of the novel is spent examining the personalities and relationships of the central characters, exploring interior states and motivations, using metaphor and allusion in an attempt to describe a deeper reality, as in this central scene when Jameson, the American with whom Joey has fallen in love, tries to explain, by means of a parable, the importance of living life in the here and now, instead of hoping for something that may never be achieved:

> 'There's an old Chinese play,' he explained softly, 'about a gardener in the Palace of a Prince who once saw the vision of the Princess walking across his lawns. He was an old man and very deaf. He never forgot that vision and he dreamt of it night and day, till it became an obsession ... '
>
> She was listening yet was looking away and did not prompt him.
>
> 'Well', he went on reluctantly, 'the word got around and the Princess got to hear of it. And she said "Give him this damask drum and let him beat on it when he wants me." And in the night, when he was alone, when he wanted to see that Princess again he hung the drum from a tree and hour after hour he beat upon it. But the drum was of damask and it made no noise and he being deaf could not understand why she never came to him. And he died, drowned in the lake, the Chinese say.'

She was silent, then she looked at him. 'So he died?' she whispered.

'He could have gone on beating for the rest of his life,' he replied, 'until for some reason or another the drum made a noise. He could have gone on beating until it thundered through the Palace, through the Kingdom, until the drum thundered through the world. As long as he himself heard it, he should have gone on beating.'

He got up. 'He beat on a damask drum,' he said, 'and he saw no vision.'

'And he died,' she repeated. 'Poor gardener.'

'The death was unimportant.' He drew her to her feet. 'Get that into your head that death is unimportant, always has been, always will be. It's what's before it, that's important, the life, the drum-beating, driven on by the current of your want, banging in your ears and no one else that counts, and up comes death, because life is all overloaded at one end, and all the things that you don't understand you want sorted out quickly. Straight away it becomes important to have knowledge of that vision. It's vital to sort things out.' (Kennedy Martin, 1959: 109)

Kennedy Martin was clearly interested in using *Beat on a Damask Drum* to explore philosophical and psychological themes, although as the novel reaches its climax he shows that he was also able to describe the reality and confusion of warfare with a visceral intensity.

Incident at Echo Six follows a similar pattern. As a studio play Kennedy Martin knew that the possibilities for action were going to be limited. The attack on the police station at the beginning of the play takes place off-screen and is heard via the shortwave wireless connecting the police station to the operations room at the army headquarters, where the first few scenes take place. By this means an element of suspense is generated as it is not clear exactly what has happened at the police station, high up in the Troodos mountains. While this was an effective method of bypassing the limitations of live studio drama, where it would have been difficult to stage a full-scale assault without the use of extensive filmed footage, it meant that a certain amount of expository dialogue was necessary in order to convey to the television audience what was happening, as in an early scene where the Commanding Officer (Allan Cuthbertson) tells the two officers he is sending to find out what has happened at the police station: 'Just remember, it's an attack on a police post three hours from nowhere, defended by a corporal, four private soldiers and a cook. An attack half an hour before dusk. A telephone message cut off as soon as the facts are passed – no details.'[4] It is only after this that it becomes clear that the police station, high up in the mountains at Laghoudera, is 'Echo Six', the base for a small army unit, and that the attack which has taken place at the beginning is the 'incident' which forms the basis of the play.

Although *Incident at Echo Six*, like most television plays at the time, was transmitted live, four sequences were filmed, in England, three weeks in advance of the live broadcast, using soldiers from the Parachute Brigade, 'just back from Cyprus and Jordan.'[5] These short telecine (TC) sequences provided location footage of soldiers running to get into trucks (TC1), which then make their way up the mountain towards 'Echo Six' (TC2), only to be blown up when they are ambushed by EOKA guerillas (TC3), with a fourth sequence towards the end showing Special Branch officers arriving at 'Echo Six' to investigate the incident (TC4). These four sequences amount to less than five minutes of the seventy-five minute play, the rest of the action being staged on sets at the BBC's Lime Grove studios. After just over two weeks of outside rehearsals the large cast (there are forty-two characters in the play) assembled in Studio G at Lime Grove for two days of technical and dress rehearsals prior to the live transmission, from 8.00–9.15 pm on Tuesday 9 December:

> *Incident at Echo Six* was shot live at the old Lime Grove Studio. Television Centre wasn't even in use at that point, I think they were building it. My recollection was that everything was dark, I think it was winter, short days, the building itself seemed very old and moth-eaten and dark but quite exciting. I was working in a studio for the first time.[6]

There are fifty-seven scenes in the play, which take place on nine studio sets, and it is not until scene twenty-two that Second Lieutenant Savage (Barry Foster) arrives at Laghoudera Police Station. Savage checks out the soldiers wounded in the attack, including the most badly injured, the unit's driver, Private Brown (played by Tony Garnett in an early acting role). The ambulance they have requested fails to arrive and Savage decides they must try to remove the bullets to save Brown's life, but he dies while they are operating. Private Brown's death is the climactic moment of the play. The (off-screen) drama of the attack which precipitated his death, the 'incident' of the play's title, is little more than a pretext for exploring how Savage and the others cope with the situation in which they find themselves, a situation over which they have little control and which they do not fully comprehend. Following Brown's death Second Lieutenant Carroll (Derrick Sherwin) tells Savage that he is going to write to Brown's girl, prompting Savage to reflect on the impossibility of describing the reality of the situation in mere words:

> *Carroll:* I'm going to try and tell her everything.
> *Savage:* Everything. Ah, it's first light, here comes the new day. What will you write in your letter? What will you write about Brown? What will you say about the night – now it's daylight? That we were ambushed,

which lasted a minute. That the ambulance never arrived. That Brown died. That daylight came and showed us sitting on our backsides. Can you write about the eight hours of nothing, nothing. The eight hours of nothing when Driver Brown died.[7]

Savage's meditation on the existential reality of the situation in which they find themselves is reminiscent of a scene towards the end of *Beat on a Damask Drum* (which had not been published when *Incident at Echo Six* was broadcast), when Joey Castle reflects on the emptiness she feels following the mission that has seen Adam Canning critically wounded while Jameson, the American she has fallen in love with, has gone off behind enemy lines to an almost certain death:

> 'Do you know what Jameson used to say? He used to say we'd find it, wherever we'd be, we'd find it. We'd find this understanding of all that's gone before and the hugeness which is to come. He asked me to have faith and I hadn't. Now he's found it and I haven't. He's found it all alone. That's the straight line you saw in his eyes. Do you know what he told me? It's the drum beating that counts, the banging in your ears and no one else's. But there's nothing in my ears. There's nothing inside me. Nothing do you understand, nothing.' (Kennedy Martin, 1959: 218)

The similarity to Savage's speech suggests a common theme in the early work of Troy Kennedy Martin: the existential struggle to make sense of tragic situations in which the participants themselves are little more than pawns on the chessboard of world events, events over which they have little control or understanding. Drawing on his own National Service experience in Cyprus, Kennedy Martin was able to dramatise an event, the 'incident' at Echo Six, and use it to communicate the reality of a situation in which young soldiers find themselves. The subject of the play had a basis in reality, as Kennedy Martin explained nearly fifty years after his period of National Service in Cyprus:

> I just saw one piece of action that formed the basis of *Incident at Echo Six*, which was that I was a Duty Officer on a night when a platoon got ambushed. It was drawn into an ambush and then it retreated, because we'd have little defended police stations on various hilltops, it's quite mountainous, and they'd withdrawn into one of these little police forts where they were being enfilade by a machine gun from somewhere, so I had to go out and have a look. A lot of other people went out but the first out was me.
>
> I think I just took some men out and there was the crossroads where they'd been actually ambushed and the bomb had gone off at the side of a road, so we had wounded and they'd been taken to this police station where there was meant to be machine gun fire going on. So I got up to the police station and there were the wounded and then there was this

thing of trying to get either an ambulance to come from Nicosia or to get extra help ... It was quite interesting, you know you notice the hesitation of people who were Majors and others who were maybe five miles away, but would they bring their troops out at night and help out ... and they wouldn't, so for the first time you began to see that sort of thing.[8]

In December 1958 *Incident at Echo Six* had a contemporary relevance, given the ongoing conflict in Cyprus, which had been the motivating factor for Kennedy Martin to write it in the first place, a quality which was recognised in a short article about the play published in the *Radio Times* a few days before its transmission:

> Documentary in its authenticity, it is a powerful play, written without sentiment and without any false glamour. For Martin has caught exactly the sense of inadequacy and the feeling of nerve-racking anxiety that must come to these young officers as they consider not only their own defensive actions against savage and unheralded attacks but the retaliatory measures that in a declared war would be straightforward and acceptable. For one false move, one ill-considered act of reprisal could become headline news throughout the world, and the subject of bitter argument for many months.
>
> Produced by Gilchrist Calder, who has been responsible for so many memorable productions in BBC Television, *Incident at Echo Six* spotlights one of the problems in Cyprus which lies beyond the pros and cons of political argument – the problem of the man on the spot. (Ayres, 1958: 5)

At a time when Cyprus was a source of world news, 'an island upon which the eyes of the whole world are nervously focused, an island which has already become the critical centre of a political hurricane' (Ayres, 1958: 5), *Incident at Echo Six* had a documentary significance, to which Kennedy Martin added drama. Producer Gilchrist Calder (in the days of live television drama the producer performed the role that would later be credited to the director) worked on a number of dramatised documentaries with the writer Colin Morris in the 1950s and early 1960s, such as *The Wharf Road Mob* (BBC, 28 March 1957), about a group of Teddy Boys, *Who Me?* (BBC, 15 October 1959), about the interrogation of three robbery suspects by a Liverpool CID sergeant, and *Jacks and Knaves* (BBC, November–December 1961), a series of four plays based on the real-life cases of the Liverpool police detective who was the inspiration for *Who Me?*. Although no recording of *Incident at Echo Six* exists it seems likely that, given the play's basis in reality, Calder would have sought to achieve the same kind of documentary realism in the drama that was a feature of his other television work.[9] Certainly the reference to the play's 'documentary authenticity' in the *Radio Times* suggests that

Incident at Echo Six was, stylistically and otherwise, in a tradition of 'serious' television drama, justifying the BBC's announcement of the arrival of 'a new and talented young author.'[10]

The Traitor (1959)

The BBC was sufficiently impressed with *Incident at Echo Six* to offer Kennedy Martin a contract as a scriptwriter/adapter and also to commission another original play from him. Prior to the transmission of *Incident at Echo Six* he had in fact received a commission to do two weeks work on a documentary on second-hand cars (nothing is known of what came of this project!) and had also received a commission to write another full-length play. At the end of December 1958 Kennedy Martin was paid a fee of 275 guineas for a sixty minute play called *Three Women*, but no play of that title was ever completed. Instead Kennedy Martin's second play went into a protracted period of development and re-writing, finally surfacing in 1961 under the new title of *The Interrogator*. The scriptwriter/adapter contract, while requiring him to take on a variety of adaptation assignments, gave Kennedy Martin the freedom to develop his own scripts and to involve himself in the creative ferment of the BBC Script Department.

It was during this period that he met other aspiring writers such as John McGrath and Roger Smith with whom he was to work very closely over the next few years. Invited to give the first MacTaggart Memorial Lecture at the Edinburgh Film Festival in 1976, John McGrath talked about the creative, if anarchic, atmosphere of the Script Department at the time: 'We all spent a lot of time talking. We were involved in the medium, committed to it, as *the* popular medium of our day. We felt, in that atmosphere of benign anarchy, that we would, eventually, get our chance to make our contribution. And we had time, and energy, to argue passionately about our craft.' (McGrath, 1977: 101). But in 1959, following the publication of *Beat on a Damask Drum*, Kennedy Martin was not yet sure whether his future resided in television or outside of it, as a 'serious writer':

> When *Echo Six* came out they asked me to stay on at the BBC and be a script editor, which was quite different from what you are now. You just worked on your own projects and gave a cup of tea to other writers and it was a much gentler experience and plenty of time for your own writing, which they encouraged. During that whole period I'm thinking 'I'm a novelist, it's great slumming here at the BBC doing this thing but I'm really a novelist ... '[11]

Having spent two years writing the novel, working as a supply teacher in London for some of the time, Kennedy Martin soon began to appreciate the advantages of being on a salary at the BBC. No doubt the enthusiasm with which his first television play was greeted and the commissions for further work were sufficient encouragement for him to set aside any dreams of being a successful novelist, for the time being at any rate, in favour of a career in television.

Kennedy Martin's first televised adaptation was a forty-five minute drama adapted from a story by Somerset Maugham called *The Traitor* (BBC, 7 August 1959). Set in Madrid, London and Geneva in 1916 the play featured Donald Pleasance as Grantley Caypor, the traitor of the title, an Englishman spying for Germany who is executed by firing squad at the end of the play. Produced by Gerald Glaister, *The Traitor* also featured Mai Zetterling as Caypor's wife and Stephen Murray as Ashenden, the man responsible for revealing Caypor's treachery:

> It's a long short story, set in Switzerland during the First World War and it's about a spy, or a traitor, and eventually he's betrayed. It's not eventually … it's just how are they going to get rid of him. His wife, or his girlfriend, is part of the whole thing … it's a rather cold-blooded thing about the killing of a guy who's past his sell-by date – and that was played by Donald Pleasance. So it had this cold edge to it … I think one was still in that slightly Graham Greene territory, that sort of semi-cynical view of espionage … Somerset Maugham wasn't a favourite of mine and when it worked I was really surprised that everyone liked it so much.[12]

According to the BBC Audience Research Report on *The Traitor* 'those who enjoyed the play appeared to have found it not only exciting as a story of Secret Service activities in wartime … but also a penetrating and interesting study of human character.'[13] As the first of many adaptations that Kennedy Martin was responsible for over the next few years, *The Traitor* was undoubtedly a success, proving that *Incident at Echo Six* was no one-off.

The Price of Freedom (1960)

The Traitor was followed in 1960 by a full-length adaptation of a stage play called *The Price of Freedom* (BBC, 3 April 1960), written for World Refugee Year by John Heron and Maureen Quiney. The play was another live studio production, transmitted from Lime Grove Studio D on Sunday 3 April 1960, 8.00–9.30 pm. This had been the *Sunday Night Theatre* slot, but *Sunday Night Theatre* came to an end on 27 December 1959, to be replaced by the *Sunday Night Play* on 6 November 1960 (when John

Osborne's *A Subject of Scandal and Concern* was transmitted). In the intervening period single plays, such as *The Price of Freedom*, continued to be shown on Sunday evenings on the BBC but without an anthology series rubric. *The Price of Freedom* was about Hungarian refugees who had been displaced by the 1956 Soviet invasion and the action was set in a refugee camp. Kennedy Martin wrote a short article for the *Radio Times* to accompany its Sunday evening transmission:

> Tonight's play is concerned mainly with love. If love was not only a private necessity (which it certainly is) but also a political virtue (which it isn't), there would be no refugee problem at all. While we in this country often get upset when one individual is hurt, we don't seem to care when whole sections of a national community are jettisoned from their homes to float and wander between twin poles of conflict – such as East and West or Arab and Jew – until, settling somewhere, they are left to rot. And by rot I mean to rot without love the way plants rot without light.
>
> You can feed a refugee, clothe him and house him, but if you do nothing else, the 'him' soon becomes an 'it', a statistic and a bore. It looks as if we would like to pay money to keep him where he is, because we don't want him to share in our own good luck.
>
> I could understand this if we were at war or if our economy was on the rocks. But it isn't. And we can act fast: witness the speed and efficiency with which the Hungarian refugees were resettled. But this only highlights just how slow we have been to help the others.
>
> In Europe, refugee camps are open places; and we like to think our own countries are open places too. But between their camps and our countries are lines of defence as efficient as any military installation, only instead of bunkers and barbed wire there are quotas and red tape. These were set up, no doubt for good reasons, to keep out the criminal, the lazy, and those with whom our economy cannot cope. But I often wonder whether these restrictions, now, just keep out everyone.
>
> In this, World Refugee Year, our own country of fifty millions has taken in six hundred refugees. This is considered very good going. Is it good enough?
>
> *The Price of Freedom* is set in one of these camps of the loveless, the lepers of our modern political society. It shows how they scratch for the little love that is around them to keep themselves alive. Naomi Capon produces and she and the cast, which contains many ex-refugees, have tried to show the humanity these people have, despite the fact that it has been frayed by the long years of waiting. John Heron and Maureen Quiney wrote the original script and I was glad to adapt something so close to my heart, as part of the BBC's programme for World Refugee Year. (Kennedy Martin, 1960: 14)

While being in sympathy with the humanitarian aims of the authors Kennedy Martin did not find the adaptation easy, as he recalled many years later: 'As far as I remember about the stage play it was just loads and loads of dialogue. It was predictable and it didn't have any style. I wasn't against the ideas behind it. It just lacked any kind of drive.'[14] No recording of *The Price of Freedom* exists but, from his comments, it seems that this was the kind of naturalistic studio drama, with 'loads and loads of dialogue', to which Kennedy Martin was soon to seek an alternative. For the time being, however, this kind of adaptation, on a subject of international concern which clearly interested him, served as a 'bread and butter' scriptwriting assignment while he was working on his own original scripts.

Element of Doubt (1961)

Element of Doubt (BBC, 17 April 1961) was another 'bread and butter' assignment, a thirty-minute adaptation of a Bernard Newman suspense story, about a film star, Myra Kane (Delphi Lawrence), who, having been accused of poisoning her husband, is acquitted because of insufficient evidence, following a trial for murder. However, at the trial of another suspect, with whom she is acquainted, she confesses to the murder of her husband in order to clear the other person, but as she has already been cleared of the murder herself, and because there is an element of doubt, both she and the other suspect are cleared. The play ends with an enigma: did George Motley (the husband) kill himself? Or was he killed?

What is unusual about the play is that it begins with the narrational voiceover of the author, Bernard Newman (played by Stephen Murray), as he reads a newspaper article about Myra Kane while sitting in a railway carriage: 'Normally murder cases leave me as cold as the corpse. But I had met Myra Kane socially, and the corpse, of course. It had been, when alive, her husband.'[15] The narration suggests immediately that this is not a live studio drama and indeed, as the *Radio Times* listing indicates, *Element of Doubt* was a 'BBC recording'. By April 1961 the studios in the new BBC Television Centre at White City were in use and *Element of Doubt* was recorded, on videotape, in Studio 4 on Sunday 16 April, the day before the play was transmitted, on Monday 17 April, 8.45–9.15 pm, scheduled between *Panorama* and *The News*.

Although the play was recorded no copy of it has survived. The new electronic recording material, 2–inch videotape, was very expensive and it was standard procedure to wipe and re-use tapes after transmission unless a request had been made for the recording to be retained for a possible repeat screening. The cost of videotapes also meant that plays were still recorded as if live, because the only way to edit a tape, until electronic editing was perfected, was to cut it, a practice which was discouraged because it rendered the tape unusable for further recordings. So even when the pre-recording of television drama was introduced, editing shots together was still done through vision mixing between several cameras in the studio (four cameras were used for the recording of *Element of Doubt*). The advantage of pre-recording the play, apart from taking some of the pressure off the actors, was that it enabled a narrational voiceover to be added in post-production, rather than having to play an audio recording of an actor's voice during a live performance (a practice which had been used in Rudolph Cartier's 1954 BBC production of *Nineteen Eighty-Four*).[16]

While *Element of Doubt* may have been a thriller it is unlikely that it proceeded at a very fast pace due to it being recorded 'as if live' in the studio. In fact, according to the camera script, the play consisted of some quite long courtroom scenes during which the mystery is unravelled.[17] Apart from its use of a voiceover, the other novelty in *Element of Doubt* was the narrative twist at the end which not only resulted in the play ending with an enigma but, as the *Radio Times* suggested, posed the question of whether such a scenario could occur in real-life: 'A totally unexpected and surprising ending is revealed which might well cause viewers to ask – could it happen?'[18] The investigative scenario and narrative strategy of *Element of Doubt* now seems reminiscent of some of the plots in early episodes of *Z Cars* which combined social comment with an investigative structure. Given that *Element of Doubt* was produced in the same year that Kennedy Martin began work on *Z Cars* the similarity seems more than coincidental, suggesting an element of continuity in Kennedy Martin's work between a routine adaptation like *Element of Doubt* and the subsequent 'ground-breaking' police series.

The Interrogator (1961)

1961 was a busy year for Troy Kennedy Martin. After *Element of Doubt* he developed a series of half-hour plays which were transmitted under the title of *Storyboard*. Five of these were adaptations, with one original script, and they represent a radical departure in Kennedy Martin's work towards the development of a non-naturalistic form of television drama (for this reason they will be discussed in the next chapter along with other work of this kind). Meanwhile he was also completing another original television play that had first been commissioned in December 1958 and which was more conventional in form than the *Storyboard* plays.

The Interrogator (BBC, 22 December 1961) was in many ways a sequel to *Incident at Echo Six*. Set on Cyprus in 1956 (the year in which Kennedy Martin was posted there) the play is based around the character of Superintendent Fallon (Bernard Lee), a Special Branch detective who has been pursuing an EOKA terrorist group in the mountains of northern Cyprus. Under suspicion of having shot a prisoner Fallon is facing suspension pending an enquiry, but on his last night he resolves to find the location of an EOKA arms dump, bringing in a group of suspects for interrogation. As with *Incident at Echo Six* the action takes place during the course of one night, during which Fallon interrogates three suspects: Kiki (Sean Lynch), who admits under interrogation that he is the group's leader, Druscilla (Tamara Hinchco), who is already known to Fallon, and Michaelis (Andreas Demetri), a teenage member of the EOKA group. All three are broken down by Fallon under interrogation and Kiki finally tells him where the arms dump is. Kennedy Martin's short outline describes the aims of the play:

> *Intention*: To examine the character of a man caught up in terrorism.
> *Theme*: The upside down scale of values and morals in terrorism. Its insanity and diseased qualities. The idea that the harder you fight terrorism the more likely you are to catch the disease.
> *Story*: How Fallon, the interrogator, commits an act of terrorism and therefore catches the disease he is fighting.
> *Plot*:
>> *Primary* – Fallon interrogates a terrorist, grows to hate him and deliberately arranges circumstances which will lead to his death.
>> *Secondary* – Fallon already under suspicion of having murdered a terrorist, although it transpires that he hasn't – but the suspicions prove to be well founded.[19]

After Kiki has told Fallon the location of the arms dump at the end of the play Fallon wants to turn him loose, knowing that the villagers will kill him. He is prevented from doing so by his colleagues, but the implication is clear: Fallon has transgressed a moral boundary and 'caught the disease' he is supposed to be fighting. The news that arrives following Fallon's 'breaking' of the suspects, that the prisoner he is rumoured to have shot has been recaptured, comes too late to admonish Fallon. The interrogation scenes have shown us he is more than capable of crossing the line in order to get results, that for him the end justifies the means no matter how morally dubious his methods.

Superintendent Fallon is an early manifestation of the maverick police detective who would reappear in many films and television dramas of the 1970s, such as Harry Callahan in the *Dirty Harry* series, Jack Regan in *The Sweeney* and Frank Pyle in *Law and Order*, law enforcers who, in varying degrees, are prepared to bend or break the rules in order to solve the crime or apprehend the criminal. More immediately, Superintendent Fallon can be seen as the precursor of Detective Chief Superintendent Barlow, the character Kennedy Martin created for *Z Cars*, who was to make his first appearance on British television within two weeks of Fallon's appearance in *The Interrogator*. Although Kennedy Martin initially conceived Barlow as 'a dreamer' he was later to write that 'the avidity with which the press greeted the concept of Barlow as the stern face of authority, the vengeful father, surprised me … ' (Kennedy Martin, 1978: 125). The dramatic context may be different, but the similarities between Fallon and Barlow suggest that the seeds of Barlow's 'stern, vengeful authority', seen on numerous occasions when interviewing suspects, reside in Superintendent Fallon's ruthless interrogator.

The Interrogator was recorded on 4 December 1961 in Studio TC3 at BBC Television Centre, two and a half weeks before its transmission. No copy of the recording has survived but the play was generally well received. In an internal BBC Audience Research Report it received an appreciation index of 68, slightly above average 'for London Studio plays broadcast during the first nine months of 1961.'[20] The response of the viewing panel was mixed, with some members feeling that 'a story with a background of terrorism in Cyprus was inappropriate and outdated now that Cyprus had gained her independence and things had settled down there' (Cyprus became an independent republic in August 1960). Other viewers noted that there was 'very little action' and that the play 'seemed plodding, long drawn out, and therefore boring', but this was a minority view and the report continued:

> The majority was favourably impressed by the play … mainly because it was a 'down to earth' story with plenty of suspense. Once it had started, it seems, viewers became involved with the characters, with the realistic situation, and with the dilemma involved. The plot was interesting and 'meaty' and well worked out, they said, and it was impossible for them not to watch till the very last moment.[21]

Although *The Interrogator* was far removed from the non-naturalistic experiments of the *Storyboard* plays that Kennedy Martin had been working on that year and different again to the social realism of *Z Cars*, which he was also developing in 1961, its theme of terrorism and psychological interrogation relates not only to some of his other early plays, such as *Incident at Echo Six* and the adaptation of *The Traitor*, but also to later work such as *Edge of Darkness* and *Red Dust*. Certainly the references in the Audience Research Report to a 'meaty' plot with 'plenty of suspense' which held the attention of viewers 'till the very last moment' could be applied to much of Kennedy Martin's work, indicating that his ability to construct engaging and suspenseful narratives was in evidence from the very beginning of his screenwriting career.

Unproduced work

In addition to the work that was produced while Kennedy Martin was working as a scriptwriter/adapter at the BBC from 1959–61 there were several other projects which never went into production. In February 1959 he received a commission to write a thirty-minute drama for a series called *Inner Circle*. Documentation in the BBC Written Archives Centre suggests that a script, entitled *Farringdon Street*, was written but that the series never went into production. *Farringdon Street* therefore became the first of a number of unproduced Troy Kennedy Martin scripts from this period.[22]

In August 1959 Kennedy Martin was approached by BBC script editor Vincent Tilsley about a play called *The Little Goat*, written by Gabriel Hahn. The play had been brought to the attention of Tilsley by Donald Wilson, script supervisor in the BBC Drama Department:

> This is a play which I would like you to read and tell me how you think it could be adapted for us. The name Gabriel Hahn disguises somebody fairly important in this Organization. My only major point is that the narration must of course come out. I am sure you will have some useful things to say. I would like you also if you will to suggest an adaptor.[23]

Gabriel Hahn was, in fact, a pseudonym for Eric Maschwitz, Head of Light Entertainment at the BBC from 1958–61. During the war Maschwitz had been in the Special Operations Executive and he drew on his wartime experience to write a play about a female agent working for the British as a spy who is found out by the Germans and interrogated. In Maschwitz's original script a flashback structure was used to reveal early on that the agent, Monique, had deliberately been given false information by the British, knowing that she would break down under interrogation, and that she was therefore being used to feed false information to the enemy. On reading the play Tilsley suggested some changes to Wilson before proposing Kennedy Martin as an adapter. One can see why Tilsley may have thought that Kennedy Martin was the right person to adapt the play for television. When Tilsley replied to Wilson's memo, on 12 August 1959, *The Traitor* had only recently been transmitted and the theme of spying and betrayal in Maugham's story was similar to that of *The Little Goat*. Furthermore, the theme of interrogation in *The Little Goat* bears more than a passing resemblance to the central theme of Kennedy Martin's second original play, which was already in development when he was asked to adapt *The Little Goat*.[24]

After reading the play Kennedy Martin wrote to Tilsley suggesting ways of developing it, but also expressing some reservations about its content: 'The idea in this play is good theatrically and from the point of view of box-office. I also find it sadistic ... I am not keen on working on a play which circles around the torturing of a woman – unless there is an idea behind it other than entertainment. At the present I don't think there is.'[25] However, Kennedy Martin did work on a script during 1959–60, although there is no more mention of it in BBC correspondence until 17 January 1961 when a report headed '*The Little Goat* by Troy Kennedy Martin' was sent from Duncan Ross to 'H.D. Tel. [Head of Department, Television] through H.S.D. Tel. [Head of Script Department, Television].' Duncan Ross's report on Kennedy Martin's script was overwhelmingly negative, concluding that the script was 'dangerous' and potentially libellous:

> I can only confirm your fears with regard to the enclosed play. It could almost certainly bring protests and, in my opinion quite rightly so, as it would do much to dishonour the most noble body of women who served us during the War. The protests could come from high places – possibly the first from the House of Lords – for the women who served in the Force referred to (the F.A.N.Y.s) are perhaps the best connected in the country.[26]

An undated reply from Troy Kennedy Martin painstakingly took issue with Ross's report, concluding:

> This play is a dramatic examination of how far expediency can go in war – the effect it has on the human beings involved – and how it can be measured morally in terms of our age. It is not a story for boy scouts. It is a better play than *Orders to Kill* – which is the only piece of writing to come out since the war which is any good, on this subject. This play will be put on sooner or later, simply because it presents the universal moral problems of mankind in terms of particular incidents which we can all understand.[27]

Ross's concerns clearly had their intended effect and *The Little Goat* did not go into production. Yet Kennedy Martin's description of *The Little Goat* as an 'examination of how far expediency can go in war' could also be applied to *The Interrogator* and given the similarity in their subject matter it seems highly likely that there was some developmental correspondence between *The Little Goat* and *The Interrogator* regarding notions of morality and expediency in wartime.

Other unproduced or aborted projects at this time include a television adaptation of Kennedy Martin's novel, *Beat on a Damask Drum*, which is first mentioned in a memorandum from Robin Wade dated 4 May 1960. However a subsequent memo dated 10 May 1960 referred to the possibility of the film rights for the novel being sold to America, which seems to have put the project on hold and on 17 February 1961 Robin Wade confirmed that the BBC was not going ahead with the adaptation.

The memo of 4 May 1960 also refers to a commission for a ninety-minute television play called *The Triangle*. This was first developed under the title of *The Boy in the Grotto*, then as *Death of a Hero* and finally as *The Triangle*. Set in Cuba, in the aftermath of the revolution, the story is based around two 'triangles' of characters. One of these triangles includes an 18 year old called Pablo, who is holed up in a cave in the hillside, a religious site known as 'the Grotto of Our Lady' (hence the original title). Pablo is in love with Maria, who is in jail for killing Carlotti, the third character in this 'eternal triangle.' The second triangle involves an army Captain, a doctor and a priest. These three figures are the main characters in the play and they spend much of the time discussing what to do about Maria and Pablo, knowing that there is a restive crowd outside the village jail, where most of the play is set, waiting to see Maria shot for killing Carlotti, a hero of the revolution. The dilemma is resolved when the Captain, the doctor and the priest contrive for the crowd to be diverted to the Grotto, where Pablo is threatening to kill himself if Maria is shot. *The Triangle* bears some resemblance to *The Interrogator*, both thematically and stylistically, and the description of it as 'Television Play III' on the front of the typescript suggests Kennedy Martin wrote it as his third original play after *Incident at Echo Six* and *The Interrogator*. Correspondence in the BBC Written Archives Centre suggests he was still working on the script in November 1961, but it was never produced.[28]

Meanwhile, in August 1961, Kennedy Martin received another commission for a television play with a wartime setting. *The Mercenaries* was to be a ninety-minute play about court martial in a prisoner of war camp during World War One and Kennedy Martin received half of the fee for this script in February 1962. However a subsequent memo, in October 1962, refers to the need to change the title because of a forthcoming Hammer horror film and *The Mercenaries* appears to be yet another uncompleted project from the early 1960s. Kennedy Martin's contract with the BBC as a scriptwriter/adapter was 'suspended' on 1 October 1961, after which, according to a memo from script organiser Robin Wade, he was 'on unpaid leave for six months' while he worked on *Z Cars*.[29] The termination of the contract represented a change in status for Kennedy Martin from a salaried BBC employee to that of a freelance writer, although he continued to work for the BBC through to 1965 and it was not until 1964 that he first wrote for an ITV company.

Another unrealised project from this early 1960s period dates from May 1962 when Kennedy Martin received a commission to adapt *Memento Mori* by Muriel Spark as a 60–75 minute drama. A script was delivered in August or September 1962 and a date was set to record the play on 23 October 1962 for transmission on 9 November 1962. However this was abandoned because, as BBC Head of Copyright R. G. Walford explained in a letter to Margaret Ramsey, Muriel Spark's agent, 'the dramatisation by Troy Kennedy Martin has not proved satisfactory.' A memo from the Assistant Head of Copyright to Robin Wade suggests that the script was not acceptable because it was co-written by Kennedy Martin and Roger Smith, when it had been commissioned from Kennedy Martin, but a subsequent memo from Donald Wilson to Robin Wade dated 9 October 1962 suggested that 'the unfortunate delay in getting it written, combined with the lapse of our rights, made it impossible to produce.'[30] Given that the script was delivered within four months of it being commissioned this does not seem like an inordinate length of time, especially in relation to the gestation of some of Kennedy Martin's other work, and it seems likely that this is not the full story.

The Man Without Papers (1965)

Following the transmission of *The Interrogator*, in December 1961, it was over three years before Kennedy Martin had another television play produced. Not that he was idle during this period. Between *The Interrogator* and his next televised play, *The Man Without Papers* (BBC 1, 9 June 1965), he was fully occupied writing episodes for *Z Cars* and the ABC series *Redcap* (see Chapter 3) and developing ideas for a new kind of television drama, which were summarised in the 1964 *Encore* article 'Nats Go Home' and realised in the six-part *Diary of a Young Man*, co-authored with John McGrath. During this period he also contributed to McGrath's experimental series *Six* and, in addition to the abandoned *Memento Mori* project, wrote an unproduced non-naturalistic drama called *Macheath – Masterspy* (see Chapter 3).

The Man Without Papers saw a return to the single play format which had occupied Kennedy Martin during his first three years in television. In fact it was the first of five single plays he had produced in 1965–6. *The Man Without Papers* was originally entitled *The Man Between* and intended for the BBC *First Night* series. *First Night* was an anthology series of contemporary single plays which ran from September 1963 to May 1964 and was the forerunner of *The Wednesday Play*. *The Man*

Between was one of two plays that Kennedy Martin was scheduled to contribute to the series, the other being *The Prodigal Son*, about which Roger Smith, the Story Editor for *First Night*, wrote to Sydney Newman in a report on work in progress for the series:

> This is an up-to-date version of the parable. It is the story of a young man who leaves home to escape the love and praise of his family and goes to the big city which he has heard is evil and where there is no love. He is stifled by the affection of a young lady he meets there. Dispirited he returns home thinking his puritan father must now disown him and give him the punishment he thinks he deserves. The father brings out the fatted calf.[31]

In the same report Smith described *The Man Between* as 'a comedy thriller of a spy who works for both sides.' The termination of *First Night* in May 1964 resulted in *The Man Between* being deferred, to be resurrected as *The Man Without Papers* and transmitted towards the end of the first season of *Wednesday Plays*. Officially *The Wednesday Play* began on 28 October 1964 with *A Crack in the Ice*, but the first six plays, transmitted from 28 October to 16 December 1964, were leftovers from a companion series to *First Night* called *Festival*, a showcase for dramatisations of literary classics which ran from October 1963 to June 1964, in parallel with *First Night*. The intention with *First Night* however, as Roger Smith hinted when he described *The Prodigal Son* as an 'up-to-date version of the parable', was to present new work with a more contemporary focus and this aim was carried over into *The Wednesday Play*, especially in the plays produced by James MacTaggart.

Kennedy Martin's intention with *The Man Without Papers* was to tap into the 1960s zeitgeist by writing a contemporary thriller, an unusual project for *The Wednesday Play*, featuring a rebellious hero in the shape of Roscoe Mortimer (Benito Carruthers), an American who, having burnt his passport as a protest against McCarthyism in the 1950s, is now a 'fugitive on the run from both the law and the lawless' (Anon, 1965a). Roscoe is 'a fast-talking hipster who can charm anything in skirts, a super-cool operator hell-bent on survival' (Mitchell, 1965b), a sort of beatnik James Bond. The play opens in Glasgow where Roscoe is being followed by a police detective, Inspector Dumphy (Charles Victor). Roscoe makes a telephone call to David Castle (James Maxwell), who Roscoe knows from their time together in a Korean prisoner of war camp. Castle now works for the Home Office and Roscoe travels to London to see him, hoping that Castle will be able to get him 'Stateless citizen's papers.' As he tells Castle: 'I've been a man without papers far too long. I'm growing old.'[32] After a long scene in Castle's office when Roscoe tries to persuade Castle to get him the papers Roscoe leaves with

Anne (Ingrid Hafner), Castle's secretary, with whom he spends the rest of the day, evading the police and unknown others who are pursuing him. After his liaison with Anne, Roscoe goes to see Marcella (Geraldine McEwan), Castle's wife, with whom he elopes, pretending to Castle that he has kidnapped her in order to blackmail Castle into providing him with the papers. The denouement takes place at a port where Roscoe is holed up in a brothel with Marcella, waiting for Castle to arrive with the papers.

In an early draft of the script Kennedy Martin wrote a long filmed sequence at the end in which Roscoe is chased by both police and gangsters at the docks, eventually escaping by swimming towards a ship, leaving the others unsure as to whether he has got away. However, the camera script does not have this chase sequence but has an 'amended' ending (pp. 125–9) – a studio sequence in which Castle, Marcella and Dumphy listen to a wireless transmission of a gunfight at the dockside as the police try to apprehend a group of gunmen Dumphy has been pursuing. Roscoe, it is implied, escapes on the ship that is preparing to sail and Dumphy decides to let him go, telling Castle: 'Do you think I want Mortimer? I got what I wanted. I don't need him.' According to this amended camera script the final telecine sequence shows the ship being pulled out of the harbour by tugs, accompanied by 'the sound of Roscoe neighing', as Castle and Marcella stand watching it sail away.[33] The problem of the ending was recollected by the director Peter Duguid, who had worked with Kennedy Martin before, on *Diary of a Young Man*. According to Duguid he had a lot of trouble getting Kennedy Martin to decide on an ending for *The Man Without Papers*:

> The story was that Troy couldn't finish it, he couldn't finish the play. It hinged on a decision that one of the main characters had to make finally, and he had difficulty in completing the script at all and that got so worrying I cleared the office next to me, which had a link door, and brought him in and I said 'You're going to have to sit there because I need the script, I can't go on without the script, I meet the actors in a week's time ... ' He never was able to finish it.
>
> So we rehearsed it and I said 'Now, I'll give you an early run through so you can decide what's going to happen at the end', because we hadn't got anything from him you see. So we put the thing together and gave him a run through about two days before the studio. He said 'Oh it's wonderful.' I said 'Whatever do you mean?' 'It's wonderful it could go either way.' I said 'Quite, but which way!' 'I can't ... I'll have to think about it', and he never came back.
>
> So I did quite a nice ending, actually ... it was a sort of reconciliation between the wife and the husband. I did it in a great long shot from the top of a massive crane, looking down on a car which she was about to go

off in ... they'd had an argument, which we did close to, and she'd go and sat in the car and he slowly walks – music over, of course, is important – and he slowly walks across and just gets into the car, long pause, and then she drives away slowly and that's the end. It didn't mean very much but at least it was an ending![34]

Duguid directed *The Man Without Papers* 'as a play of action, achieving a good deal of excitement' (Anon, 1965b). The production included twenty telecine sequences, filmed in April 1965, a few weeks before the studio recording on 12 May 1965, with editing and dubbing taking place from 14–21 May. A BBC TV Film Library Retention Form, completed by James MacTaggart, requested that the play be retained for two years from its transmission date, until 9 June 1967, for a 'possible repeat', but the play was not repeated and only part of it has survived.[35]

Kennedy Martin's intention with *The Man Without Papers* was clearly to produce a fast-moving contemporary thriller. The camera script lists ninety-three studio scenes containing 399 shots, plus the telecine sequences. In a seventy-five minute play this suggests a very fast pace, something which was commented on in newspaper reviews: 'the script had all the pace and the punch that one has come to expect from its writer' (Anon, 1965a); 'Here he deployed all his native and acquired craft; his gift for pace, space and anything but grace. As an entertainment on the simple (but uncommon) level of sheer watchability, this was *Z Cars* with bells on' (Wiggin, 1965). The pace of the drama was also commented on in the BBC Audience Research Report: 'The production made a satisfactory impression on the whole. There were occasional accusations of 'too gimmicky photography' and 'abrupt' switches of scene, but viewers were well pleased with settings that looked very authentic, they said, and continuity that apparently moved at a good, brisk pace.'[36] Opinions among the BBC viewing panel were mixed regarding the success of the play with many finding it both 'baffling and compelling at one and the same time.' Some viewers objected to the 'loutish manners and motives' of Roscoe and while some admitted that the play contained 'an interesting thread concerning liberty and freedom of the individual' this did not counteract 'the revulsion they felt for the chief character of the story.'[37]

An interesting footnote to *The Man Without Papers*, illustrating its 1960s cultural kudos, was the inclusion of contemporary pop music by groups such as The Pretty Things and The Yardbirds, as well as original music by Ben Carruthers' own group The Seeds, for whom Bob Dylan wrote specially commissioned songs. The credentials of Ben Carruthers for playing the rebellious Roscoe were emphasised in the *Radio Times*:

Born into a generation of protest, involved with the New York *avant-garde* in theatre and art, connected with a hip scene which stretches from San Francisco to Paris, Carruthers epitomises the best in the young footloose 1960s artists who care more for life than money.

This is also the world of the phenomenal Bob Dylan, currently winding up his record-breaking concert tour, who has specially written the songs his old friend Ben Carruthers sings in tonight's production. (Anon, 1965c: 35)

Apart from its contemporary cultural relevance *The Man Without Papers* marks an interesting development in Kennedy Martin's career. After the early television plays, the excursion into popular drama series with *Z Cars* and experimental drama with *Diary of a Young Man*, *The Man Without Papers* was not simply a return to the traditional form of the single play but an attempt at a fast-paced thriller. As such it anticipated the movies that Kennedy Martin was soon to write – *The Italian Job* (1969), *Kelly's Heroes* (1970), *The Jerusalem File* (1971) – and the filmed television thrillers of the 1980s and 1990s: *Reilly – Ace of Spies* (1983), *Edge of Darkness* (1985) and *Hostile Waters* (1997).

The Pistol (1965)

The Pistol (BBC 1, 16 June 1965) was the next play to be shown in *The Wednesday Play* series following *The Man Without Papers*. An adaptation of a novel by the American author James Jones, whose other novels include *From Here to Eternity*, *Some Came Running* and *The Thin Red Line*, *The Pistol* was a very American project. Not only was it about an American platoon of GIs based in Hawaii immediately before the attack on Pearl Harbor, it featured an all-American cast and was directed by James Ferman, an American living in Britain who was later to become Head of the British Board of Film Censorship.

Roger Smith, who was working as Story Editor on *The Wednesday Play*, collaborated once again with Kennedy Martin on the adaptation, renewing a working partnership which had begun in 1961 on the *Storyboard* series. The play, like the novel, takes its title from a pistol that has been requisitioned to Private First Class Mast (Clive Endersby) while on duty in Hawaii and which he is unable to return to the Arms Sergeant when confusion breaks out following the attack on Pearl Harbor. Suddenly, as the soldiers await an invasion by the Japanese, the illicit pistol becomes a much sought-after weapon. As Roger Smith explained in the *Radio Times*:

A pistol can be useful. It can save you from the Samurai sabres of the Japanese officers that will split you down the middle, that all the other troops are talking about. And when Mast's company is sent off to Makapuu Point, the furthermost and bleakest part of the island, where there is nothing but rock and mud and a deafening wind, to wait for the Japanese to invade, suddenly everyone becomes interested in the pistol. Everyone wants it. And they'll go to any lengths to get it. They'll cheat, they'll deal, they'll bribe, they'll fight for it. And nineteen-year-old Mast learns that he must do everything to defend it. (Smith, 1965: 39)

This is the basis for the drama and, with its focus on a group of soldiers in a crisis situation, it was familiar territory for Kennedy Martin, reminiscent of his very first play, *Incident at Echo Six*, but this time with American soldiers and a different island. No recording of the play has survived, despite the fact that this was an expensive production (£10,000) which one might have thought would merit its preservation, regardless of any artistic value. In fact the drama received some good reviews: 'The careful direction by James Ferman turned the play into that rare thing, a convincing slice of America created in Britain. Yet the chief joy of *The Pistol* was the neat, crisp dialogue by Troy Kennedy Martin and Roger Smith and the acting of the American cast' (Barnes, 1965). 'Who could have forecast that the American characters and big canvas of the story would translate happily to television? But it worked, conveying plenty of the atmosphere of a group of frightened men convinced that they were about to die' (Usher, 1965). 'The pistol was loaded with other ammunition as well ... good acting, good writing, good production' (Eastaugh, 1965). The ambitious nature of the production was emphasised in several reviews, with one critic noting in his preview that James Ferman 'has tried to make this drama look more of a film production than a TV play' (Green, 1965). The BBC Audience Research Report noted that:

> The acting and production, especially the production, were both admired. If a small group of viewers could not forget that (as they had read in *Radio Times*) the actual location was Hastings, not Hawaii, the 'realism' of it all impressed many considerably. The production was called both lavish and enterprising, with much film unobtrusively integrated with studio scenes, with convincing 'outdoor action' and a fight scene that seems to have been strikingly authentic-looking and exciting.[38]

Both *The Pistol* and *The Man Without Papers* seem like rehearsals for the larger-scale action-based dramas that Kennedy Martin was to go on to write and the reference to James Ferman trying to make *The Pistol* 'look more of a film production than a TV play' provides a clue as to where his ambitions were heading. *The Man Without Papers* and *The Pistol* may have been single plays but they were far removed from many of the studio-based dramas being televised in the mid 1960s. As Kennedy Martin said in a typical throwaway remark about *The Man Without Papers* in 1986, 'that was just a sort of early movie.'[39]

The Successor (1965)

Three months after *The Man Without Papers* and *The Pistol* were transmitted Kennedy Martin had an altogether different script televised. *The Successor* (Anglia, 13 September 1965) was an adaptation of a play by Reinhard Raffalt and Steven Vas about the election of a Pope. As a production for television it betrayed its theatrical origins, being entirely studio based, apart from some archive footage at the beginning of the play of tanks rolling into a city and riots in the streets, evoking the Russian invasion of Hungary in 1956. The pre-title sequence also shows a bricklayer walling up the Cardinals in the Vatican, referring to the ancient tradition of the Conclave when the Cardinals are locked up until they elect a new Pope, and ends with archive footage of an atomic explosion to underline the troubled background of recent world events against which the election of the Pope is taking place.

Apart from some short telecine sequences during the course of the play – archive footage of crowds in St Peters' Square awaiting the result of the election; shots of a chimney issuing smoke, which was the signal for whether a new Pope had been elected or not – all of the action takes place in a limited number of studio sets, representing rooms within the Vatican and the Sistine Chapel (recreated on a somewhat smaller scale!). The drama has an all-male cast of sixteen, mostly Cardinals from cities around the world who have gathered for the election, and the opening scene indicates the impasse at which they have arrived, after three weeks of trying to elect a Pope, with yet another vote ending in a tie between the two leading candidates for the succession. The remainder of the play, in three acts, is concerned with debating the way forward, with the traditional and progressive wings of the Church arguing their respective positions. The debate centres on the role of the Church in the modern age and the need for religion at a time when much of humanity has abandoned it for its 'new toys', a reference to the weapons of warfare and the atomic bomb. Eventually a compromise is arrived at and a middleway proposed. Following the request of the dying Cardinal of Toledo that they choose the 'simplest man', the affable Cardinal of Bologna (Rupert Davies, better known at the time for playing Inspector Maigret in the BBC series) is proposed as the solution to their problem. At first reluctant, he is finally persuaded to assume the responsibility of the succession, to become the new leader of the Catholic Church.

Competently, if unimaginatively, directed by John Jacobs, *The Successor* is entirely dialogue-led, a surprisingly naturalistic production for the author of 'Nats Go Home' and a marked contrast to Kennedy Martin's two *Wednesday Plays*, with their more elliptical, action-oriented plots. The difference between the plays in many ways highlights the difference in the mid 1960s between the plays being produced by the BBC and those of the ITV companies. Both *The Successor* and the following year's *The New Men*, another Kennedy Martin adaptation for Anglia Television, were transmitted under the ITV *Play of the Week* umbrella, an anthology play series which, together with *Armchair Theatre*, was the showcase for the single play on the commercial network, screening mostly adaptations rather than original television plays. Anglia was one of four ITV companies, along with Associated-Rediffusion, ATV and Granada, contributing plays to the networked series.

The Midas Plague (1965)

Another genre switch followed with Kennedy Martin's next televised play. *The Midas Plague* (BBC 2, 20 December 1965) was screened as part of BBC 2's *Out of the Unknown* science fiction anthology series. The series was produced by Irene Shubik, not only one of the few women producers working in television in the 1960s but someone who thought that science fiction was legitimate material for television drama, not a view widely shared at a time when the single play had more 'highbrow' connotations. Shubik had been responsible for the first adult science fiction series on television when she persuaded Sydney Newman to let her put *Out of This Earth* together for ABC in 1962, an anthology series of thirteen science fiction stories from authors such as Isaac Asimov and Philip K. Dick, adapted for television by writers such as Clive Exton, Leon Griffiths and Terry Nation.

When Newman became Head of Drama at the BBC Shubik followed him as part of the expansion of staff needed for BBC 2, becoming Story Editor on the anthology play series *Story Parade* (BBC 2, 1964–5) before being given the chance to produce the first two seasons of *Out of the Unknown* (1965–7). Leon Griffiths and Terry Nation were again among the dramatists she brought in to adapt stories by Asimov, Ray Bradbury, John Wyndham and other science fiction writers, while Kennedy Martin was commissioned to adapt Frederick Pohl's *The Midas Plague*. Pohl's story was a satire about a futuristic society in which robots serve as slaves to humankind, producing endless consumer goods for their human masters to enjoy. In this society humans are no longer rewarded for how much they produce but for how much they consume, the more 'successful' consumers having the volume of goods they need to consume reduced, while for the less successful the volume is increased. Morrey (Graham Stark) is the central character, an underprivileged and unsuccessful consumer who is forced to consume more and more until he is overwhelmed by the amount of goods being forced on him. Morrey rebels and takes steps to change the system, making an illegal adjustment to his robots so that *they* have to consume the goods. The plan works and he begins to climb the social ladder, until one day one of his robots explodes through overwork. Morrey discovers that the robot was, in fact, a spy robot and he is arrested and taken before the Prime Minister, only to discover that the Prime Minister is also a robot and that robots have been running the country for years.

The Midas Plague was recorded on 26 October 1965 and directed by Peter Sasdy, who the previous year had directed Asimov's *The Caves of Steel* for *Story Parade* and who went on to direct a number of Hammer horror films in the late 1960s and early 1970s as well as the classic Nigel Kneale television drama, *The Stone Tape* (BBC 2, 1972). Like the other dramas in the *Out of the Unknown* series *The Midas Plague* was a sixty-minute studio drama with some telecine sequences. Whereas some of the other dramas were more 'serious' in their subject matter *The Midas Plague* was clearly a satire, offering the opportunity for plenty of comic moments: such as the burglar who breaks into Morrey's home, not to steal things but to offload yet more goods, and the scene in which Morrey gets his robot servants drunk on whisky, so that they start acting like humans. Yet at a time when new technology was an important feature of 1960s modernity – this was only two years after Harold Wilson's famous speech in which he called for a new Britain 'to be forged in the white heat of a technological revolution' (Wheen, 1982: 61) – *The Midas Plague* presented a satirical warning against the excesses of the consumer society and any future dependence on robots as slave labour.

Clearly a departure from previous work, this episode of *Out of the Unknown* gave Kennedy Martin the opportunity to work in a less 'serious' genre, affording the opportunity to make a statement about the British class system and social mobility in a humorous and light-hearted manner. As such it was a complete contrast to the ITV plays and the episodes of *Redcap* that he wrote in 1965–6, while being significant as his first excursion into science fiction and his first satire. In this respect it has something in common with his adaptation of Angus Wilson's futuristic allegory *The Old Men at the Zoo* (1983), while humour was to become increasingly evident in subsequent scripts for *The Italian Job, If It Moves, File It, The Sweeney* and *Edge of Darkness*.

The New Men (1966)

Troy Kennedy Martin's last televised play was another *Play of the Week* for Anglia Television. *The New Men* (Anglia, 8 November 1966) was an adaptation of the novel by C. P. Snow, about a team of scientists in England, during the latter part of the Second World War, and their efforts to develop the first atomic bomb. The play was previewed in the *TV Times* by Sarah Snow:

> The year is 1943. The place – an atomic research establishment in England. The people – a team of young nuclear scientists headed by Walter Luke (Michael Bryant) and Martin Eliot (Lyndon Brook). Martin's elder brother Lewis (Marius Goring) is in charge of scientific personnel at the Ministry, the job C. P. Snow held himself at that time during the war. Their objective – plutonium and the first atomic bomb before the Germans get it. Before the Americans get it, too, for that matter. Hence the atmosphere – urgent and dedicated. For, as Luke says, 'I'd rather we got it first – so that we should have some influence in case some other maniac in the U.S. wants to drop the damn thing.' A safe demonstration, the scientists believe, will end the war. Fervently they agree the Bomb must *never* be used – the consequences would be appalling. (Snow, 1966: 9)

Like *The Successor*, *The New Men* was a studio play which used some archive film to provide historical context. It had the same production team – director John Jacobs and designer Michael Wield – that had worked on *The Successor* and, despite the different subject, there is a stylistic similarity between the two productions – a slow narrative development with an emphasis on dialogue and debate rather than action. Yet *The New Men* has a much more contemporary feel to it, even though the events described are set more than twenty years before. In 1966 nuclear weapons were still very much on the political agenda and the Campaign for Nuclear Disarmament (CND) was still very active. In 1965 Peter Watkins' dramatisation of a nuclear attack on Britain, *The War Game*, had been banned by the BBC, ostensibly because it was 'too shocking' to be shown on television, although there was clearly also a concern that it made CND's case only too well.[40]

Now, with *The New Men*, Kennedy Martin had the opportunity to dramatise for television the subject of C. P. Snow's 1954 novel, the attempt by a group of British scientists to develop the first atomic bomb so that it can be used as a threat to force the Germans to agree to peace. These scientists are 'the new men' of the novel's title, many of them with left-wing sympathies who are working on the bomb 'to stop Adolf Hitler getting in front and using it to destroy the kind of freedom they're fighting for' as Lewis Eliot tells a Special Branch officer who is inves-

tigating suspected 'communist sympathisers' at the research establishment.[41] But then an accident occurs in the laboratory, exposing Walter
Luke, the chief research physicist working on the bomb, to a lethal
dose of radiation, and news arrives that the Americans have developed
an atomic bomb at Los Alamos. Act Two closes with Sir Hector Rose
(Richard Vernon) telling Lewis Eliot: 'There are times when events get
too big for men.'[42]

Part Three of the play begins with telecine footage of the first atomic
explosion in New Mexico and discussion among the British scientists
about American plans to use the bomb on a Japanese city. They decide
to send a delegation to America to protest against the plan, but to no
avail, and another telecine sequence shows the bombs being dropped
on Japan in 1945. Lewis Eliot's brother, Martin, threatens to send a letter
to *The Times* deploring the dropping of the bombs, but is dissuaded by
his brother. Martin Eliot's final speech underlines the responsibility that
the scientists must bear for the events that have occurred: 'We split the
atom in two and made a bomb – the bomb's gone bang and split the
world in two.'[43]

The New Men is clearly dealing with themes Kennedy Martin would
return to twenty years later with *Edge of Darkness*. Not only does the play
debate the ethics and the dangers of atomic fission, as *Edge of Darkness*
was to do in the mid 1980s when nuclear politics was once more back
on the political agenda, but its dramatic highpoint, the accident in 'the
hot lab' when Luke is exposed to a lethal dose of radiation, anticipates
the dramatic highpoint of *Edge of Darkness* when Craven and Jedburgh
break into the 'hot cell' in the nuclear reprocessing plant, Northmoor,
where they both receive lethal doses of radiation. Both dramas show
a willingness to deal with one of the biggest issues of the twentieth
century and while *Edge of Darkness* was to do this on a grander scale (and
a bigger budget) in the 1980s *The New Men* represents the culmination
of Kennedy Martin's engagement with world issues in the plays written
for television between 1958 and 1966.

From *Incident at Echo Six*, which dealt with the consequences of a
'terrorist' attack in Cyprus, to the development of the atom bomb in
The New Men, via plays such as *The Price of Freedom* (the fate of Eastern
European refugees), *The Interrogator* (the interrogation of 'terrorists'
by a colonial power) and *The Man Without Papers* (the hounding of a
conscientious objector), Troy Kennedy Martin showed a predilection for
subjects that are as relevant today as they were in the 1950s and 1960s.
While these plays were not the only television dramas he worked on
during this period they provided a firm foundation for his subsequent
work, not only the feature films for which these single plays were a

rehearsal but the major drama serials of the 1980s, in which many of the themes first developed in these early plays were to find their fullest expression.

Screenplays (1969–71)

The transition from writing plays for television to writing screenplays for the cinema was a logical one for Troy Kennedy Martin, especially given his advocacy of film over studio drama, and he was not the only television dramatist to gravitate towards the cinema in the late 1960s. Both John McGrath and Roger Smith followed the same trajectory: McGrath with screenplays for *Billion Dollar Brain* (1967), *The Bofur's Gun* (1968), *The Virgin Soldiers* (1969) and *The Reckoning* (1970), and Smith with the screenplay for *Up the Junction* (1967), previously produced as a *Wednesday Play* at the BBC. The film version of *Up the Junction* was the second film to be directed by Peter Collinson, who also directed Kennedy Martin's first screenplay, *The Italian Job* (1969).

Prior to writing *The Italian Job* Kennedy Martin did some rewriting on *Darling* (1965), a 'swinging sixties' film directed by John Schlesinger from an original screenplay by Frederick Raphael. Kennedy Martin thinks what he did was not used, which may be why he was not credited, but *Darling* was an early introduction to the movies, at a time when he was still writing plays for television. When he started work on *The Italian Job*, however, his work for television ceased. After *The New Men*, in 1966, he devoted himself, for the next few years, to writing screenplays, with only occasional work for television. Yet there is an interesting correspondence between his work for television and his screenplays, with some of the themes and characterisation of his television scripts also emerging in the movies he worked on.

The origins of *The Italian Job* reside in a play written for television by Ian Kennedy Martin, which he submitted to the BBC:

> They bought it but they never made it. It was called *Ritual for the Steal*. There were two elements in it, one – which became *The Italian Job* – was a guy who is just coming out of jail. He is still in jail and is contacted by a villain, who is then killed, and so the guy in jail knows that there's a big job out there which is already arranged. He's a wheels man and usually the driver is the last person to be contacted, so he knows that this man has a big job out there. Computerised traffic lights had just come into central London, so I put the MacGuffin, the big robbery, in central London, with green lights all the way out and creating traffic jams. I think the BBC felt that this would be too expensive to do, you know it was

just ludicrously expensive to try and do this in London. So Troy bought these, it was two plays actually, and turned them into *The Italian Job*.[44]

Troy Kennedy Martin took his brother's basic idea and developed it, setting the heist in Turin instead of London. In doing so he made a decision which led to *The Italian Job* becoming one of the great cult movies in cinema history. His other major contribution to the development, and subsequent cult status of the film was to persuade Michael Caine to take the role of Charlie Croker, the brains behind the heist. Kennedy Martin had known Caine since the early 1960s, when he appeared in one of the *Storyboard* plays, *Tickets to Trieste*, and Caine was part of the package Kennedy Martin took to Paramount when he was trying to interest a major Hollywood studio in the project. Paramount's Head of Production, Robert Evans, initially wanted Robert Redford to play the leading character, but was persuaded to offer the part to Michael Caine, who Kennedy Martin always had in mind to play the character when he was writing the script (Field, 2001: 22).

The Italian Job highlights some significant differences, from the writer's point of view, between the television play and the cinema film. Whereas the television dramatist was invariably considered the 'author' of the single play, in film it is the director who is considered the '*auteur*', with the writer generally having a much lower profile. This authorial confusion is highlighted in Steve Chibnall's chapter on *The Italian Job* in *The Cinema of Britain and Ireland*, one of a series of books on national cinemas 'foregrounding the work of the most important directors and their exemplary films' (McFarlane, 2005: iv). In accordance with the remit of the series, Chibnall begins his chapter on *The Italian Job* by referring to it as 'Collinson's film' while suggesting that the film displays many of the conventions of the war film: 'the planning, preparation and execution of the raid conforms precisely to the generic conventions of the "special operation" behind enemy lines depicted in countless films about the Second World War' (Chibnall, 2005: 145). Chibnall then complicates matters, as far as the film's authorship is concerned, by pointing out:

> If there remains any doubt that *The Italian Job* is a war movie in disguise it should be dispelled when we realise that the next film by its writer, Troy Kennedy Martin, was *Kelly's Heroes* (Brian G. Hutton, 1970) in which a disreputable platoon of American soldiers, with a resourceful leader (Clint Eastwood) steels [sic] gold bars from a bank in Nazi-occupied France. Does this plot sound familiar? (Chibnall, 2005: 145)

In terms of theme, structure and character therefore, what Chibnall seems to be suggesting is that *The Italian Job* is actually Troy Kennedy

Martin's film, not Peter Collinson's. Yet, during the course of production, Kennedy Martin's original conception of the film as a political satire about Britain's relationship to Europe – at a time when Britain was applying to be a member of the European Economic Community – was transformed in the hands of Collinson, taking on a lighter tone and a more stylised appearance:

> Kennedy Martin had conceived a very different film: a more realistic underworld story with undertones of social and political criticism, more in sympathy with the contemporary rage on the streets of Paris than the patriotic chanting of the terraces at Wembley ... the allegorical intentions of the film were present from the beginning: but the tone in which they were handled would change considerably in the transition from script to screen. Collinson would play up the satire of English chauvinism already evident in the screenplay, and add a dose of camp excess that was not entirely to the author's taste. As the sexual proclivities of characters like Croker and Professor Peach were exaggerated for humorous effect, Kennedy Martin's critical drama became Collinson's comic book. (Chibnall, 2005: 147)

Chibnall's suggestion that 'Collinson's film ... was not entirely to the author's taste' highlights a contradiction in terms of the ascription of authorship in *The Italian Job*. In his more anecdotal account of the various contributions made by *The Italian Job* production team Matthew Field also, implicitly, problematises the issue of the film's authorship by suggesting, in effect, that it was 'authored' by at least three people: Kennedy Martin, Peter Collinson and producer Michael Deeley. While Collinson took the edge off Kennedy Martin's 'critical drama', Deeley is credited with devising the (literal) cliffhanger ending for the film, after Kennedy Martin's several versions of the end 'were rejected by Paramount's head of production Robert Evans' (Field, 2001: 88).

The fact that Kennedy Martin wrote a number of different endings for *The Italian Job*, none of which were considered satisfactory by Paramount, is interesting with regard to some of his other work, where the writing of a satisfactory ending, or any ending at all, was clearly a problem. Field devotes a chapter in his book to the problem of the ending of the film, even reprinting 'the ending that featured in Kennedy Martin's final shooting script' (Field, 2001: 88–98). Michael Deeley's reflection on the problem of the ending recalls Peter Duguid's story about Kennedy Martin's difficulties with the ending of *The Man Without Papers*: 'It was a real let's-get-out-of-this-jam issue. Here we were making a picture and running out of time. We didn't have an ending. The script just fizzled out. It was an embarrassment, after this great chase' (Field, 2001: 98). Deeley himself came up with the ending – the coach containing the stolen gold bullion suspended precariously on the edge of a cliff – and his ending was approved by Robert Evans, although not by Peter Collinson, with the result that it was handed to Second Unit Director Philip Wrestler to film. Kennedy Martin thought it was a good ending, but made this ironic observation: 'It had to be written by a studio executive because if a writer had written it, they would have just laughed, torn it up and thrown it in the bin' (Field, 2001: 98).

Four decades after the film was made Kennedy Martin attributed the rejection of his ending (or endings) for *The Italian Job* to budgetry constraints and offered some further thoughts on the 'problem' of endings, making a distinction between narrative closure and difficulties which sometimes arise because of the contemporary nature of the plot:

> Regarding endings and *The Italian Job*, there was nothing wrong with the endings I submitted – I suspect their real problem was that the film was vastly over budget and Bob Evans wanted an ending which could be filmed on the spot, as it were, shortly after the abandonment of the Minis on the mountain. Filming my ending would have meant taking the entire unit to Geneva with additional expense etc. The ending suggested by Evans and Deeley, the producer was, essentially, a cost-cutting exercise.
>
> The problem I've occasionally had in finding the last third of a script, occurs when it has a very contemporary plot and the outcome of events is not yet resolved in real life. For instance, a screenplay called *The Warming* [see Chapter six] about global warming that was begun at some point in the late eighties, did not come to a satisfactory conclusion because the end game wasn't apparent until 2005. Similar concerns made me hesitate about the closure of the Black Panthers movie [see below] where the pressures for a commercial end vied with political considerations, which weighed more with me. It's possible that sometimes the ideas you have are ahead of their time. At other times, they slip and fall behind. Getting it right is as much a matter of luck as judgment.
>
> This sort of challenge should not be confused with the actual closure of scripts, where I never had a problem in producing a series of outcomes, any of which would do. With *The Italian Job*, had the budget been kept to, then the original ending (which is built into the script and which can be evidenced in parts of the film) would have allowed the move to Geneva and the ending as written. However, there is no doubt that the ending which was used has been a great success. Much of that had to do with the brilliant way it was done.[45]

Kennedy Martin also provides an interesting observation on what he describes as the 'change of temperature' in some of his work, when the lighter mood he has created suddenly changes to take on a much darker hue. He describes how he intended this to happen in *The Italian Job*, only to see it undermined by Peter Collinson's determination to turn his political satire into a 'comic book':

> There is, in some of my work at least, a moment where there's a change of temperature. In *The Italian Job*, which was quite jokey in the scripts – the problem is that it looks far too pretty and juvenile the way Peter did it – there comes a point where they attack the actual bullion convoy in Milan or Turin and it's really a very brutal attack and he could never come to terms with that. What I was doing was saying right well that was the first half of the thing and we laughed at them and we thought these cheerful cockney chappies, like the people who did the Great Train Robbery, all artful dodgers, but now this is reality, the reality is that there's blood on the pavements and then it went on to the second half … they found great difficulty in taking that on board and they did their absolute best to choreograph the fight and stylise the violence.[46]

Something similar happened with Kennedy Martin's next screenplay, for *Kelly's Heroes* (USA/Yugoslavia, 1970), a war movie for Metro-Goldwyn-Mayer starring Clint Eastwood and Telly Savalas. As Steve Chibnall points out, *Kelly's Heroes* reworks the plot of *The Italian Job* by having a ramshackle group of American soldiers, led by a rebellious mastermind, venture into enemy territory to steal a consignment of gold bullion from a foreign bank. If *The Italian Job* is, as Chibnall suggests, 'really a war film', then *Kelly's Heroes* is really a heist movie, in which Kelly's renegade 'heroes' are the bank robbers while the guards defending the gold bullion are the German army.

Although *Kelly's Heroes* reworks the plot of *The Italian Job* its origins can be traced right back to Kennedy Martin's 1950s war novel, *Beat on a Damask Drum*, which had a renegade group of soldiers venturing behind enemy lines to retrieve priceless works of art. But the psychological realism of *Beat on a Damask Drum* is given a Hollywood makeover in *Kelly's Heroes*, with Hollywood stars and plenty of humour for light relief. Some of the realism remains, but Kennedy Martin once again wanted the film to be 'darker' than it turned out to be:

> Half way through *Kelly's Heroes*, which again was a sort of Hawksian thing with lots of cheerful chatter and macho guys, they're caught in a minefield behind enemy lines … One of the guys gets blown up, which is bloody enough. There's a bull in the field and they know he won't tread on a mine so they have to follow the way he goes and they're all townsfolk, except for one, and they're all terrified of the bull, and then coming towards them is this convoy of Germans. They've heard the explosion and they've come up from the local home guard post and they're all trundling down on these German trucks. Clint Eastwood and the others have got behind a stone wall and in the original script the Germans who are coming towards them are all the kind of people that they threw into

the home guard, they were all over sixty years old and there were a couple of kids. By the time they get to where the minefield is there's only two of them left in the field, beside the dead man, and they shout out in German 'Can we help?' and they are cut down, there's a sort of blood craze. When it's over everybody involved wants to give up the operation and go back, they're absolutely shattered, completely demoralised, their own friends have died in this field as a result of all this mayhem, they've got all these dead old Germans. So of course that was all changed, they had to be modern Nazis and they all had to have great machine guns. Eastwood's leadership only takes place after the demoralisation takes place, that's when he actually takes over, and we see how ruthless he is and the real steel that's behind him. There also was a little bit of alienation to say to the audience, don't get too sucked in to this.[47]

With *Beat on a Damask Drum* there was no commercial pressure to cause Kennedy Martin to alter his downbeat, realist war story, but with *The Italian Job* and *Kelly's Heroes* he found himself having to compromise on his original intentions. Where *The Italian Job* had been conceived as a political satire about the Common Market, *Kelly's Heroes* was conceived as 'a sort of anti-Vietnam movie':

> Way in the background there were all these ideas, and if people wanted to use ideas, to actually hang performances on or give some focus to the direction, but in the hands of Peter Collinson and Mike Deeley they were only interested in the top level, they weren't interested in going any deeper. The same thing with *Kelly's Heroes*. The thing is I'm quite a good action writer and also I use humour a lot and then people think 'Oh God, this is just about gags', but *Kelly's Heroes* was again a tougher thing which was softened and *The Italian Job* was a harder piece than Collinson made it.[48]

What seems clear is that because of the greater commercial pressure, and perhaps also because of the egos of the people involved in movie production, the writer has far less control over the finished product than he or she had with the television play in the 1960s and 1970s. Whatever the original intentions of the screenwriter, his or her 'vision' for a movie is often eroded during the process of rewriting for production, altered, revised and amended as the other principal members of the production team make their individual contributions and help to reshape the original material. If Kennedy Martin felt his original idea for *The Italian Job* was 'softened' by Peter Collinson, he also felt the same way about *Kelly's Heroes*:

> I was really disappointed with what they did. It's very interesting that Clint Eastwood says in his biography that he really liked the script, the first script, when he got it and then he committed to it and when he

saw the rewrites he determined never to work for another production company again which wasn't his own and after *Kelly's Heroes* he founded Malpaso.[49]

Kelly's Heroes does at least contain much of Kennedy Martin's trademark humour, even if it was not realised as the 'anti-Vietnam movie' he originally envisaged, but his next screenplay did not really lend itself to a humorous treatment. *The Jerusalem File* (USA/Israel, 1971), was a thriller set in Israel (where it was also filmed) in the aftermath of the Six Day War. Produced by Metro-Goldwyn-Mayer *The Jerusalem File* seems like quite an intriguing production for a Hollywood studio. Featuring three British actors in leading roles: Donald Pleasance, Nicol Williamson and Ian Hendry, with Raoul Coutard, the leading French New Wave cinematographer, responsible for the photography, Kennedy Martin's screenplay was an attempt to explore another contemporary issue: the Arab–Israeli conflict.

Unlike *The Italian Job* and *Kelly's Heroes*, this was no allegory but a contemporary thriller about an attempted rapprochement between Israelis and Palestinians when a group of Jewish students persuade a young American with an Arab contact to act as a mediator by arranging a meeting between the two groups. Unfortunately there is a lack of clarity in the exposition which leads to some confusion about what is going on for much of the film and uncertainty about who is responsible for the attacks and killings that occur. Even at the climax, when the young Israelis turn up for a meeting with the Palestinians in the desert, only to be gunned down, it is not entirely clear who is responsible, although it is implied that another, hard-line, Palestinian group may have been responsible for the killings. This narrative confusion may be partly to do with the inexperience of the American director, John Flynn, who was directing only his second film, together with the fact that he was in charge of a very cosmopolitan production team, with an Israeli producer, a British screenwriter, a French camera team, an English sound crew, Israeli technicians and English, American and Israeli actors, filming in Israel in the wake of a war when tensions were still running high.

It was also an audacious project, to address the possibilities of a rapprochement between the two sides so soon after the Six Day War, and one which MGM may have been uncomfortable with. Reviews of the film were almost universally negative, with the following example being fairly representative of the response most reviewers had to the film, although Christopher Hudson in his *Spectator* review did at least acknowledge that this was an attempt to make a political film in Hollywood:

> Political films have as a rule to be fiercely partisan if they are to be
> successful. *Z* and *The Battle of Algiers* are examples of a semi-documen-
> tary approach in which the story is there to colour the political message
> rather than to gloss or dilute it. *The Jerusalem File*, about an attempt at
> Arab–Israeli conciliation after the six-day war, is a failure on two counts.
> It is politically indeterminate, in that we are not allowed to identify with
> one or other of the contesting groups; and, as a costly, large-scale produc-
> tion, it cannot manage to observe events without seeming artificially to
> recreate them.
>
> This would not matter if John Flynn, the director, had been content to
> turn *The Jerusalem File* into a straightforward political thriller. But as an
> admirer, apparently, of Costa-Gavras he has decided to film as efficiently
> as the rather feeble script will allow, and leave us to draw our own conclu-
> sions. This approach may pay dividends when there is a clear distinction
> between Us and Them: but here it has the effect of leaving us one step
> behind whatever is going on, so that much of the heavily significant
> dialogue and action appears merely cryptic. (Hudson, 1972)

The problems with *The Jerusalem File* illustrate the difficulty of trying to
make a contemporary political film in the form of a Hollywood thriller.
The combination of politics and entertainment is a difficult mix for
Hollywood, and political comment is sometimes more easily achieved
through allegory than through a direct engagement with contemporary
events. In this respect *The Jerusalem File* was an interesting failure.

Kennedy Martin wrote three more screenplays in the early 1970s:
One More Time (while under contract to MGM), *Johnstone in Exile* and
Crazy Joe. None were produced. According to Kennedy Martin they were
all about the Black Panthers, suggesting he was still trying to engage
with contemporary political issues within the mainstream of popular
Hollywood cinema:

> They nearly got produced but for every script that gets produced there's
> a hundred that don't. Really they couldn't find black actors that were
> bankable. There was Harry Belafonte but that fell out because politically
> he hated the Panthers. The modifications he wanted to the scripts were
> too much. It was a very dangerous area. Again it was done through a
> popular genre.[50]

Eventually Kennedy Martin cut his losses and returned to England,
resuming writing for television with episodes for popular series, rather
than single plays, and a screenplay for the second *Sweeney* feature film.
The time he devoted to screenwriting in the late 1960s and early 1970s
certainly established him in Hollywood, but his attempts to deal with
contemporary political issues within popular cinema were of limited
success. Ultimately the experience was a chastening one and Kennedy
Martin did not work in Hollywood again until the late 1980s:

You find out that the more popular the corridor down which you're going, or the avenue, then the more it is controlled ... All writers get fucked over really. It's just the whole business of making a film, the amount of money involved and the entrepreneurial people who get involved on the business side of it, the desperate need to maintain authority which the director's have. It's a very tough business, it takes a long time to learn how to relax in it.[51]

A footnote to this period of screenwriting is that Kennedy Martin also worked on a screenplay for a Yugoslavian film called *67 Days: The Republic of Uzhitze* (*Uzicka republika*) (Yugoslavia, 1974), directed by Zivorad 'Zika' Mitrovic, about the Yugoslav Resistance during the Second World War, when the Partisans held out against the invading German army for sixty-seven days. Kennedy Martin received no screen credit for his contribution to this all-Serbian production: 'I wasn't that interested in the credits since the whole thing seemed quite mad at the time. I spent less than a month on the draft and no doubt Mitrovic took it on from there.'[52] How Kennedy Martin got involved with *67 Days* is unclear, although *Kelly's Heroes* had been filmed in Yugoslavia and it may be that Mitrovic was hoping Kennedy Martin could do for the Partisans what he had previously done for Kelly's renegade heroes![53]

Notes

1 British Film Institute Library, London (hereafter BFI), Troy Kennedy Martin Special Collection (hereafter TKM Collection), Item 15, BBC Press Release, 'The Story of a National Serviceman in Cyprus Today', undated.

2 See Robert Stephens, *Cyprus: A Place of Arms* (London: Pall Mall Press, 1966)

3 Troy Kennedy Martin, interviewed by the author, 25 September 1998.

4 BFI, TKM Collection, Item 15, *Incident at Echo Six*, Camera Script, p. 12.

5 BFI, TKM Collection, Item 15, BBC Press Release, 'The Story of a National Serviceman in Cyprus Today', undated.

6 Troy Kennedy Martin, interviewed by the author, 25 September 1998.

7 BFI, TKM Collection, Item 15, *Incident at Echo Six*, Camera Script, p. 82.

8 Troy Kennedy Martin, interviewed by the author, 4 April 2003.

9 Making a second payment (of 275 guineas) to Kennedy Martin for *Incident at Echo Six*, Robin Wade, Script Organiser at the BBC, wrote in a memo dated 17 October 1958: 'It is in order to telerecord and repeats will be at two thirds of the initial sum if given within 15 months of the date of the first performance' (BBC Written Archives Centre, T48/351/1). If *Incident at Echo Six* was telerecorded no copy of it has been preserved and it was never repeated.

10 For a discussion about 'serious' television drama see Caughie (2000: 3–7)

11 Troy Kennedy Martin, interviewed by the author, 4 April 2003.

12 Ibid.

13 BBC Written Archives Centre (hereafter BBC WAC), Audience Research Report, *The Traitor*, 27 August 1959.

14 Troy Kennedy Martin, interviewed by the author, 4 April 2003.

15 BFI, TKM Collection, Item 32, *Element of Doubt*, Camera Script, p. 1.

16 See Cooke (2003: 16) on the use of voiceover in *Nineteen Eighty-Four*.

17 There are seventeen scenes in the play, an average of nearly two minutes per scene, and a total of 189 shots, giving an average shot length of 9.5 seconds.

18 *Radio Times*, 'Tonight's Thriller', 13 April 1961, p. 23.

19 BFI, TKM Collection, Item 3, *The Interrogator*.

20 BBC WAC, Audience Research Report, *The Interrogator*, 15 January 1962.

21 Ibid.

22 BBC WAC, T48/351/1, *Inner Circle*. An anonymous note, probably sent by Script Organiser Robin Wade to an unidentified recipient, dated 26 January 1960, refers to Kennedy Martin wanting to know 'if it's worth doing his revisions to the script.' A handwritten reply on the note reads 'Not at the moment. The series will not be scheduled before July.'

23 BFI, TKM Collection, Item 7, *The Little Goat*, memo from Donald Wilson to Vincent Tilsley, 11 August 1959.

24 It is not clear whether Tilsley was aware in August 1959 of the subject matter of Kennedy Martin's second original play, which would eventually become *The Interrogator*, or indeed whether Kennedy Martin had yet developed *The Interrogator* along these lines, but given that *The Interrogator* and *The Little Goat* were both in development from 1959–61 it seems quite possible that the theme of interrogation in *The Little Goat* influenced the development of *The Interrogator*. It is not until 24 January 1961 that *The Interrogator* is first mentioned in BBC correspondence and on 15 February 1961 Script Organiser Robin Wade informed the Assistant Head of Copyright at the BBC that *The Interrogator* was to be the new title for a play called *Three Women*, which had been commissioned at the end of December 1958, shortly after the transmission of *Incident at Echo Six*. It seems curious however that *The Interrogator* would originally have been named *Three Women* as there is only one central female character in *The Interrogator*, suggesting that if it did evolve from *Three Women* the script must have undergone a considerable transformation between December 1958 and December 1961, when *The Interrogator* was transmitted.

25 BFI, TKM Collection, Item 7, *The Little Goat*, memo to Vincent Tilsley, 4 September 1959.

26 BFI, TKM Collection, Item 7, *The Little Goat*, memo from Duncan Ross to Donald Wilson, 17 January 1961.

27 BFI, TKM Collection, Item 7, *The Little Goat*.

28 BBC WAC, T48/351/1, memos from Robin Wade to Head of Copyright, 4 September 1961 and 13 November 1961. *The Triangle* is mentioned once more in BBC correspondence when a note dated 12 August 1965 refers to it being written off Roger Smith's list, which suggests that it was being considered as a *Wednesday Play* more than five years after it was originally commissioned. I am grateful to Troy Kennedy Martin for providing me with a copy of the script.

29 BBC WAC, T48/351/1, memo from Robin Wade to Head of Copyright, 4 September 1961.

30 BBC WAC, T48/540/2, correspondence in the file on Muriel Spark.

31 BBC WAC, T5/2, 081/1, '*First Night* – General', memo dated 14 April 1964.

32 BFI, TKM Collection, Item 13, *The Man Without Papers*, typescript, p. 21.

33 BBC WAC, *The Man Without Papers*, Camera Script, pp. 128–9.

34 Peter Duguid, interviewed by the author, 28 November 2003.

35 The BBC Film Library has one 16mm reel containing the first 47 minutes of *The Man Without Papers* – unfortunately the ending is missing! I'm grateful to Christine Slattery at the BBC for letting me know of its existence and to Veronica Taylor for arranging a private viewing at the National Film Theatre, attended by

Peter Duguid and Troy Kennedy Martin, in May 2004.
36 BBC WAC, Audience Research Report, *The Man Without Papers*, 9 July 1965.
37 Ibid.
38 BBC WAC, T5/1, 787/1, Audience Research Report, *The Pistol*, 9 July 1965.
39 Troy Kennedy Martin, interviewed by the author, 27 March 1986.
40 In the late 1970s Troy Kennedy Martin wrote an article about TV censorship in which he discussed the banning of *The War Game* (see Kennedy Martin, 1979).
41 BFI, TKM Collection, Item 30, typescript of *The New Men*, p. 29.
42 Ibid, p. 44.
43 Ibid, p. 61.
44 Ian Kennedy Martin, interviewed by the author, 19 March 2004.
45 Troy Kennedy Martin, email to the author, 21 November 2005.
46 Troy Kennedy Martin, interviewed by the author, 27 March 1986.
47 Ibid.
48 Ibid.
49 Ibid.
50 Ibid.
51 Ibid.
52 Troy Kennedy Martin, email to the author, 21 September 2005.
53 *67 Days: The Republic of Uzhitze* (*Uzicka republika*) was released in America in a shorter version (it was originally 170 minutes long) under the title *Guns of War*. See the Internet Movie Database for more on the film: www.imdb.com/title/tt0067920 (accessed 21 September 2005).

Experiments in television drama 3

> Television drama at the moment is going nowhere fast. Informed management believe it is so bad it can't get worse. They are wrong. It can and will destroy itself unless a breakthrough in form is made, substantiated and phased into the general run of drama programmes. Not an art set-up like the Langham group to be propitiated on the altar of prestige, but a working philosophy which contains a new idea of form, with new language, new punctuation and new style. Something which can be applied to mass audience viewing. Something which can re-create the direction, the fire, and the ideas which TV used to have. Something which can provide, for the first time, an area of theory, experiment and development which TV drama has never had and which it needs so badly. (Kennedy Martin, 1964: 21)

Troy Kennedy Martin's famous polemic, 'Nats Go Home', subtitled 'First Statement of a New Drama for Television', was published in the theatre magazine *Encore* in March 1964. Its opening paragraph set the tone for an article which was to stir up a hornet's nest in television drama circles at the time and which has become one of the most cited articles in the history of television studies. In his book *Television Drama: Realism, Modernism and British Culture*, John Caughie devotes ten pages to it, noting how 'the underlying insistence of the article is not simply that television drama needs this or that practice, but that television drama needs a greater degree of theoretical elaboration and that this requires a greater degree of theoretical debate' (Caughie, 2000: 93). 'Nats Go Home' was the product of debates which had been going on in the Drama Department at the BBC for some time, involving the new generation of scriptwriter/adapters recruited in 1959–61. Kennedy Martin remembers an atmosphere of creativity in the department, despite some differences in outlook between the old guard and the new 'young Turks':

> Donald Wilson was the Head of the Script Department at the time and he ran this little department with about eighteen or twenty writers in it

... It was wonderful and he was a very avuncular man ... he was always like a headmaster ... He'd been in the army during the war – he'd been a Captain or a Major or something – and then he eventually went off and did *The Forsyte Saga* ... we were young Turks and he did give us our heads, but they didn't really understand where we were coming from ... "[1]

The fact that Wilson eventually went off to produce *The Forsyte Saga*, an ambition he had long cherished, while his protégées went on to produce more radical and innovative work, such as *Z Cars*, *Diary of a Young Man* and *The Wednesday Play*, underlines the difference between the older and younger generations as the BBC embarked on a new era, for it was Kennedy Martin and other young writers such as Tom Clarke, John Hopkins, John McGrath and Roger Smith – soon to be joined by a host of creative talent including Tony Garnett, Ken Loach, James MacTaggart, Dennis Potter and Ken Trodd – who were to forge the new drama at the BBC in the 1960s.

However, they were not the first group of people at the BBC to show an interest in experimenting with the form of television drama. In 1956, well before the 'young Turks' arrived at the BBC, a proposal had been made to set up a group to 'chew over the problem of experimental Television programmes'[2] and in December 1958, the same month in which Kennedy Martin was taken onto the staff at the BBC, a 'Drama Experimental Unit' was formed. This unit subsequently became known as the Langham Group, as a result of it being based at the BBC's Langham House, and it was this group that Kennedy Martin referred to as an 'art set-up' in his 'Nats Go Home' article six years later. The remit of the Langham Group was to consider the potential for experimentation in television and in its short existence (the group disbanded in 1960) it was responsible for three productions: *The Torrents of Spring* (BBC, 21 May 1959), *Mario* (BBC, 15 December 1959) and *On the Edge* (BBC, 16 July 1960). In a letter to BBC Head of Drama Michael Barry in 1960, Anthony Pelissier, a leading member of the group, summarised what he felt they had achieved:

> The Langham Group's real contribution has been, it seems to me, *to question* ... the validity of present-day story and drama construction, the soundness of old-fashioned theatrical design, Acting as 'projected' for proscenium presentation, cutting for cutting's sake ... the possibility that there are [sic] more than one level of consciousness at which a programme may be appreciated and found stimulating and, finally, the intellectual 'West End' attitude of mind – a parochial and 'conditioned' point of view ...[3]

What the Langham Group was 'questioning' was the 'theatrical' tradition in BBC drama whereby plays would be staged for television with little regard for their televisual possibilities. Yet their choice of plays – stories by Turgenev and Thomas Mann and a wartime 'adventure story' – did not suggest a radical departure in television drama but an attempt to modernise traditional storytelling, hence Kennedy Martin's criticism of the group as 'an art set-up ... propitiated on the altar of prestige.' Moreover, Pelissier's assessment of the group's 'contribution' suggests a limitation in its ambitions: the 'questioning' of certain tenets in television drama production rather than a radical departure from them.

The radio and sound pioneer Charles Parker, responsible for a number of impressionistic *Radio Ballads* in the 1950s and 1960s, was one of those attracted by the experimental ambitions of the Langham Group, but according to his BBC colleague Philip Donnellan the experimental work of the group turned out to be a creative dead end:

> Charles and I were told we really ought to be going into television and asked what we wanted to do. Charles wanted to go into drama but with a very purist attitude to television style that I had no interest in at all. In 1958 he joined the Langham Group (Michael Barry's experimental drama group) and he did a production of *Torrents of Spring* on one camera in one continuous take. But that led him into a blind alley and he never got any further. (Gilbert, 1983: 10)[4]

The achievements of the Langham Group may have been limited but the work of the group did have some influence and it may have been a spur to the experimental ambitions of the 'young Turks' in the BBC Drama Department. One person said to have been influenced by the work of the group was James MacTaggart, a producer/director working at BBC Scotland whose production of Jack Gerson's *Three Ring Circus* (BBC, 2 February 1961) was cited by John McGrath as the forerunner of the experimental work with which he and Kennedy Martin were involved in the early 1960s:

> The *ur*-drama from that whole line was *Three Ring Circus*, which was done in Glasgow and directed by Jimmy MacTaggart, and it was on the basis of *Three Ring Circus* that Jimmy was brought down to London to direct, and one of the first things that happened was, of course, that we all nobbled Jimmy because he was trying to do something, and Troy worked with Jimmy very closely on that ... what were they called ... *Storyboards* ... You see what Troy brought to it which the Langham Group didn't have, Troy was very good at attracting a mass audience. His storylines were commercial in today's parlance.[5]

MacTaggart, who was a few years older than the 'young Turks', was to become the catalyst around whom they all gathered, producing most of the innovative drama that came out of the BBC in the next few years, including the first season of *The Wednesday Play*. One of the first productions he worked on after arriving at BBC Television Centre was *Story-board* (BBC, July–September 1961), a series of six experimental plays written and adapted by Troy Kennedy Martin.

Several months before *Storyboard* however, and before MacTaggart's arrival, Kennedy Martin had already demonstrated an interest in experimenting with the form of television drama in a short script written as an exercise for a BBC training course. The course was one which all new staff in the Drama Department were required to complete and it was designed to teach the basics of television production, culminating with a 'Practical Production Exercise' where the participant was required to produce/direct a short play in the studio.[6] For his exercise Kennedy Martin produced a short drama, from his own script, called *Mac*. The title refers to a character who does not appear in the drama but whose escape from a mental hospital motivates the action, posing a real or imagined threat to Mary, the central character, played by Tamara Hinchco in the telerecorded production.[7] The half-hour drama is set in the small flat where Mary lives with her husband, Bill (Ronald Wilson), and their baby, Caroline. Bill does not appear until towards the end and the baby is asleep in a pram so Mary is the main focus of attention for most of the drama. Nearly all of the action takes place in the living room, with four short scenes in which Mary goes into the kitchen or out into the hallway. This suggests a conventional one-room studio drama but the play is actually about Mary's growing paranoia on learning, from a telegram sent by Bill, that Mac, an old friend of Bill's and ex-boyfriend of Mary's, has escaped from a mental hospital: 'Mac escaped. Secure windows and doors don't answer phone, do nothing till I get back. Do as I say, darling. Love – Bill.'[8]

What makes the drama unusual is the extent to which it is about what is going on in Mary's head as she reacts to the news in the telegram. With only one person on set for nearly all of the drama most of the 'action' is concerned with Mary's growing unease, which is conveyed through an interior monologue. This necessitated the use of extensive pre-recorded voiceovers as Mary worries over the implications of the news about Mac's escape: hearing an echo of his voice threatening to kill her, remembering (or imagining) a conversation with the psychiatrist who admitted Mac to hospital, and overhearing a conversation between two women walking in the corridor outside her flat. Mary becomes increasingly agitated as she imagines Mac returning to carry out his threat, and she ignores the ringing telephone in case it is him. To emphasise her growing anxiety the script, at one point, gives the instruction for the sound of a heartbeat which 'begins in the distance and gradually increases in volume. Mary stands transfixed in the centre of the room.'[9] The amplified heartbeat accompanies her subjective monologue, heightening as she hears the sound of the lift in the corridor outside the flat until: 'The lift clangs open and the two women come out still talking about "My Fair Lady". She sits down, half dressed, defeated. All the noises recede to nothing.'[10] Finally, resigning herself to the situation and the possibility of Mac returning, she takes the baby out of the pram and locks her in a cupboard. When the sound of the lift announces someone's arrival it is Bill, not Mac, who emerges. Shortly after his return a telephone call brings the news that Mac has been killed, knocked down by a butcher's van while under the influence of drugs. Noticing the absence of the baby, Bill is then horrified to discover Mary has locked her in the cupboard.

In his 'Nats Go Home' polemic, written more than three years after *Mac*, Kennedy Martin launched a stinging attack on naturalism in television drama, arguing that:

> Since naturalism evolved from a theatre of dialogue, the director is forced into photographing faces talking and faces reacting. The director faced with a torrent of words can only retreat into the neutrality of the two- and three-shot where the camera, caged from seizing on anything of significance, is emasculated and only allowed to gaze around the room following the conversation like an attentive stranger. This enslavement of the visual element is too binding. (1964: 25)

In *Mac* Kennedy Martin was already experimenting with ways to subvert naturalism and avoid the 'enslavement of the visual element'. His solution was to use narration, exploring the inner anxiety of the central character through the extensive use of voiceovers (there are twenty-nine cues for voiceovers in the thirteen-page script and eighty per cent of the dialogue is communicated through voiceovers). It was the first step towards the development of a new non-naturalistic drama.

Storyboard (1961)

The next step took the form of a six-part series of half-hour plays, transmitted under the title of *Storyboard* (BBC, July–September 1961). Elwyn Jones, a key figure in the Drama Department at the BBC in the early 1960s, introduced the series in a short article in the *Radio Times*:

> To tell a story in visual terms: that, and simply that, is the aim of *Storyboard*; to take the work of accomplished writers and translate it to the screen. The six stories chosen all have a strong narrative thread. They have character and atmosphere certainly, but they are not mere mood pieces. All of them have plots, a firm story-line, sometimes hard and direct, sometimes twisting and turning, but always distinct, always in evidence.

The range, in time and place, is wide, from the nineteenth-century America of tonight's *The Gentleman From Paris* to the present-day capitals touched on in *A Trip To Trieste*, which will be the fourth programme. And the range of action will be wide too: from the matrimonial machinations of Bernard Malamud's *The Magic Barrel* to the gangster threatenings of Raymond Chandler's *I'll Be Waiting*.

Two young writers are responsible for the television versions – Troy Kennedy Martin and Michael Imison working in close collaboration with an equally young producer, James MacTaggart. Their enthusiasm and precise technical skills combined with stories which have already passed the scrutiny of editors and readers should make for exciting viewing. (Jones, 1961: 51)

The six *Storyboard* plays were transmitted live and while Elwyn Jones may have seen the scripts he may not have been fully aware of the extent to which Kennedy Martin, Michael Imison, Roger Smith, designer Richard Wilmot and producer James MacTaggart were planning to break the conventions of naturalism in the series. Even the running order was to change because *A Trip To Trieste* was not shown as the 'fourth programme' in the series but the sixth, under the title of *Tickets to Trieste*.

In his 1986 MacTaggart Lecture (named in honour of James MacTaggart, who died in 1974, and delivered annually at the Edinburgh Television Festival) Kennedy Martin described the 'mission' to 'destroy naturalism' that he and the other young writers in the BBC Script Department were on in the early 1960s. He likened the situation in the Drama Department when they arrived to a 'Garden of Eden' in which the old guard 'had an indefinable confidence, some might call it complacency' (Kennedy Martin, 1986: 9). While Elwyn Jones was ten years older than most of the new recruits Kennedy Martin clearly did not see him as part of the old guard:

There was, of course, a Lucifer in this Garden of Eden, whose name was Elwyn Jones. Elwyn, a Welsh intriguer, ran the Documentary Drama Unit from what looked like a phone booth on the fifth floor of the new Television Centre. From the beginning, in his sardonic way, he had provided the only alternative to the broad theatrical synthesis which prevailed at the time. He had, for instance, commissioned *Z Cars* and was gathering a nucleus of young writers about him whose only thought was to wreck the proscenium-arch theatre, which was the basis of their elders' world ... When I suggested to Elwyn that we produce a series of stories aimed specifically at breaching the naturalist monopoly, he jumped at it. He called Jimmy McTaggart [sic] in Glasgow and asked if he would come to London to produce it. (Kennedy Martin, 1986: 9)

It is a sign of the creative ferment within the BBC Drama Department at the time that Kennedy Martin was working on both *Storyboard* and *Z Cars* in 1961 (and possibly several other projects as well including *The Interrogator*, *The Triangle*, *The Mercenaries* and an early draft of the *Diary of a Young Man* scripts) and that Elwyn Jones, while responsible for the Documentary Drama Unit, was a catalyst for some of the non-naturalistic experiments that Kennedy Martin and others were pursuing. Roger Smith was keen to stress how important Elwyn Jones was in encouraging young writers like himself: 'He was hugely influential. He brought me in, got me the job and said lad go and do it. I have a lot of time for him, he's very much a kind of unsung ... I know there are lots of unsung heroes at that time, but he really was and they were from an older documentary tradition, people like Robert Barr, etc.'[11]

The first of the six *Storyboard* plays was *The Gentleman From Paris* (BBC, 28 July 1961), adapted from a story by John Dickson Carr about the search for the will of a rich woman who lies dying in one of the rooms of an old house in New York in 1849. Played out in eighteen scenes on two studio sets the play received a very mixed response from the BBC Viewing Panel with some finding it 'slow and dull' while others found it 'unusual, mysterious ("the ingenious hiding of the will, and the deductions leading to its finding were masterly"), gripping right up to the unexpected denouement, and well written ... '.[12] Its share of the television audience was small, but then it was up against ITV's *No Hiding Place*, one of the most popular series on television at the time. Without being able to see the original production it is difficult to know how 'experimental' *The Gentleman From Paris* was.[13] However, Kennedy Martin's description of the second play, *The Magic Barrel* (BBC, 4 August 1961), does give some indication of the way in which they were exploring new ideas with the series:

> Because we had neither the facility to post-record music, nor the money to commission it even if we had, we scored large chunks of the scripts directly to sound, which is, of course, the opposite of what usually happens. I remember scripting the whole of a Bernard Malamud story, 'The Magic Barrel', to the guitar music of *Fantasy for a Gentleman*. And how pleased we were when the bride-to-be slowly walked across the studio towards her lover, with the music sweeping around her, its modalities altering with every hesitation in her eyes. It was so on target that we might have been excused for thinking that Rodrigo himself had been commissioned to score it. Of course, it could be argued that in our looney way we were trying to anticipate film, trying to insert into our Heath Robinson pre-production process the kind of items which would have been at the tips of our fingers in any facility-house today. This is true, but we were also trying to work out specific ways of dealing with

and exploiting the limitations of the medium. (Kennedy Martin, 1986: 9–10)

The Magic Barrel was taken from a collection of stories by the American writer Bernard Malamud which won the National Book Award in 1959. It told the story of a young man, studying to become a Rabbi, who thinks he will command a better congregation if he has a wife, so he applies to a marriage broker to help him find one. Like all the *Storyboard* plays, the challenge in trying to be innovative and break away from the naturalistic form of 'proscenium-arch theatre' in productions like *The Magic Barrel* was that they were trying to achieve effects which might have been achievable with film, where shots are edited together and music dubbed in post-production, but which were far more difficult to achieve live in a television studio:

> *Storyboard* was really going to be experimental insofar as we'd try and do without these proscenium arch sets ... it was a move towards making movies with live television really, using more expressionist sets and shadows and being more spare and I guess trying to arrange cuts that would be edits in a movie but which were more difficult to arrange in terms of TV.[14]

The ambition of the series was most clearly evident in the third play, an original script by Kennedy Martin called *The Middle Men* (BBC, 11 August 1961). The story was unusually complex for a half-hour drama, involving wheeling and dealing on the stock market and the possibility for the 'middlemen' to exploit a shortage of steel in world markets: 'A sudden demand for steel ... the amount is huge, a fortune is involved. From all over the world come the middlemen – some sincere, some scheming, some scurrilous' (*Radio Times*, 3 August 1961: 53). Not only was the subject matter unusual, it was matched by a complexity in the structure of the drama. Fifteen actors play twenty-one different characters in a drama which cuts swiftly from one international location to another: Tokyo, New York, Milan, Barcelona and London, with scene changes often motivated by telephone calls between the 'middlemen'. As in *Mac*, where Kennedy Martin made extensive use of voiceovers in an attempt to escape from the straitjacket of naturalism, *The Middle Men* used telephone conversations for a similar purpose.

In order to realise the fast pace of the narrative six cameras were used and the camera script indicates a total of 130 scenes in the thirty-minute drama. With a total of 156 shots many of these 'scenes' clearly comprised only one shot, often of an actor speaking on the telephone, before cutting to a different location and a different scene. At 156 shots *The Middle Men* had an average shot length of about eleven seconds, but as the drama reaches its climax the cutting between cameras accelerates, culminating with a montage sequence that was extremely audacious for live studio drama. The last seven pages of the camera script lists thirty-eight shots and with each page of the sixty-page script representing about thirty seconds of screen time this suggests an average shot length of about five seconds for this three minute montage sequence.

Not only was *The Middle Men* innovative in the speed of its cutting but the montage sequence is almost wordless as the drama cuts between five different locations, with big close-up (BCU) shots of a clock to chart the passing minutes, as a 3.00 am deadline approaches. During this sequence time is compressed, another objective of the new drama on which Kennedy Martin expounded in 'Nats Go Home'. In shot 123 the direction on the camera script is for a character to look at an alarm clock, showing the time of seven minutes to three. Two shots later there is a BCU of a clock to establish the time. During the course of the montage sequence that follows there are several BCUs of the clock to indicate the passing time until shot 143 when a close-up indicates the time of one minute to three, followed by the clock chiming three o'clock in shot 145. In other words seven minutes of story time are compressed into about ninety seconds of screen time through the use of elliptical editing:

> [T]ime on television can be manipulated with the ease and freedom that it attains in a poem or novel. With a *new* punctuation, Time can go back, forward, jump or be distorted in a manner as acceptable to viewers as it is, through sentences and paragraphs, acceptable to a reader.
>
> There is a lot of work to be done on the development of the new grammar. There is also a lot of opposition to be overcome, for this idea of Time and Structure demands editing and the recording of production down to the minutest detail. (Kennedy Martin, 1964: 28–9)

The montage sequence in *The Middle Men* may have been one of the first attempts to incorporate a form of Eisensteinian montage into television drama – Kennedy Martin also acknowledged the influence of Eisenstein's montage theories in 'Nats Go Home' – but to attempt to achieve this in a live studio drama illustrates the aesthetic ambition of the production. Whether the sequence was actually realised on the day of transmission is a matter for conjecture. It is possible that during the course of the live broadcast the camera operators and vision mixer may not have been able to achieve all of these rapid shot transitions. A note on page twenty-eight of the camera script anticipated a similar problem in a scene in which a telephone conversation between two characters was apparently intended to be shown by means of superimposition, with each character being framed separately using two cameras with the images superimposed, the characters being positioned on either side of the frame. As if this was not complicated enough the camera showing 'Julie' was to start on a close-up and slowly pull out to a long shot, while the camera framing 'Johnny' was to start on a medium shot and gradually move in to a close-up. The sequence was to end with the image of Julie being faded out to leave Johnny framed in close-up. The note on the script – which was probably James MacTaggart's instruction to the camera operators and vision mixer – reads: 'If the following sequence doesn't come off we'll intercut as usual.'[15] A more conventional way to show this kind of telephone conversation would have been by using a split screen, but it may be that the equipment needed to achieve this was not available for this production so MacTaggart was forced to improvise.

The unorthodox and ambitious nature of *The Middle Men* was clearly appreciated by some members of the audience who were 'most cordially disposed towards the author's invention of a story that was, various viewers said, up-to-date as to theme, unorthodox in approach and with a fresh and brisk treatment.'[16] Other viewers, however, found themselves 'out of their depth' because of the financial machinations of the plot, while the fast pace of the production 'seems to have been of no help in easing the bafflement of viewers who felt bemused by the rapidity of the telephone calls.' As one viewer commented, 'pace? I've heard of the rat race; now I know the meaning of it.'[17]

The fourth play in the *Storyboard* series, *The Long Spoon* (BBC, 18 August 1961), was an adaptation of a story by John Wyndham, about a devil who materialises from a tape recorder to turn the lives of a young couple upside down. In contrast to *The Middle Men* this was a surreal comedy and it was received much less favourably by the BBC's viewing panel, some of whom were 'exasperated at being presented with such "nonsensical piffle" which was too pointless and "daft" and too fantastic to be at all amusing, merely serving, it was said, to waste half-an-hour in a boring and juvenile fashion.'[18] A small minority were more positive, finding the play 'a novel, light-hearted and diverting fantasy, with an amusing topical slant too ... in view of this particular devil's interest in football pools.'[19] Although studio-based, the rehearsal script lists three short telecine sequences, one of which was to show crowds entering a football stadium prior to a match where Chelsea thrash Fulham 60–0, with another telecine sequence showing a montage of the goals:

> *Commentator:* And it's a goal, another goal, another goal, goal, goal, goal, goal, goal, goal, goal, goal, goal, goal.
> (Fade out sound and mix to:)
> *Brian C:* You'll see more of that in Sports Special at ten-thirty this evening. Now we have here in the studio, Billy Wright and Eric Maschwitz, Head

of BBC Light Entertainment to discuss with you why is football today so dull and what can be done to make it brighter.[20]

Clearly intended to be a zany comedy *The Long Spoon* was radical in pre-empting the surrealist comedy of the Monty Python team by several years. Formally, however, it was less innovative than *The Middle Men*, being described by viewers as 'competent, if unremarkable.'[21]

I'll Be Waiting (BBC, 25 August 1961), the fifth play in the series, was adapted from a story by Raymond Chandler. Its scenario was evocatively described in the *Radio Times*: 'Midnight. In a hotel on 'Sunset Strip' a redhead waits for her man. Outside in the darkness killers wait … in the quiet of the hotel corridors Tony the house detective also waits' (*Radio Times*, 17 August 1961). According to the *Radio Times* the story was 'Dramatised for television by Troy Kennedy Martin and Michael Imison' but the rehearsal script attributes the adaptation to Kennedy Martin and Roger Smith. Recollecting the drama nearly forty years later Smith was quite clear about his involvement:

> I wrote *I'll Be Waiting* with Troy … we had the designer in and we designed the studio before we'd written the script, which was absolutely unheard of. We had the story, but it was important how we could do it in the studio and how the set would be. I remember we had this wonderful kind of balcony and then the black drapes … Richard Wilmot was the designer and he did little fairy lights so it looked like the city, if you see what I mean. Jimmy was very keen on wide-angle lenses and they had very great, long depth of field … It was written and worked out in no time I have to say.[22]

Smith had previously written a play for the Granada series *The Younger Generation* called *Our Ted* (Granada, 21 July 1961) and, after becoming a script editor at the BBC, was to emerge as a key figure in the development of *The Wednesday Play*, commissioning Dennis Potter's first scripts and recruiting both Tony Garnett and Ken Trodd to the series as script editors. Smith had an acting role in the second *Storyboard* drama, *The Magic Barrel*, as a blind banjo player and he also appeared in the final *Storyboard*, *Tickets to Trieste*, alongside an aspiring young actor called Michael Caine.

Tickets to Trieste (BBC, 1 September 1961) exemplified the modernity of the *Storyboard* series which, apart from the nineteenth century setting of *The Gentleman From Paris*, was resolutely contemporary in its settings, subject matter and style. Written by Ken Wlaschen and dramatised for television by Kennedy Martin, *Tickets to Trieste* was a crazy story featuring three beatniks (two of whom were played by Michael Caine and Roger Smith) who get involved in an international espionage situation when they attempt to rescue a beautiful woman in distress.

Kennedy Martin introduced it, as the final play in the *Storyboard* series, in a short article in the *Radio Times*:

> Tonight *Storyboard* – a series of six dramatised stories – comes to an end with *Tickets to Trieste*, a crazy romp through Europe by Ken Wlaschen, the American poet. Wlaschen, pacing his studio in, of all places, Guildford, England, surrounded by bull-fighting weapons and walls covered with rejection slips, told me the story through a blare of jazz.
>
> 'It's about this guy Ackerman,' Wlaschen explained. 'He is a beatnik from San Fran who pads in Paris. He decides to rescue a Red chick in Trieste. Don't you understand man? It's all part of the plan to start World War III – or stop it – depending on which way you look at it.'
>
> 'Look at what?' I asked.
>
> 'At *Tickets to Trieste* of course!'
>
> I won't go any further, But if you add a beautiful agent named 'Mother,' an assortment of Central European spies, some dancing, some music, and a happy ending you'll get some idea of this fairy story. It's one way of letting off steam at the end of a series! (Kennedy Martin, 1961: 50)

In the first MacTaggart Lecture, delivered at the 1976 Edinburgh Film Festival, John McGrath cited *Tickets to Trieste* while describing the non-naturalistic drama that the 'young Turks' were trying to achieve at the BBC in the early 1960s:

> I shall never forget the end of *Tickets to Trieste*, a comic and directorial *tour de force*, all done in the studio, when the three agents, led by a young Michael Caine, lost their all in Trieste, shrugged, turned, and hipped together to the music of the Limelighters off the set and along a huge sky-cloth going round the studio past a continuous cartoon drawing of their journey back to London drawn all the way along it. That shot said: this is the story of what happened. The movement told you that they didn't care, the music that they would keep on merrily. The cartoon told you: you're in a studio, really, but we don't care if you know that, and the music should have told you anyway that we *enjoy* being in this particular studio ... (McGrath, 1977: 103)

Lacking any visual record of the programme McGrath's description gives as good an account as we are likely to get of the non-naturalistic style of the *Storyboard* plays: the use of the camera to reveal rather than conceal the artifice of the studio, the communication of narrative information through gesture rather than dialogue, the use of music as an important element in the narrative, not just an emotional support, and the use of set design as an integral part of the narrative, economically facilitating the telling of the story while at the same time revealing the artifice of it.

At a time when BBC television drama was trying to shake off its fustian postwar image and win back some of the viewers lost to the shiny new populism of ITV, *Storyboard* was an early manifestation of the new spirit of adventure emerging within the BBC under its new Director General, Hugh Carleton Greene, who took up his post on 1 January 1960. As the final play in the series, *Tickets to Trieste* attempted to tap in to the zeitgeist of the early 1960s with its 'hip' language and trendy new characters (beatniks *and* spies – a year before Sean Connery's appearance as James Bond in *Dr No* and four years before Michael Caine shot to fame playing Harry Palmer in *The Ipcress File*) and it is not difficult to detect a resemblance between this and Kennedy Martin's 1965 *Wednesday Play, The Man Without Papers*, in which the American beatnik Roscoe Mortimer is caught up in a shady world involving duplicitous government agents.

As a 'lost' series the significance of *Storyboard* has perhaps been overlooked in the history of British television drama, but Roger Smith, for one, acknowledges its importance: 'It was terrific getting the feel of the possibility there was in television ... *Storyboard* was predominantly Troy, I only wrote one of the scripts, but I was heavily influenced by that and out of that came *Studio 4* ... '[23] James MacTaggart and Roger Smith both worked on *Studio 4* (BBC, January–September 1962), the next BBC series to experiment with a new approach to television drama, but Kennedy Martin (who was not involved in the series) was less than enthusiastic about its achievements, as he wrote in 'Nats Go Home':

> *Studio 4* was the next series associated with narrative drama. It was a failure. Its aims were confused and made more so by the introduction of 'nat' plays within the format. It was not until the third series – *Teletale* – came out this autumn that one could see the faint emergence of a form, despite the fact that it was handled by novice directors in pocket-sized provincial studios. (Kennedy Martin, 1964: 32)

Roger Smith wrote a short drama for *Teletale* (BBC, November 1963–March 1964) called *Catherine* (BBC, 24 January 1964), which saw the directorial debut of Ken Loach and an acting role for Tony Garnett, playing the estranged husband of the central character. Later that year Smith was the story editor on *First Night* (BBC 1, September 1963–May 1964), a series of contemporary dramas by new writers, produced by James MacTaggart, which was the forerunner of *The Wednesday Play* (BBC 1, 1964–70), on which MacTaggart was the producer for the first two seasons (January–December 1965) when a number of innovative plays were produced.[24] With Kennedy Martin, Loach, MacTaggart, McGrath and Smith all involved in the production of *Diary of a Young Man* in the summer of 1964 there was clearly a continuity in the development of innovative contemporary drama at the BBC in the early 1960s, from *Storyboard* in 1961 through to *The Wednesday Play* in 1965, involving the nucleus of the group Kennedy Martin describes as the 'young Turks' in the BBC Drama Department.

Nats Go Home (1964)

The article which Kennedy Martin wrote for *Encore* in the spring of 1964 is arguably as important in his oeuvre as any of the dramas and films he has written in his career, both for the influence it had at the time and its continuing currency in debates about the aesthetics of television drama. John Cook and Glen Creeber, in their respective books on Dennis Potter, each refer to the article as having a profound influence on Potter's ideas for a non-naturalistic drama. Glen Creeber notes how 'Inspired by Martin's article, *Stand Up, Nigel Barton* can be seen as Potter's attempt to use the television technology of the day to create a new grammar for television drama – moving away from the portrayal of *external realities* and presenting the *internal workings* of the human mind' (Creeber, 1998: 54). John Cook, additionally, highlights the influence the article had on *The Wednesday Play* as a forum for innovation in television drama: 'Its importance for *The Wednesday Play* cannot be overstated for, appearing less than a year before the launch of the new play slot, it undoubtedly had an influence over the latter's stylistic direction' (Cook, 1995: 27).

Although 'Nats Go Home' was published in March 1964 it is likely Kennedy Martin wrote it before the end of 1963, as the reference in the article to the appearance of the *Teletale* series 'this autumn' suggests. The provocative nature of the article is announced in its title, as John Caughie has noted:

> The phrase 'Nats go home' in 1964 echoed with the call of postcolonial struggles for independence, 'Brits go home': Kennedy Martin and his allies in the BBC Drama Department (Jimmy McTaggart [sic], John McGrath, Roger Smith, Tony Garnett, Kenith Trodd) as freedom fighters, shaking off the yoke of a colonizing power and demanding self-determination. (Caughie, 2000: 92)

It is a sign of the extent to which Kennedy Martin had been politicised while working in the BBC Drama Department in the early 1960s, having only a few years before been part of a 'colonising power' when he was a Second Lieutenant in the Gordon Highlanders in Cyprus, that he was now able to write an article which would nail his radical credentials to the mast. The object of his attack was naturalism, a form which he felt was outmoded and unsuited to a vital new medium like television. What was needed, he argued, was a revolution in television drama to overthrow the tyranny of the naturalist form: 'The key to this revolution lies in taking a long look at Naturalism to find out why it was, and is, the wrong form for drama for the medium' (Kennedy Martin, 1964: 21). He traces the origins of naturalism in British television to 1950s America and the emergence of the Paddy Chayefsky school of naturalistic drama in American television, a form which was influenced by the work of the Actors' Studio, the teachings of Stanislavsky and the prominence of Freudian ideas in American culture, all of which

> combined to create a vital theatre full of psychological motivation which could be adequately photographed with the available techniques at the disposal of the directors. It was a theatre of dialogue, a theatre of performance. It was a writer's theatre. But first and foremost, which one tends to forget – it was still theatre. (Kennedy Martin, 1964: 21)

This form was imported into Britain when Sydney Newman, who had been working for the Canadian Broadcasting Corporation following a spell in American television, was recruited in 1958 by the British independent television company ABC to work on their anthology play series, *Armchair Theatre*. Having seen John Osborne's *Look Back in Anger* at the Royal Court Theatre, Newman was enthusiastic about the new wave of working-class realism in British drama and began commissioning a new generation of playwrights to write for *Armchair Theatre*. Kennedy Martin is complimentary about the work of some of these playwrights, including Clive Exton and Alun Owen, whose plays, such as *No Fixed Abode, After the Funeral* and *Lena, O My Lena* 'were genuine dramatic masterpieces more representative of the decade than many of the more celebrated films and theatre plays' (Kennedy Martin, 1964: 22).

Yet by 1960, he argues, things had already started to change: 'Some of the good writers, tired of the limits of the naturalist form had taken to fantasy. Others had opted out. [...] the public and the critics became dissatisfied with the single shot drama spot' (Kennedy Martin, 1964: 22). The time was ripe for a 'long look at the dying TV drama form', but a number of factors had prevented this happening, not least the popular success of drama series such as Kennedy Martin's own *Z Cars* which, ironically, had helped to revitalise naturalism and shift the emphasis away from the single play towards drama series. Kennedy Martin's critique of naturalism in television drama was no doubt partly a consequence of his disenchantment with *Z Cars*, which had caused him to leave before the end of the first series (see Chapter 4):

> One of the reasons why I didn't go overboard about *Z Cars*, which I had a lot to do with and put together the first scripts and invented the idea and was the script editor on it, was that I felt all I was doing was contributing to what I thought then was the death-throes of naturalism ... they all said it was a breakthrough but I didn't really think it was. All I think it did was that it used more modish and up-to-date styles of acting and just things like everyone spoke in a Lancashire accent.[25]

As we have seen, Kennedy Martin's first non-naturalistic experiments in television drama predated *Z Cars* and the motivation for his attack on naturalism had been brewing while he worked on the scripts for *Diary of a Young Man* in 1962–3, an extract from which was used in the article to illustrate the fundamentals of the new drama.

Following his explanation of why naturalism has such a stranglehold on current television drama the manifesto-like nature of 'Nats Go Home' becomes evident in the listing of three 'statements' which act as a clarion call to action:

> FIRST. The deep-rooted attitude shared by artists, critics and executives within the industry alike that naturalism is synonymous with TV Drama must be got rid of.
> SECOND. All drama which owes its form or substance to theatre plays is OUT ...
> THIRD. Naturalist series from *Dixon* through to *Z Cars* and *It's Dark Outside* can be separated. They are folk drama – excellent of their kind but can serve the new drama's purpose only as a school where young writers learn the fundamentals of TV ... (Kennedy Martin, 1964: 24)

This third statement admonishes *Z Cars* to some extent by reclassifying it as 'folk drama', suggesting that popular drama series can serve a purpose, acting as a training ground where new writers can learn the craft of writing for television, 'giving in return their fire and their zeal and their social commitment: qualities that series should always be in need of.' There was undoubtedly a personal note to this statement which expressed Kennedy Martin's equivocal feelings towards *Z Cars*, implicitly acknowledging that the series did have a social agenda and some 'fire' in its early days. These three manifesto statements are followed by an analysis of the ingredients, or 'common denominators', of naturalism:

> The common denominator in all 'nat' plays is that they tell a story by means of dialogue. Naturalism deals with people's verbal relationships with each other ... The second common denominator is that naturalism works within a strict form of natural time – studio time equals drama-time equals Greenwich Mean Time. Fades equal a long lapse of time, dissolves a short lapse and cuts immediate time. (Kennedy Martin, 1964: 24–5)

The application of these elements to television, a 'makeshift bastard born of the theatre and photographed with film techniques', has two major consequences which are at the heart of Kennedy Martin's critique of naturalism:

> ONE. Since naturalism evolved from a theatre of dialogue, the director is forced into photographing faces talking and faces reacting. The director faced with a torrent of words can only retreat into the neutrality of the

two- and three-shot where the camera, caged from seizing on anything of significance, is emasculated and only allowed to gaze around the room following the conversation like an attentive stranger. This enslavement of the visual element is too binding.

TWO. Since naturalism visually evolved from Hollywood film techniques (no matter how far it has developed since then), there is still retained a deep-rooted belief that the close-up of an actor's face somehow acts subjectively on the viewer. We, therefore, get the spectacle of writer, actor and director all combining to somehow involve the viewer emotionally in a character's predicament by close-up writing, acting and shooting. This attempt to evoke subjective emotion similar to the Hollywood cinema of the 40s is on a direct collision course with the objectivity of the camera. (Kennedy Martin, 1964: 25)

Having analysed the shortcomings of naturalism as a dramatic form, Kennedy Martin proceeds to present his solution, listing the three objectives of the new drama:

to free the camera from photographing dialogue
to free the structure from natural time and
to exploit the total and absolute objectivity of the television camera. (Kennedy Martin, 1964: 25)

These objectives are then explored in detail, using an extract from the script of what was to become episode four of *Diary of a Young Man* as illustration. The solution to the 'enslavement' of the camera which, in naturalist drama, is 'forced into photographing faces talking and faces reacting', is to remove dialogue from the screen. Kennedy Martin's proposal is to replace it with a new 'narrative' form of drama which would substitute 'visual story telling' for the old naturalist form of exposition through dialogue. This new form of narrative drama would also have the advantage of freeing up the time structure and enabling a more 'objective' use of the camera.

A long extract from 'Diary Four: The Night of the Long Knives' is used to illustrate the potential of this new narrative drama, with descriptive passages indicating how the camera might be freed from photographing dialogue and sequence cuts indicating the potential for freeing the structure from natural time. In addition, stills sequences and voiceovers indicate the techniques which might be used to subvert naturalism. The script extract exemplified the new form of 'visual story telling' Kennedy Martin was proposing where, far from the visuals being subservient to the dialogue as in naturalist drama, the visuals contain or 'distil' the narrative information:

Despite what everyone may say to the contrary, naturalism is not a visual form. The bulk of the dramatic information rests on the dialogue and the visuals do nothing but supplement it. In a narrative sequence such as this, the visuals do not supplement, nor restate information, they, in fact, distil it. (Kennedy Martin, 1964: 27)

The new form would also enable time to be compressed through elliptical editing, or in some cases, as in the *Diary* extract, through stills sequences, circumventing the tendency in naturalism, especially in live drama, to show the action unfolding in real time. An inventive use of editing could also extend time to show, as in Kennedy Martin's example in the article, a dramatic moment such as the Death of a Hero through a montage of shots rather than in the real time it might take for him to fall to the ground:

> This could be done by recording the actor falling a dozen times with four cameras around him taking shots of his face, his feet, his buckling knees, his amazed eyes, ground shots of him tumbling like an oak tree, shots of his back, turning shots, swift pans moving up his body as it collapses downwards.
>
> Twenty-five cuts could be edited together to record the fall. The five seconds of the natural fall could be lengthened by seven or more and because of the fast cutting the viewer would not be aware of the lengthened time, rather he would *experience* it, and think the fall as short as the natural one. (Kennedy Martin, 1964: 28)

This description clearly shows an awareness of the montage theories Sergei Eisenstein applied to films such as *Battleship Potemkin* and *October* in the 1920s. That such innovative editing techniques had not been applied to television drama was largely a consequence of the fact that most television drama was transmitted live up to the end of the 1950s and, even when pre-recording became possible in 1958, continued to be recorded as if live for several years because of the difficulties of editing videotape. This was the situation at the time Kennedy Martin was writing and was why directors such as Ken Loach were eager to get out of the electronic studio and start shooting television drama on film, on location. Kennedy Martin's article anticipates this development, seeing the potential in it for a new form of narrative drama that would only be fully realised with the transition to film:

> There is a lot of work to be done on the development of the new grammar. There is also a lot of opposition to be overcome, for this idea of Time and Structure demands editing and the recording of production down to the minutest detail. This cuts across the myth of the live transmission producing a spontaneity in the actor's performance, which is still held sacred in many quarters of television. (Kennedy Martin, 1964: 28–9)

Perhaps the most difficult aspect of Kennedy Martin's argument for a new drama was the need 'to exploit the total and absolute objectivity of the television camera.' The key to understanding this is to see the involvement that viewers have with the television image as being diametrically opposed to the involvement viewers have with the image on the cinema screen. In the latter case, Kennedy Martin argues, the involvement is an emotional, subjective one, whereas with television, the peculiar quality of the electronic image results in what he describes as an 'objective' involvement:

> As a general rule, a viewer's involvement is induced to move along an index of increasing interest. It is then directed towards one of two goals, one being an objective involvement which stimulates mind and imagination; the other an emotional one, where the aim is to directly disturb the senses. The emotional one is the more difficult to achieve on TV. (Kennedy Martin, 1964: 30)

One way to achieve an 'objective' involvement was to use self-reflexive or distanciation techniques, as in Brecht's theatre or Resnais' new wave cinema (to cite two examples Kennedy Martin gives) where 'both have distorted their medium's structure to produce new kinds of objectiveness' (Kennedy Martin, 1964: 29). Yet in television, the quality of the electronic image was such that it had, for Kennedy Martin, a naturally objectifying quality, a cold distancing quality resulting from the relatively primitive technology in use at the time (black and white electronic tube cameras recording in high-level lighting conditions and broadcasting on 405 lines) compared to the high-resolution image of the 35mm film cameras used for cinema films.

There is some confusion in the argument at this point regarding 'objective' and 'emotional' involvement which clouds the issue, with the suggestion that the viewer's *emotional* involvement can be increased through exploiting this 'objectifying' element of the electronic camera ('if the viewers' involvement is to be directed towards the second goal, that of empathy, the element of objectivity within the camera itself should be analysed'), while a little further on this 'objectifying' quality of the TV camera is referred to as 'the true beginning of *mental* involvement' (Kennedy Martin, 1964: 30). The argument is further complicated when 'editing for involvement' is introduced and an example given of a form of Eisensteinian montage which 'if it is good enough obtains total involvement of an emotional kind' (Kennedy Martin, 1964: 31). The lack of clarity in the analysis obscures an interesting argument about the 'distancing' quality of the electronic television image in the early 1960s which was soon to be circumvented by two technological developments: the introduction of 16mm film as a more versatile and 'liberating' medium for making television drama and the move to transmission on 625 lines, first on BBC 2 and then subsequently on BBC 1 and ITV.

Reflecting in 1986 on the arguments for a new aesthetic in television drama that he had proposed in 'Nats Go Home' Kennedy Martin sought to clarify his argument, acknowledging that it may have been superseded by subsequent technological developments:

I didn't know anything about the cinema in those days so in fact these things to a certain extent came about when they moved to film – Tony Garnett and *The Wednesday Play* moved over to film. I don't think you get the same kind of objectivity in film as you do in video. It's something to do with the smallness of the image that you get on the screen. It's to do with the lack of focus. You got a kind of pornography effect, which is that if you saw somebody the pimple on the nose stood out. You could never actually focus it in such a way that small effects were in any kind of way matted out.

A lot of the desire to talk over what was going on on television or to point or to laugh or to have a feeling of superiority was because the image never really held you and there was a tendency to move into close-ups on the part of directors who thought that they were able to get the same sort of effect in a close-up as you would in the cinema. So if someone was crying, or has lost his daughter as in the Bob Peck scenes [in *Edge of Darkness*], if you actually have big close-ups, with the equipment we had then, somehow the audience would be able to empathise with him, but I don't think that this was the case because the camera just objectified everything. It wasn't able to take the place of the viewer who in a theatre would be able to allow his eyes to block out the edges of the set and to be able to suspend his disbelief. The camera didn't suspend anyone's disbelief and you were then presented with what the camera gave you. So the idea then was to turn it around and say well if this is the case what can you do with this kind of objectifying view of drama and of course it really fell completely into the ideas of Brecht and all that sort of stuff. So the thing was if you wanted to get some sort of emotion going you had to really go to all sorts of collages and montages and things like that to kind of arrest him intellectually.[26]

The suggestion is that there was the potential, at least in 1963–4, to exploit 'the total and absolute objectivity of the television camera' for a non-naturalistic purpose, to use it to achieve a Brechtian distanciation effect. Correspondingly, montage editing, another departure from naturalism at the time, could be utilised to achieve a new kind of narrative drama that would engage the viewer through a form of 'objective involvement', stimulating the mind and the imagination. In contrast to the 'passive' involvement of naturalist drama Kennedy Martin sought an 'active' emotional and intellectual involvement which would be achieved through a combination of montage editing (freeing the camera from photographing dialogue while also freeing the structure from natural time) and 'objectifying' camerawork (exploiting the naturally alienating quality of the electronic image).

The new drama clearly needed to embrace a new grammar and new forms of technology and it is often assumed that Kennedy Martin was making a case for the use of film (this was how Allan Prior interpreted it in his response to the article in an issue of *Screenwriter*).[27] However, at the time of writing, Kennedy Martin clearly thought the new drama could be achieved with video rather than film, both in the studio and in the form of the new mobile video equipment that had recently come into use:

> If this new drama is ever to get off the ground it must create a new grammar, especially in relation to editing. It must employ new techniques, like Mobile Ampex. It must develop new designs leading to maximum fluidity in the studio by doing away with the old box sets and creating acting areas specifically through the use of lighting. (Kennedy Martin, 1964: 31–2)

The *Storyboard* plays had attempted to use the television studio in new ways and the experience of doing them had convinced Kennedy Martin of the possibilities for a new drama. While the new grammar would eventually be achieved more easily with film there was, nevertheless, the potential with the electronic studio to achieve some of the elements of the new drama. However, the *modus operandi* in studio drama was naturalism and it would have needed a revolution in attitudes to effect a change in production techniques:

> The degree of editing was much more flexible on film, although you can actually run your hands across the editing machine in the studio like a sort of fugue. Often you'd have four to eight cameras maybe on a big production and you'd see the mixer cutting between them for no other reason than just to flex his hand and the wonderful energy of the picture coming up in the middle which he was only half aware of was never actually used in any kind of artistic way.[28]

What the new drama needed were creative directors like James MacTaggart, John McGrath and Philip Saville, people who might be prepared to use the technology in new ways. Kennedy Martin did not disguise the fact that he saw the new drama as a director's medium, an unusual argument for a writer to make and one which won him few friends among the screenwriting community: 'The Screenwriters Guild had a meeting, to which I wasn't invited, where they almost kind of lynched me because they felt that's what I was doing and it's absolutely true, I really did think that it was a director's medium. I've sort of modified my view about that now but that's what I was saying.'[29]

'Nats Go Home' hit its intended targets and drew considerable response, with eight pages of 'Reaction' in the subsequent edition of *Encore* and further responses in the Spring edition of *Screenwriter*, which also reprinted the article under the heading 'Television Drama – Is This The Way Ahead?'[30] The *Screenwriter* responses were predictably hostile to the contention that the new drama would be a director's medium, not a writer's medium, although Allan Prior, an erstwhile colleague of Kennedy Martin's on *Z Cars*, was more sympathetic to the argument, drawing the conclusion that the future for television drama resided in film rather than the television studio.

In *Encore* the Head of BBC Television Drama, Sydney Newman, responded to Kennedy Martin's contention that the BBC did not know what to do with the new drama by citing his appointment of James MacTaggart as the producer of the new *First Night* series, implying that, as Head of Drama, he was actively encouraging the new drama by appointing someone who had been central to the early 1960s experimental series – *Storyboard*, *Studio 4* and *Teletale* – on each of which MacTaggart was the producer. The former Head of BBC TV Drama, Michael Barry, gave the article a guarded welcome, while Dennis Potter, who at the time was the television critic on the *Daily Herald*, was concerned that Kennedy Martin was too dismissive of naturalist drama and 'the kinds of experience which can be well conveyed by this means, providing the dialogue is good enough and the writer genuinely has something to *say*.' Yet Potter was largely supportive of the thesis, adding:

> Kennedy Martin suggests that his ideas will 'not suffer the didactic gladly'. If by this he means the great wodges of propaganda, he's right, thank God. But the sort of didacticism we need, passionately concerned to present all sorts of evidence, constantly infiltrating all our defences, is ideally suited to the narrative method. (Potter, 1964: 40)

The longest response came from Tony Garnett, then an actor but soon to join the BBC staff as a story editor on *The Wednesday Play*. Garnett took issue with the suggestion that naturalism was mainly a theatrical form, arguing that 'Films and television drama rely more on Nat. conventions than the theatre ... Indeed the Nat. vogue in our theatre was a short one. Its main traditions and its present interests are elsewhere.' But he did agree that television is 'most unsuited' to naturalism (Garnett, 1964: 44). Garnett was generally in agreement with Kennedy Martin and he took the opportunity to extend the theoretical discussion of television as a medium for the communication of ideas, concluding:

> The tasks ahead for those who wish to see the creative development of television drama are threefold. Firstly, the deadwood of Nat. and the

confused dependence on the theatre must be cleared away. Secondly, by refusing to countenance any taboos the first steps towards a definition can be made by asking the right questions, and attempting to answer them by taking creative and technical risks, actually on the screen. Thirdly, out of this work, a theory of television drama will gradually emerge which will provide terms of reference for the critical attention it will then deserve. (Garnett, 1964: 47)

The following year Garnett, working with Ken Loach, was able to put some of this theory into practice with the groundbreaking *Up the Junc-tion* (BBC1, 3 November 1965), the first *Wednesday Play* to make exten-sive use of 16mm film for location shooting and to apply film editing techniques to scenes recorded in the studio.[31] Using handheld camera-work and an elliptical editing style *Up the Junction* was enthusiastically endorsed by Kennedy Martin in an article published in *Contrast* shortly after its transmission:

> *Up the Junction* provoked a lot of complaints about its content; but I don't think anyone phoned in to say that its form was highly uncon-ventional, that four sound-tracks were playing simultaneously, that ends of sentences were overlaid, and jump cuts took you back and forth till you were lost in time. In fact these very techniques brought about a quicker response than ever from the audience, because Ken was getting them to feel rather than to think – which brings me back to the ques-tion of whether you simply state your case (or dramatic intention) to the audience, or whether you should aim to set them emotionally on fire. (Kennedy Martin, 1965/66: 140–1)

Yet while *Up the Junction* was a revolutionary development in television drama, kick-starting the shift to film as the preferred medium for social-realist film-making in the 1960s and 1970s, naturalism continued to be the dominant form, as John McGrath observed in 1976 in the inaugural MacTaggart Lecture at the Edinburgh Festival. Analysing the structural changes in British television since the early 1960s, which had seen a liberal broadcasting system replaced by a more conservative and censo-rious one, McGrath acknowledged that 'naturalism has flourished as the dominant mode of television drama. The excitements now are not about the *form* of the drama, but about its content; with no realisation that the naturalistic form *is* the content, that it distorts what the writer is trying to say, contains it within safe limits' (McGrath, 1977: 105).

As an example, McGrath cited the Loach/Garnett/Allen *Days of Hope* (BBC 1, September-October 1975) as a potentially radical drama where the message had become 'blurred' because of the adoption of a natural-istic form. The example highlighted the extent to which Loach's style had shifted from the impressionistic modernism of *Up the Junction* towards a cinematic naturalism in *Days of Hope*. Yet it was in a drama recorded a year before *Up the Junction* that Loach first realised the advantages of getting out of the studio and onto the streets, breaking taboos and taking the 'creative and technical risks' Tony Garnett had called for in his response to 'Nats Go Home'. That drama was *Diary of a Young Man*.

Diary of a Young Man (1964)

In his response to 'Nats Go Home' the Granada Television producer Philip Mackie wrote that when he came to the long extract from the 'sample script' in Kennedy Martin's article he suddenly understood what the purpose of the article was: 'It is a prospectus for his new series which he wants someone to put on' (Mackie, 1964: 44). In fact the BBC had allocated project numbers to six episodes of *Diary of a Young Man* in March 1963, a full year before 'Nats Go Home' was published[32] and in a memo to the Assistant Head of Copyright at the BBC, dated 13 March 1963, Elwyn Jones implied that the negotiations over the scripts had been going on for some while: 'I know how tiresome this set of negotiations have become for you. We are anxious, though, not to give these wild young men any grounds for thinking us completely inflexible ... from what we have already seen we would be reluctant to lose them [the programmes] completely.'[33] The memo hints at the strained relationship that existed between the Corporation and Kennedy Martin/ McGrath (the 'wild young men') following their resignation from *Z Cars*, but Jones's memo also acknowledges that the BBC recognised the potential in the new scripts and wanted to produce them.

Kennedy Martin has suggested that he may have been working on *Diary of a Young Man* as early as 1961.[34] Certainly he would have had time to work on the scripts after he left *Z Cars* in the spring of 1962 for, apart from one episode of *Z Cars* which was transmitted in July 1962, he had nothing produced between April 1962 and August 1964, although he did work on the aborted *Memento Mori* script with Roger Smith in the summer of 1962 (see Chapter two).

According to John McGrath, the original idea for *Diary of a Young Man* lay in an unperformed play called *Jack* that he wrote for the Royal Court Theatre in 1960, which was subsequently reworked on three occasions – as *Diary of a Young Man* in 1964, as a stage play called *The Life and Times of Joe of England*, produced by McGrath's 7:84 Theatre Company in 1977, and again in 1980 as a two-part *Play for Today* called *The Adventures of Frank*:

Diary of a Young Man was based on a stage play of mine, called *Jack*, and then we did *Diary of a Young Man* and then in 7:84 I did a thing called *Joe of England*, so his name went through various transformations, and then based partly on that, partly on the original play, partly on *Diary of a Young Man* I wrote *The Adventures of Frank*.[35]

In his posthumously published book, *Naked Thoughts That Roam About: Reflections on Theatre*, McGrath supported his claim that *Diary* had its origins in his stage play by reprinting the opening song from *Jack*, a 'musical' on which he collaborated with Dudley Moore (McGrath, 2002: 18–19). The verses are almost identical to those that come at the beginning of the first episode of *Diary of a Young Man*, except that in *Diary* the age of the narrator is changed from sixteen to nineteen, perhaps because it was more appropriate for the age of the central character, Joe.

Kennedy Martin, however, disputes McGrath's claim that *Diary of a Young Man* was based on *Jack*, insisting he had no knowledge of the play when writing *Diary*. According to Kennedy Martin, the division of labour on *Diary* was originally going to be that he would write the scripts while McGrath directed, which had been their working relationship on *Z Cars*. However, McGrath subsequently changed his mind about directing the series and Peter Duguid and Ken Loach, two recent graduates from the BBC Directing Course, were brought in to direct three episodes each:

> When we agreed to do *Diary* it was always I was going to write it and he was going to direct it, but I felt that the directing should carry with it some kind of money or whatever … and at that point the writer was always thought of as more important than the director and I felt this wasn't right. But when I actually wrote it John would come round and I'd say what about this and what about that and he'd say yea that's good, or whatever, but it was the kind of input that I felt a director should put into it.
>
> I didn't think he was a writer on it and then towards the end … getting towards number five or six he began to sort of look a bit humped, you know you could tell something was going on, and eventually he said, 'I want to have a writing credit on this' and of course I didn't really realise that he thought of himself as primarily a writer as he'd had a couple of plays on and he'd been a writer at Oxford and all the rest of it, so … I was absolutely astonished at that. I think there was like one where it could be agreed that he could have had a co-writer's credit. Anyway, so we kind of broke off relations … I handed it in and then said we've got this disagreement about the writing … In the end I kind of relented and I also thought well if we're going to do this together he should really get a co-writing credit on each of them.[36]

The extent of the disagreement between Kennedy Martin and McGrath over the authorship of *Diary of a Young Man* is evident from a letter sent to McGrath, in October 1963, from Gareth Wigan, his (and also Kennedy

Martin's) agent, in an attempt to intervene in what had clearly become a serious rift which threatened the production of the series:

> The essence I feel, as I did when the dispute first emerged, is that it is irresponsible now that the series has been written that it should risk being unproduced because Troy and you are unable to agree over the division of credits and money ... Clearly it would not seem likely that you should ever collaborate together again, whatever happens to this one, but nobody can persuade me that it is worth seriously considering, for any longer than the month that has passed, the possibility of abandoning a finished work over a dispute about something so comparatively trivial, and because the resolution of that dispute may effect the future.[37]

Kennedy Martin's conciliatory gesture was to agree to a joint writing credit for the whole series, even though he thought there was really only one episode 'where it could be agreed that he could have had a co-writer's credit'. With McGrath deciding not to direct (perhaps as a way of forcing the issue) it seems likely that the series would not have gone ahead had Kennedy Martin not agreed to the joint credit. Fortunately an agreement was reached, enabling the production of this seminal drama series to go ahead, but the dispute highlights how seriously the question of authorship in television drama was taken at a time when the writer was considered to be the unequivocal author of the work, while the director was merely a member of the production team, albeit one whose role, in practice, was crucial.

Episode one of *Diary of a Young Man*, 'Survival, or They Came to a City' (BBC1, 8 August 1964), relates the experiences of Joe (Victor Henry) and Ginger (Richard Moore) following their arrival in London. At the beginning of the episode Joe recites the following verses, over images of a suitcase being packed, photographs of his mother and himself as a young boy and of Joe at an orphanage after his mother has died:

> When I was only seven years old
> My father went to war
> He sent my mother no money so
> She turned into a whore
>
> He lived the life that soldiers lead
> Before they go to hell
> In Singapore and Tokyo
> And the Suez Canal as well.
>
> When I was only nine years old
> My mother died of pox
> They burned her up in an oven
> And covered the ashes with rocks

> So I was put in this orphanage
> Here as you can see
> And now I'm almost nineteen years
> They're going to set me free.[38]

The style of this pre-title sequence sets the tone for this determinedly non-naturalistic drama. The opening six shots of a suitcase being packed as Joe prepares to travel to London are edited together in a series of jump cuts so that what might have taken several minutes to show in a naturalistic drama is compressed into just fifteen seconds of screen time, the verse-like narration and accompanying drum roll providing both continuity and momentum to the images. A brief montage of suitcases being piled up by railings is followed by still images illustrating the story Joe narrates in the verses, culminating in a live action shot of a train travelling along a railway line and a still image of Joe and Ginger standing in front of a sign reading 'Euston', holding their suitcases. The drum roll stops as the series title appears on the screen over a still image of Joe, foregrounding him as the protagonist in the drama, and a jazzy music track accompanies the modernist design of the title sequence.

The narrative economy of the pre-title sequence, communicating Joe's life story from the age of seven to 'almost nineteen' in the form of verse narration accompanied by photographs, with both live-action and still images describing the preparations for a journey and then the journey itself as Joe and his friend Ginger travel from the north to London, encapsulates the new form of 'narrative drama' Kennedy Martin had argued for in 'Nats Go Home', distilling narrative information into just forty-two seconds where a naturalistic drama might have taken several minutes.

As they leave the platform at Euston station Joe's narrated 'diary', delivered in an expressionless monotone, takes up the story: 'We arrived in London on a wet foggy morning. All we wanted out of life was a bird, a pad and some money.' The narration continues throughout the episode as Joe describes their first few days in London as they try to find somewhere to stay, get a job and earn some money. Studio scenes are interspersed with exterior filmed sequences and montages of stills, the latter invariably accompanied by music and Joe's narration. While the dialogue-led studio scenes slow the narrative pace the stills sequences and exterior scenes quicken the tempo, the different forms combining to achieve a new kind of narrative storytelling.

The first episode was directed by Ken Loach, who also directed episodes 3 and 5 while Peter Duguid directed episodes 2, 4 and 6.[39] As Loach explained to Graham Fuller in the late 1990s:

In *Diary of a Young Man* we cut to music, used sequences of stills, and voice-overs – all the things that, rather curiously, were taken up by commercials more than anything else. That series was mostly a laboratory to see how you could disturb that very formal, traditional way of making and shooting TV drama in a studio. (Fuller, 1998: 8)

A full panoply of techniques was used to 'disturb' the traditional way of making television drama: photographs and live action accompanied by music and/or voiceover, freeze frames, superimposition, jump cuts, montage sequences and collage effects, such as the superimposition of the faces of Ringo Starr, George Harrison and Alec Douglas Home onto the heads of statues at the Albert Memorial. While studio scenes were still used in *Diary of a Young Man* the ambition to achieve a new realism by getting out of the studio and onto the streets resulted in a far greater use of film than was usual in television drama: thirty-three film sequences in episode one compared to ten studio sequences, although the studio scenes are generally much longer than the film sequences.

It was not only the style that made *Diary of a Young Man* radical. The intention to break with naturalism and take 'a realistic look at what's going on in London now' resulted in the breaking of some social taboos regarding the portrayal of sexuality and the use of language.[40] This brought forth some predictable criticism, such as the vicar in Radcliffe-on-Trent who wrote to the Postmaster-General (the government minister responsible for broadcasting) protesting about the 'filth and depravity' in the drama (Anon, 1964). BBC Head of Drama Sydney Newman was a little concerned about the 'bloodies and the bed scenes' in episode one but he was otherwise very enthusiastic about the drama, as he indicated in a memo to James MacTaggart:

> The first episode of *Diary of a Young Man* will be regarded in the years to come as a major breakthrough in television story telling as *No Trams to Lime Street* was five and a half years ago. From what I understand of the remaining five episodes, this is a dead cert.
>
> I could be wrong, but for sheer variety in the total use made of live action, film and stills combined with the highly original and imaginative use of words, music and sound effects, this is television of the first order.
>
> If you watch the 'bloodies' and the bed scenes, etc. – in short avoid getting into trouble over irrelevancies as you prepare your single plays for the next calendar year, we will win, hands down, in the single play drama stakes.[41]

In episode two, 'Money' (BBC 1, 15 August 1964), Joe sets out to achieve his third ambition – having found a 'bird' (Rose) and a pad – to make some money. In episode three, 'Marriage, or For Better or for Worse'

(BBC 1, 22 August 1964) Joe and Rose get married, further estranging Ginger, while in episode four, 'Power, or The Night of the Long Knives' (BBC 1, 29 August 1964), Joe is working in the city, learning how to survive in the cut-throat world of big business, while Ginger is thriving in the more humble and honest trade of window cleaning. Jean Marsh makes a guest appearance as 'Fred' in episode five, 'Life, or A Girl Called Fred' (BBC 1, 5 September 1964), a suicidal young woman who works in the advertising agency where Joe works. Joe tries to find the meaning of life for Fred, a quest that results in a number of surreal sequences, imaginatively directed by Ken Loach. Finally in episode six, 'Relationships' (BBC 1, 12 September 1964), Joe is in prison for failing to pay maintenance to Rose. On getting out he finds that Rose is now in a relationship with Ginger. Joe persuades them that they need to go out into the country to 'sort out their relationships' and after a series of bizarre encounters the episode ends with Joe leaving England on a ship. As the ship sails away Joe ends his diary:

> (Voiceover) Since I came down from the orphanage I have learned that even in a civilised country, power and money are the most important things. Even in a civilised country you have to fight tooth and nail for your home. Even in a civilised country, loneliness, sorrow, suicide and heartbreak haunt many of its people. When I come back, I hope I won't hate England. When I come back I shall have another look at it. Maybe things will have changed. Or both of us. (He turns into shot, he is crying). Tomorrow I'll be twenty-one, so here endeth my diary as a Young Man.[42]

The six episodes of *Diary of a Young Man* cover two years in Joe's life. Although it is based on the experiences of Joe and Ginger from the moment they arrive in London to Joe's departure at the end of episode six, *Diary* is not a conventional serial with a continuous narrative but more an episodic series in which events involving Joe and Ginger (but mainly Joe) are played out as if chapters in Joe's diary. The conception and realisation of the series made it a worthy illustration of the New Drama as outlined by Kennedy Martin in 'Nats Go Home'. Innovative in form, taboo-breaking in content, *Diary of a Young Man* was a radical experiment in television drama in the early 1960s, all the more remarkable for the fact that it was broadcast on BBC 1 on a Saturday evening, scheduled variously between 9.30 pm and 10.15 pm against more eclectic fare on BBC 2 (ranging from a programme featuring Joyce Grenfell to a programme about music in Brecht's drama).

Yet *Diary of a Young Man* was not a blueprint for the future of television drama. It may have been a 'dazzling debut', as Peter Black described the first episode in the *Daily Mail* (10 August 1964), but it was an experiment in television drama that was not followed up, apart from the modernist experimentation of *Up the Junction* and John McGrath's video reworking of *Diary* in *The Adventures of Frank*. The extensive use of film for location shooting in *Diary* eventually led Ken Loach towards documentary-drama rather than non-naturalism, and the rush to embrace film and get out of the studio meant that the experimental techniques explored in *Diary of a Young Man* were not pursued. Television drama became polarised between naturalistic studio drama, which flourished despite Kennedy Martin's intervention, and the more 'realistic' aesthetic afforded by film.

Unproduced work

Diary of a Young Man was not the only experimental drama Kennedy Martin worked on in 1962–4. In September 1964 Michael Bakewell, BBC Head of Plays, acknowledged receipt of an undisclosed number of scripts which he referred to as the *Macheath* scripts.[43] The reference was to *Macheath – Masterspy*, a six-part serial involving an ex-spy called Macheath, loosely based on the character from John Gay's eighteenth century satire *The Beggar's Opera* which Bertolt Brecht adapted in 1928 as *The Threepenny Opera*. Given the interest in Brecht at the time, whose alienation theories clearly influenced Kennedy Martin's 'Nats Go Home' polemic, it seems likely that *The Threepenny Opera* was the main stimulus for *Macheath – Masterspy*.

Although Michael Bakewell acknowledged receipt of the scripts after the final episode of *Diary* had been transmitted, *Macheath – Masterspy* appears to be another product of the post-*Z Cars* period when Kennedy Martin's inclination to experiment with other forms was leading him further and further away from naturalism.[44] In the case of *Macheath* the result was more surreal, rather in the style of *The Long Spoon* in the *Storyboard* series, a comic strip-style updating of *The Threepenny Opera* featuring characters such as 'Otto von Bogle, the famous German spy, Colonel Eczema of the British Secret Service, Lord Two Nations Brown, the nouveau riche capitalist, Doppleganger, the sinister figure from Transylvania (if you see his face you die!!!).'[45]

As in *Diary of a Young Man*, the first episode of *Macheath* opens with the voice of a narrator and although the narration delivered over the opening titles is not in verse its presentation in the script emphasises the heightened melodrama of the opening scene, setting the tone for the drama that is to follow:

<u>NARRATOR</u>: Macheath on the trail of the arch fiend, Doppleganger, finds himself in a refrigerator car on a railway siding outside Glasgow.
At last!
He can dispatch the said foul fiend to his doom!
But
Consternation!!!
Doppelganger is not there.
And as the car is shunted out of the siding, with a series of jerks
Macheath is thrown,
Stunned
And in a state of concussion, he staggers about
Until
Tragedy!
He is caught upon a hook.
He struggles but it is to no avail.
The doors close.
The car gets colder and colder.
He is trapped!!
Soon the train whistle blows – our hero is hauled off to his frozen fate…
The meat-pie markets of the metropolis of London.

INT. REFRIGERATOR CAR. (STUDIO)
MACHEATH, NOW WHITE WITH FROST AND ALL FROZEN STIFF SWINGS ON A HOOK AMONGST ALL THE OTHER LUMPS OF BEEF, LOOKING VERY SILLY.
THERE ARE GOODS YARD AND MACHINERY NOISES.
OVER THIS – TITLES:
"THE SMITHFIELD MARKET MYSTERY!"
or
"MACHEATH MURDERED!!!"
FANFARE ENDS WITH TWANG OF A JEWS HARP.[46]

As in *The Man Without Papers* (in what may be an autobiographical allusion), *Macheath – Masterspy* opens with the central character travelling down from Glasgow to London, where most of the subsequent action takes place. The use of narration and such non-naturalistic techniques as characters speaking to camera, the appearance of expressions like 'Ouch' and 'Wham' in bubbles onscreen, comic-strip style, plus techniques such as a reverse motion telecine sequence in which 'The train which was disappearing into the distance stops and comes whizzing backwards', all testify to the experimental nature of the drama. With their outlandish, surreal scenarios the scripts made no concessions whatsoever to naturalism or realism and the BBC clearly had no idea what to do with them. In 1964 there was no real precedent for this kind of anarchic comedy-drama and it was another three years before comedy programmes such as *At Last the 1984 Show* and *Do Not Adjust Your Set* paved the way for the surrealism of *Monty Python's Flying Circus* (BBC 1, 1969–74). Kennedy Martin was disappointed that *Macheath* was never produced:

> I wrote a series of scripts called *Macheath – Masterspy*, which never got made, which was a sort of early *Monty Python*, very, very loosely based on the old Macheath characters and with no real homage to Brecht, but which were really much in advance of their time and I think that it was to their eternal shame that they never did them. The drama people were into doing heavy serious stuff and the comedy people couldn't handle the drama things. There was a character called Doppelganger ... if you see his face you die ... and he would be hijacking Polly Peachum, tying her to railway lines and everyone would go down to rescue her on the train which was going to run her over. It was a thirties pastiche, with trains everywhere. They'd run through the Houses of Parliament, wreck the Houses of Parliament and then Macheath would be tried for treason and he'd be put up in the court and then the train would actually run through the court. So they would do silly things like send to the Design Department saying how much would it cost to run a train through the Houses of Parliament. But there was a lot of that kind of humour and I spent six to nine months writing those, on spec ... I thought that was in line with the New Drama in that it was very anarchic.[47]

Not long after this Kennedy Martin wrote another script which was similar in tone and style to *Macheath*. *Great Scott, It's Matilda!* (originally *Good God It's Matilda*) was commissioned as a half-hour drama for the BBC's *Thirty-Minute Theatre* anthology play series. Subtitled 'A murder mystery featuring Tonks of Her Majesty's Mounted Railway Police', the play was a parody of a Victorian murder mystery in which Inspector Tonks attempts to solve the mystery of the death of Matilda, the wife of the Chief Constable of Police, who falls from a fifth floor window at the beginning of the play. 'Great Scott, it's Matilda!' is the first line of the play, uttered by Chief Superintendent Grobe when Matilda lands at his feet, as he and Chief Superintendent Biggs are approaching the building in which a Policeman's Ball has been taking place. Both Grobe and Biggs are carrying bunches of flowers, having the same intention to court Matilda, but despite this Tonks treats them as suspects, along with the Chief Constable and Chief Superintendent Yardarm.

In the course of solving the murder all four suspects are killed, three by falling from the fifth floor window, while Biggs is hit by a flowerpot thrown from the window in a re-enactment of the crime. Tonks concludes that the Chief Constable was responsible for the death of his wife and that Yardarm was implicated because he was trying to kill the Chief Constable, whose job he was after. The plot hinges on the unlikely coincidence of the Chief Constable bending down to tie his shoelace at precisely 12.05, knowing that his wife would come rushing into the room at precisely that moment (in fact she was pushed by Yardarm), trip over him and fall through the open window.

Ingeniously, if implausibly, plotted the drama was clearly intended to be played for comedy and there are many farcical scenes, including Tonks falling from the fifth floor window (and surviving) in a re-enactment of the crime. As in *Macheath – Masterspy*, the 'cartoon' nature of the drama is illustrated by the inclusion of onscreen captions, silent cinema-style. In one scene, Tonks explains that a grandfather clock has been primed to explode when a soprano hits top C, causing a brandy glass to break and initiating a chain of events which culminate with buckshot being fired at anyone in the vicinity of the piano – the device having been set by someone, Tonks deduces, who hates music. Tonks then accidentally sets the device off and the subsequent explosion, according to the script, was to be accompanied by captions reading 'Bang', 'Stars' and 'Good Grief!!', followed by a cut to smoke.[48]

At fifty-three pages the script was clearly too long for a half-hour drama, which was probably one reason why it was never produced for *Thirty-Minute Theatre*. According to a BBC memo sent by Ken Trodd to the Assistant Head of Copyright in October 1966 the play was 'an enjoyable piece' and he added: 'Harry Moore's enthusiastic intention was to open the Autumn series with it ... I hope the new regime will not neglect it.'[49] However, the response from Shaun MacLoughlin of the Plays Department was that *Matilda* was 'good but overlength and requires filming', adding that Kennedy Martin did not want to rewrite the play and had gone to America.[50] *Great Scott, It's Matilda!*, therefore, became yet another script to add to the list of unproduced dramas written by Troy Kennedy Martin in the 1960s.

The Chase (1964)

While *Diary of a Young Man* was in production John McGrath was also developing a series of 'experimental' films for BBC 2, called *Six*, for which Kennedy Martin wrote *The Chase* (BBC 2, 19 December 1964) with Michael Elster, who also directed it. McGrath described the aims of the series in a BBC Press Release:

> We do not have the equivalent in English of 'film d'auteur'; I suppose the nearest is a 'personal film' – anyway, that is what these films are meant to be. We want the conventional categories of producer, novelist, scriptwriter, script-doctor, adaptor, screenwriter, director, and editor to

> be broken down; we want the film to be allowed to come through as the clear expression of one person's deepest and most intimate thought. In other words, we want the film to attain the artistic status of the poem or the novel ... [51]

The films, varying in length from 28–59 minutes, included contributions from Ken Russell, Philip Saville and McGrath himself and were shot on 35mm film, making them more expensive to produce than studio drama and more expensive than if they had been shot on video.[52] *The Chase* was one of the most expensive of the films made for the series because of the variety of locations used, plus the fact that it included some aerial photography filmed from a helicopter. Apart from wanting to encourage 'personal' films there was no real theme to the series and the films ranged from Ken Russell's silent film parody of George and Weedon Grossmith's novel *Diary of a Nobody* (BBC 2, 12 December 1964) to Philip Saville's *The Logic Game* (BBC 2, 10 January 1965), an obscure film engaging with then fashionable ideas about existential psychoanalysis. McGrath described the series as 'an opportunity for making experiments, not for making experimental films' (Robinson, 1965: 50) and the freedom given to the film-makers reflected the adventurous spirit of the new BBC channel, as David Robinson noted in an article in *Contrast* called 'Nursing the Avant-Garde':

> Mrs. Wyndham Goldie and Huw Wheldon were favourably disposed to the idea, which was handed over to Michael Peacock at BBC-2 (since clearly he was more likely to be sympathetic than Donald Baverstock, then head of BBC-1). The resulting series of six films, ranging in length from about half an hour to one hour, seem to have sufficiently satisfied the expectations of their sponsors to open the way for a further group of films. (Robinson, 1965: 50)

McGrath, who produced *Six* and the subsequent series, was not too happy with the series title however: 'It was pathetic. They wouldn't let me call it *Short Circuit*, which I wanted to call it. They said "Oh it will sound like a fuse". So I said fine, but no, they came up with a wonderful title, *Six*, and then the following year it was called *Five More!*'[53] With the decision taken to shoot on film the role of the director inevitably became more important. Whereas television drama was seen as a writer's medium film was seen as a director's medium and the aim to make a series of 'personal' films meant, in effect, that the *auteurs* here would be the directors. Indeed *The Chase* was listed in the *Radio Times* as 'A film by Michael Elster' (*Radio Times*, 17 December 1964), not a film by Michael Elster and Troy Kennedy Martin.

The Chase was the second film shown in the series. Originally called *Bowles Day Off* it begins with Frank Bowles (Ken Jones) accidentally reversing his car into a parked motorbike, knocking it over. He drives away, unaware of what he has done, and is bemused when he is soon being pursued by four motorcyclists. The 'chase' takes him out into the country and he eventually ends up in Northampton, where he books into a hotel in an attempt to evade the final motorcyclist who is still pursuing him. During the chase an accident occurs and one of the bikes runs off the road, leaving just one biker to pursue Bowles. The film ends enigmatically, with a freeze frame of Bowles looking out of the hotel window as the biker rides off, having made a telephone call and learnt that one of his mates has died as a result of the accident.

What is unusual about the thirty-five minute film is that there is very little dialogue, the script consisting mostly of a description of the chase. Presumably intended to be a suspense drama the film does not really achieve the level of tension necessary for it to be effective, partly because the four bikers lack any real sense of menace (the gang leader is played by one of *The Likely Lads*, Rodney Bewes) and partly because the film lacks pace – much of the chase occurring in real time. Consequently *The Chase* suffers in comparison to the narrative economy of the far more elliptical *Diary of a Young Man*. While it may have been 'a virtuoso film exercise' (Robinson, 1965: 51) on behalf of Michael Elster (who had just spent four years at the Polish Film School) and an experiment for television which would not have been made within the commercial film industry, *The Chase* is not a manifestation of the New Drama. Rather, it was an exercise in 'personal' film-making which expressed Michael Elster's vision and technique rather than that of Kennedy Martin.

'Opening up the Fourth Front': The MacTaggart lecture (1986)

Although *Diary of a Young Man* and *The Chase* were contemporaneous (both were produced in the summer of 1964) *Diary* was a more radical experiment in narrative storytelling than *The Chase*, which inclined more towards documentary realism in its aesthetic, suggesting that film was not *inevitably* the way forward for television drama. The radical montage of styles in *Diary of a Young Man* was a more innovative mix which seemed, at the time, to offer a genuine alternative to the stagnancy of much naturalist drama. Yet the model offered by *Diary of a Young Man* was not embraced by others working in television at the time and naturalism continued to dominate. Kennedy Martin later reflected on the reasons for this:

> We were getting towards it [a new form of drama] with photomontages and things like that but it had a really long way to go and the other thing

was that I really thought of it in terms of much shorter periods. I wasn't really thinking of it in terms of thirty minutes or forty-five but really much more in terms of what the pop promo is now, five or ten minutes, and using maybe hundreds of edits in that time and really trying to give you a real experience of whatever it is you're trying to do ... So the idea of somebody working in a garret with all sorts of editing equipment and with no thought of how much they cost and with all the facilities at his disposal and just producing a very personal piece of work, all on his own, that was the sort of thing I was getting at. So the promo is the nearest thing to it and we didn't really achieve that. I think that what would have happened is that if we'd stayed in video, if film didn't exist, then there would have had to have been some kind of breakthrough, but what happened was that film got introduced into the BBC through Tony Garnett and Sydney Newman coming in, through the back door as it were.[54]

It was these ideas about short mini-dramas 'using maybe hundreds of edits' that Kennedy Martin developed in his MacTaggart Lecture, delivered at the Edinburgh Television Festival in August 1986. Acknowledging the part that James MacTaggart had played in the development of a new drama when Elwyn Jones brought him down from Glasgow to produce the *Storyboard* series, Kennedy Martin proceeded to analyse why the early 1960s period of experiment and innovation, begun with *Storyboard* and culminating with *Diary of a Young Man*, did not destroy naturalism as they had hoped:

> When Ken Loach, Jimmy McTaggart [sic], Peter Duguid and John and myself finished *Diary of a Young Man* – which was a kind of statement of all we had learnt – I did think that we had set the agenda for the next ten years. But it was not to be; it was the naturalism of *Z Cars* and the realism of the *Wednesday Play* which were going to do that. (Kennedy Martin, 1986: 10)

1965 was the 'watershed' year when film and pre-recorded drama began to take over from live drama, which, for all its limitations, did have the advantage of being less vulnerable to editorial control, simply because no one could preview the programme. As John McGrath later remarked: 'having tape and being able to pre-record and being able to spin in scenes and then subsequently having cameras that got lightweight and you could take out, that was all terrific, but it also brought with it the possibility of surveillance of what you were doing. The technology of censorship was there ... '[55] 1965 was also the year in which *The Wednesday Play* began to redefine the nature of television drama. Yet while *The Wednesday Play* was responsible for some ground-breaking plays its success, according to Kennedy Martin, proved counter-productive as far as the development of a new aesthetic in the mainstream of television drama was concerned:

> I do believe that the *Wednesday Play*, by its very success, effectively pre-empted the debate on television drama. In the process of doing so, the crude but interesting speculation about a native television style got swept to one side.
>
> While the Plays Department at the BBC went from strength to strength, the Series and Serials went down the drain. After *Diary* there was no new controversial material. There seemed to be an unconscious pact between the two departments – a sort of pact with the devil, in which Plays took on all the radical drama and Series became middle-of-the-road. (Kennedy Martin, 1986: 10)

Furthermore, the technological revolution of pre-recorded video, light-weight film cameras and post-production editing, which Kennedy Martin saw as essential to the development of a New Drama, brought the unconsidered outcome of greater editorial control, ushering in a new era of drama production in which the work of progressive writers became subject to various degrees of censorship and control:

> [T]here was a growing realisation that as a result of the new post-production techniques, at least some of the writers' input could now be done by producers and script-editors, and that any mistakes – the mistakes that the writer was originally employed to see did not happen in live television – could now be rectified in the cutting-room. As a result, a new media-ocracy began to develop in popular television. Out of which grew, not the power of the director (which I had forecast in the *Encore* article), but that of the producer and his script-editor. And with the safety-net of skilled technicians to cushion their errors, the creation of stories gradually became the responsibility of committees. Thus the miracle of post-production, which was going to bring such magic to television, became an institution which blunted talent and hid the incompetence of management and essentially reinforced the safe, the conservative and the bland. (Kennedy Martin, 1986: 10)

Making reference to the inaugural MacTaggart Lecture, in which John McGrath had criticised *Days of Hope* and *Bill Brand* as potentially radical dramas whose messages had become blurred because of their adoption of a naturalist form, Kennedy Martin argued that:

> What he failed to realise at the time, and what we can see with hindsight, was that these two series were not the end of the road for a genre which had begun with the *Wednesday Play*, but the first sign of a revival in Series, which, over the next five years, was to give us such pieces as *Rock Follies, Gangsters, Out, Pennies from Heaven, Law and Order* and *Boys from the Blackstuff*. These original television drama series moved in to fill the vacuum caused by the crisis in single plays. (Kennedy Martin, 1986: 11)

He might also have added *Edge of Darkness*, screened at the end of the previous year, to this list, for it was undoubtedly the success of *Edge of Darkness* that had brought the invitation for Kennedy Martin to deliver the MacTaggart Lecture that August. Yet the reference he did make to *Edge of Darkness* was to relate an experience during the filming of it which had caused him to reflect on the need for a new kind of television drama to provide an alternative to the existing forms. The time was ripe, he felt, to open up 'a Fourth Front, alongside Plays, Series and Serials, which would deal specifically with micro-drama ... ' (Kennedy Martin, 1986: 11).

The possibilities for innovative drama in the mid 1980s, Kennedy Martin argued, resided in a new form of micro-drama, modelled on the pop video and commercials, mini-dramas lasting only a few minutes 'in which time is fractured and naturalism goes out of the window. The great success of videos has been the torpedoing of naturalistic continuity and style, and the replacement of it with every kind of alternative' (Kennedy Martin, 1986: 11). The advantage of this new form was that it would be cheaper and quicker to produce than expensive long-form dramas (like *Edge of Darkness*) which could be in production for several years. Also, new technology – lightweight video cameras and more sophisticated editing systems – and a new, younger generation of film school graduates, weaned on TV commercials and music videos, meant that:

> [W]e have the technical resources and the talent to make stunning short imaginative dramas, and we have the models on which these micro-dramas could be based [...] Given that there is a need for feedback and that the technology, the talent and the resources are available, what would happen if they were used to construct short bursts of energy, micro-dramas, in which the content was not dictated by the need to sell either music or beer, but reflected an exuberant social, political or aesthetic point of view? (Kennedy Martin, 1986: 12).

Kennedy Martin saw these new dramas as 'a conduit for unrepresented forces' and a way of putting pressure on the existing channels for 'faster and more fragmented shows' (Kennedy Martin, 1986: 12). In this he was picking up on postmodern ideas about a 'three-minute culture' in which attention spans have grown shorter, especially among younger viewers, and narrative forms have become more fragmented. Central to this thesis is the ability of the viewer to use the television remote control to change rapidly from one channel to another, a development highlighted by Kennedy Martin in his lecture:

> The arrival of the remote-control button is but one of the technical developments which has already had a major impact ... It has also brought about a change in viewers' perceptions. They are now able to cut from

one image to another with an ease once given only to vision-mixers. The result is that an element of fragmentation is being built into the viewing pattern at the viewer's end. Like it or not interactive television is emerging. And it is going to become more interactive as technology progresses. Programme-makers on popular channels must eventually take this into account, and zapp before they are zapped. This is the environment in which the four-minute drama will become important, since they should be, by definition, zapp-proof [...]

Looking to the future, I can see a bifurcation coming. On the one hand, a small screen with a segmented, fragmented, post-modernist style. On the other, the wall screen, in which television reaches its optimum size, bringing it in line with cinema, with spectacle and with Peacock. (Kennedy Martin, 1986: 12)

Twenty years later Kennedy Martin's speculations seem remarkably prescient. Developments in technology have brought a bifurcation similar to the one he envisaged, with miniature screens available on mobile telephones and on palmtop computers, while widescreen televisions with cinema surround-sound cater for viewers wanting to see the latest Hollywood blockbuster or the lavish television serial on a much larger screen. Meanwhile a proliferation of digital television channels has brought more choice for the viewer and the remote control has become an essential instrument in the new multi-channel, interactive broadcasting environment.

While music videos have flourished, with digital channels now specialising in the form, the concept of a 'fourth front' of micro-dramas, opening up a new radical frontier, has not yet come to pass. Instead the pace of series drama has quickened and storylines have multiplied as drama producers have responded to the increased competition for the viewer's attention. Innovation is occasionally evident in series and serial drama, while single dramas sometimes engage with social and political issues, but naturalism remains the dominant form.

In his consideration of 'Nats Go Home', Kennedy Martin's 'first statement of a new drama for television', John Caughie remarked: 'if this was the "first statement" we seem still to be waiting for the second' (Caughie, 2000: 92). Yet in its attempt to intervene in television drama debate in the mid 1980s and to theorise on the need to open up a 'fourth front' in television drama, Troy Kennedy Martin's 1986 MacTaggart Lecture had a familiar polemical thrust and a manifesto-like quality to it. Coming twenty-two years after 'Nats Go Home' this was Kennedy Martin's 'Second Statement of a New Drama for Television'.

Notes

1 Troy Kennedy Martin, interviewed by the author, 17 April 2003.
2 BBC WAC, T31/292, memo to Anthony Pelissier from Ian Atkins, 22 February 1956.
3 BBC WAC, T31/292, letter to Michael Barry from Anthony Pelissier, 22 February 1960.
4 *The Torrents of Spring* comprises a series of long takes, not just one long take as Donnellan implies. Charles Parker contributed a complex, multi-layered soundtrack to the drama. (A viewing copy of *The Torrents of Spring* is held by the National Film and Television Archive).
5 John McGrath, interviewed by the author, 27 April 2000.
6 The term 'producer' was still being used to describe the work of the TV director at the BBC at this time.
7 The schedule for the day of the production, Tuesday 27 September 1960, involved preparing the set and lighting in the morning, with camera rehearsals from 5.00–8.30 pm followed by 'Closed Circuit Transmission and Telerecording' from 9.00–9.30 pm (BFI, TKM Collection, Item 10, *Mac*, General Television Training Course: Practical Production Exercise).
8 BFI, TKM Collection, Item 10, *Mac*, Practical Production Exercise, p. 2.
9 Ibid, p. 9.
10 Ibid.
11 Roger Smith, interviewed by the author, 26 April 2000.
12 BBC WAC, Audience Research Report, *Storyboard: The Gentleman From Paris*, 14 August 1961.
13 The only evidence that any of the plays were telerecorded is a note on the rehearsal script for *I'll Be Waiting*, suggesting it was due to be telerecorded off transmission, but if it was the recording has not survived.
14 Troy Kennedy Martin, interviewed by the author, 4 April 2003.
15 BFI, TKM Collection, Item 51, *The Middle Men*, Camera Script, p. 28.
16 BBC WAC, Audience Research Report, *Storyboard: The Middle Men*, 31 August 1961.
17 Ibid.
18 BBC WAC, Audience Research Report, *Storyboard: The Long Spoon*, 7 September 1961.
19 Ibid.
20 BFI, TKM Collection, Item 52, *The Long Spoon*, Rehearsal Script, p. 33.
21 BBC WAC, Audience Research Report, *Storyboard: The Long Spoon*, 7 September 1961.
22 Roger Smith, interviewed by the author, 26 April 2000.
23 Ibid.
24 *The Wednesday Play* began in October 1964 with six plays left over from Peter Luke's *Festival* anthology series (BBC, October 1963–June 1964).
25 Troy Kennedy Martin, interviewed by the author, 27 March 1986.
26 Ibid.
27 Allan Prior, 'If only they'd film it!', *Screenwriter*, No. 15, Spring 1964, pp. 25–6. See also Jamie Sexton, ''Televerite' hits Britain: documentary, drama and the growth of 16mm filmmaking in British television', *Screen* 44:4, Winter 2003, pp. 439–443.
28 Troy Kennedy Martin, interviewed by the author, 27 March 1986.
29 Ibid.
30 'Reaction: Replies to Troy Kennedy Martin's attack on naturalistic television drama', *Encore*, May–June 1964, pp. 39–48; 'Television Drama – Is This The Way Ahead?', *Screenwriter*, No. 15, Spring 1964, pp. 18–35.

31 Ken Loach subverted the usual studio recording procedure on *Up the Junction* by getting the camera operators to film the studio scenes in such a way that they needed editing. As it was not possible to edit the videotape there was no option but to use a 16mm telerecording of the studio material, made as a safety back-up, to edit with. By this means Loach was able to apply film editing techniques to the studio scenes as well as the location footage. (For more on this see Cooke, 2003: 69–75)

32 BBC WAC, T48/351/1, 6 March 1963.

33 BBC WAC, T48/351/1, memo from Elwyn Jones to the Assistant Head of Copyright, 13 March 1963.

34 Interview with the author, 4 April 2003.

35 John McGrath, interviewed by the author, 27 April 2000. A checklist of McGrath's work in *New Theatre Quarterly*, Vol. 1, No.4, November 1985, also refers to *Jack* as the 'basis for TV series *Diary of a Young Man*' (p. 401).

36 Troy Kennedy Martin, interviewed by the author, 4 April 2003.

37 BFI Library, John McGrath Special Collection, Box 9, Item 1, Letter from Gareth Wigan to John McGrath, 24 October 1963.

38 From episode one of *Diary of a Young Man: Survival or They Came to a City* (BBC 1, 8 August 1964).

39 The National Film and Television Archive has viewing copies of episodes one, five and six. Episodes two, three and four no longer exist.

40 In an article introducing *Diary of a Young Man* in the *Radio Times*, James MacTaggart was quoted as saying of the two protagonists: 'Their adventures are based firmly on a realistic look at what's going on in London now – seen from the cool, appraising viewpoint of their sharply independent generation. The series is essentially a new kind of writing for television, exploring the possibilities of the medium in a rather more extreme way than we've tried before.' *Radio Times*, 6 August 1964, p. 5.

41 BBC WAC, T5/630/1, memo from Sydney Newman to James MacTaggart, 13 August 1964.

42 BFI, TKM Collection, Item 1, *Diary of a Young Man*, Rehearsal Script.

43 BBC WAC, T48/351/1, letter from Michael Bakewell to Gareth Wigan (Kennedy Martin's agent), 16 September 1964.

44 It is possible that *Macheath – Masterspy* was written before *Diary of a Young Man* as an early draft of episode five of *Diary* has *Macheath Masterspy II* written on the cover and crossed out.

45 From the treatment for *Macheath – Masterspy*. I am grateful to Troy Kennedy Martin for providing me with a copy of his treatment and the scripts for *Macheath – Masterspy*.

46 Transcript for *Macheath – Masterspy*, episode one: 'The Smithfield Market Mystery', pp. 1–2.

47 Troy Kennedy Martin, interviewed by the author, 27 March 1986.

48 I am grateful to Troy Kennedy Martin for providing me with a copy of the script for *Great Scott, It's Matilda!*

49 BBC WAC, T5/1, 648/1, memo from Ken Trodd to the Assistant Head of Copyright, 20 October 1966.

50 BBC WAC, T5/1, 648/1, memo from Shaun MacLoughlin (Organising Assistant in the Plays Department) to the Assistant Head of Copyright (copied to Ken Trodd), 20 October 1966.

51 BFI Library, John McGrath Special Collection, Box 10, Item 5, BBC Press Release, *Six*, undated.

52 The first television dramas to be filmed on video, on location, appeared in 1964. Philip Saville used an Outside Broadcast unit for an innovative production of

Hamlet at Elsinore (BBC 1, 19 April 1964) and an Outside Broadcast unit was used on a Granada series called *The Villains* (Granada, 1964–5).
53 John McGrath, interviewed by the author, 27 April 2000.
54 Troy Kennedy Martin, interviewed by the author, 27 March 1986.
55 John McGrath, interviewed by the author, 27 April 2000.

Drama series 4

By the early 1960s series drama was the most popular form of drama on British television. ITV had largely been responsible for this, for while the BBC had two very popular series, *Dixon of Dock Green* and *Maigret*, ITV dominated the ratings with a combination of imported American series, such as *Dragnet*, *Rawhide* and *Wagon Train*, and homegrown series, such as *Emergency – Ward 10*, *No Hiding Place* and *Coronation Street*. Such was ITV's popularity as the new decade dawned that BBC programmes rarely appeared in the twenty top-rated programmes.

In 1960 the BBC appointed a new Director General, Hugh Carlton Greene, and it was Greene who was to lead the fightback as the corporation embarked on a new era. The BBC's cause was helped by the Pilkington Committee, set up by the government in 1960 to consider the impact of ITV on British broadcasting. When Pilkington reported in 1962 the committee criticised the 'low standards' of ITV and recommended that the new third channel be given to the BBC. Yet by the time of the Pilkington Report the BBC had already begun to respond to the challenge of ITV, recruiting a new generation of enthusiastic young programme makers, including the 'young Turks' in the BBC Drama Department, who were responsible for a number of innovative and popular new programmes in the early 1960s. *Storyboard* was one of the first manifestations of the new era at the BBC, but in 1962 a whole new range of programmes was introduced, including *Compact* (1962–5), *Dr Finlay's Casebook* (1962–71), *Steptoe and Son* (1962–5), *That Was The Week That Was* (1962–3), *Studio 4* (January–September 1962) and *Z Cars* (1962–78).

Z Cars (1962–78)

Z Cars not only led the BBC fightback against ITV in the weekly ratings charts, it also marked a significant departure for the BBC in terms of popular programming. Launched on 2 January 1962 the series marked the arrival of a new kind of police drama, one conceived and developed in response to the cosy, reassuring image of policing represented by the BBC's own *Dixon of Dock Green*. Some sources suggest that *Z Cars* was inspired by a four-part BBC drama-documentary series called *Jacks and Knaves* (November–December 1961), based on the real-life cases of Liverpool police detective Bill Prendergast. However Troy Kennedy Martin started work on *Z Cars* in April 1961, several months before *Jacks and Knaves* was broadcast, even before the *Storyboard* plays were produced. He described the genesis of *Z Cars* in an article written in 1978:

> I was lying, annoyingly ill, in 1961 monitoring police messages to pass the time and occasionally coming across incidents where it was obvious that the police were not coping. They seemed confused, lost and apparently young and inexperienced. The world that filtered through these fragmented calls was so different from that of *Dixon* that I took the idea of a new series to Elwyn Jones, who was then head of a small but influential section of the BBC Drama Department. (Kennedy Martin, 1978: 126)

Elwyn Jones was in charge of the Documentary Drama Unit within BBC Drama, producing dramatised documentaries such as *Who Me?* (1959), *Scotland Yard* (1960) and *Jacks and Knaves* with writers and directors including Robert Barr, Gilchrist Calder and Colin Morris. Having developed links with the Lancashire Constabulary during the production of *Who Me?* and *Jacks and Knaves*, Jones was keen for Kennedy Martin's new police series to be set in Lancashire and he arranged for him to spend time researching the series in the Liverpool area:

> I was originally going to set it in London and it was Elwyn Jones who thought of setting it in the north, because he'd already got an agreement to do these four plays [*Jacks and Knaves*] ... some people say that I was influenced by them, but I didn't see them before I'd written the first six or so [episodes of *Z Cars*] ... I do think setting it in the north made a huge difference and gave it the same sort of edge that you get now with these films that are coming out in the north.[1]

The origins of *Z Cars* within the Documentary Drama Unit, together with Jones' insistence that it be set in the north, were key factors in the success of the new series. Its development as a documentary drama helped to make the series more authentic than *Dixon*, which was a BBC Light Entertainment production, and the northern setting helped to reinforce the series' claim to be more realistic. The new wave of northern drama, seen in films such as *Room at the Top* (1959) and *Saturday Night and Sunday Morning* (1960) and in television series such as Granada's *Coronation Street* (1960), had introduced a new realism into British culture at the turn of the decade and the BBC had Elwyn Jones to thank for seeing the opportunity to develop a new kind of northern-based police series which would enable the BBC to respond to the popular success of ITV series such as *Coronation Street*. Jones asked David Rose, who was also working for the Documentary Drama Unit, to produce the series:

> Elwyn simply said to me 'Look David, would you produce a police series? I've been to the Lancashire Constabulary and they say they've got these things called "Z cars", which is rather new, crime patrol, two police within the car.' Then he said 'I think John McGrath would be great for first director, so let's get hold of him.' Troy had been up there by then and said that he would like to write the first episode at least – six were asked for, six episodes of fifty minutes ... [2]

Jones was instrumental in getting the *Z Cars* team together, also bringing in Robert Barr to take responsibility for 'ensuring the programme's documentary credentials' (Laing, 1991: 127). Initially Kennedy Martin and the Lancashire-born writer Allan Prior, whose previous credits included a four-part drama-documentary called *Man at the Door* (BBC, 1960) which David Rose had directed, were asked to write three episodes each, but by the end of September 1961 Rose was referring to 'a series of thirteen 45-minute episodes to be transmitted live' in a memo sent to Robert Barr, Elwyn Jones and Kennedy Martin.[3] Of these thirteen episodes Kennedy Martin wrote six, Prior five, and Michael Ashe and Robert Barr one each. When the programme proved to be an immediate critical and popular success, with viewing figures rising from an initial nine million to fourteen million within the first few weeks, a further thirteen episodes were commissioned.[4] Eventually the first series of *Z Cars* ran for thirty-one episodes, from 2 January to 31 July 1962.

Although Kennedy Martin may have had the original idea for the series, David Rose's account of his conversation with Elwyn Jones suggests it was Jones who saw the potential for basing the series around police operating in patrol cars, a new development in policing in the early 1960s and a distinct departure from the portrayal of George Dixon as the friendly 'bobby on the beat' in *Dixon of Dock Green*. This change in methods of policing was prompted by an increase in social problems in the 1960s as new towns began to replace inner city slums and it was the impact of these social and environmental changes that Kennedy Martin and John McGrath wanted to explore in *Z Cars*. As McGrath later admitted, they were not interested simply in making a new kind of police series but wanted:

> [T]o use the cops as a key or way of getting into a whole society ... . And it was very cleverly worked out ... the two kinds of communities these

cops were going to work in. The first was called New Town, which was roughly based on Kirkby. The other was Seaport, which was based on the sort of Crosby-Waterloo water front. The series was going to be a kind of documentary about people's lives in these areas, and the cops were incidental – they were the means of finding out about people's lives. (Laing, 1986: 170)

In this respect *Z Cars* differed from *Coronation Street*, which was based on a concept of a close-knit northern community that was, in reality, rapidly becoming outdated. Far from wanting to create a community-based drama Kennedy Martin and McGrath wanted to focus on the lack of community feeling in new towns such as Kirkby and to explore, through the work of the new crime patrols, the kind of social problems that were occurring as a result of social and environmental change in the early 1960s. Kennedy Martin thought popular drama could and should be used to explore these issues and it was this which excited him about developing a new drama series for the BBC:

> The main purpose of a series is to hold a mirror up to English life as it is at the moment. This is something which television series have obviously failed to do. The pictures most of them have drawn have been patently untrue. I also wanted to break down the dominance of the story line and put in its place character and dialogue. I wanted to reassert the funda-mental values of life. Death, for instance. We planned to have no more than one murder in the first 13 episodes and when death occurred it was to be, as it should be, terrifying. (Kennedy Martin, 1978: 311–13)

The series began, in fact, with a death. A policeman has been killed while investigating a robbery and his death is the catalyst for the intro-duction of crime patrols at Newtown police division. Detective Chief Inspector Frank Barlow (Stratford Johns) puts Detective Sergeant John Watt (Frank Windsor) in charge of 'finding the crews', Kennedy Martin's working title for episode one before it became 'Four of a Kind' (2 January 1962). Most of the first episode is spent introducing the main characters as Barlow and Watt find their four crime patrol men from the ranks of the ordinary police constables: Fancy Smith (Brian Blessed), Jock Weir (Joseph Brady), Bert Lynch (James Ellis) and Bob Steele (Jeremy Kemp).

Character certainly dominates story in the first episode, most of which is spent establishing the traits of the main characters, as one might expect in the opening episode of a new series. Kennedy Martin knew that audiences would be engaged by interesting characters speaking realistic dialogue – once the audience was involved with the charac-ters the storylines and social issues he and McGrath wanted to explore would follow. For Kennedy Martin this meant showing the police as ordinary human beings with human attributes, men who smoke, bet on the horses, even abuse their wives – as in a controversial scene in the first episode where it is made clear that Janey Steele's black eye is the result of a fight with her husband the previous evening.

The Chief Constable of the Lancashire County Constabulary, which had assisted with the research and preparation for the programme, was horrified at the police being portrayed in such a way and immediately demanded that the Controller of BBC Television Programmes, Stuart Hood, take the series off the air. Hood defended the programme and the only thing that was taken off was the credit at the end acknowledging the help of the Lancashire County Constabulary. What was offensive to the Chief Constable was for many viewers a refreshing change from previous representations of the police, as the BBC Audience Research Report on the first episode indicated:

> [M]any viewers were pleased with the way 'Four of a Kind' set the scene for *Z Cars*. According to comment, the script gripped their attention from the outset, developing the story on intriguing lines, and while the episode itself came to a clear-cut conclusion, there was plenty of interest and excitement for the future. Nor, apparently, was there any feeling here that the programme had shown the police in a poor light. On the contrary, it was praised as breaking new ground in presenting a constabulary who were neither brutal nor benign, but thoroughly human and down-to-earth, whether at home or at work. This new slant on the 'arm of the law' ('making one see the police as they are – men who have their qualities and failings') apparently struck a number of viewers as a most refreshing feature of the programme. Not only that, but the whole script was described as written in an agreeably lively as well as realistic vein. Though some members of the large group who had taken to the idea of *Z Cars* may have valued the documentary aspects of the programme most, it was clear that many more had enjoyed the characterisation of 'Four of a Kind' and found real entertainment in following the adventures of the quartet of young policemen who, in the course of the story, are selected to man the Newtown crime car patrol.[5]

The combination of documentary realism and Kennedy Martin's fictional characterisation of the police undoubtedly contributed to the critical and popular success of *Z Cars*. In an early article on the series, Peter Lewis observed how the blend of documentary and drama was responsible for the series' distinctiveness, despite, or rather because of, the creative tensions between Kennedy Martin, whose background was in drama, and Robert Barr, whose background was in documentary. Lewis pointed out that for Kennedy Martin, after his earlier single plays and the *Storyboard* series:

Z Cars was completely fresh ground. As a natural fiction writer he found himself forced into what the BBC regarded as primarily a job of documentary writing, under the control of a group producer, Robert Barr, with a distinguished documentary reputation. The resulting friction between them made the series what it is. Both men, with a rueful regard for each other, are prepared to admit that it wouldn't have been as good without the fighting. 'One of the qualities of *Z Cars*,' says Barr, 'comes from a constant war between me, who wants it to be documentary, and Troy, who wants to write fiction.' (Lewis, 1962: 309–10)

The success of *Z Cars* also owed much to the ambition of Kennedy Martin and John McGrath to introduce a new style into television drama. Not only did they want to make the series more realistic, they also wanted to make it much faster than most studio drama. Consequently they were always pushing to use film as much as possible, both to enhance the realism of the series but also to achieve a faster narrative pace. Even in the studio scenes they sought a faster pace than was usual in live studio drama of the time. John McGrath explains what they were trying to achieve:

When I did *Z Cars*, certainly for the first time for me, I had six cameras to work with and a big studio, and designers and writers who worked together with the director to make it possible to have maybe twenty-five or thirty sets in a studio ... The idea was to design ... which is Troy's phrase really ... to design for the camera, rather than to design for the stage, and the writing was such that there were a lot of small scenes ... you know there were two scenes a page, where before you would have had one scene for fifteen pages, and as a writer and as a director, particularly a director at that time, I was very excited by the idea of giving television some of the speed, the pace, of film, because that was also the time of the *nouvelle vague* and *A Bout de Souffle* where people cut-cut-cut, and this 'but we mix between scenes' – no we don't, we cut![6]

While the exposition in episode one is slower than in some subsequent episodes, because of the need to introduce the characters, the increased use of film is evident right from the beginning, when Barlow and Watt are seen at the graveside of the murdered police constable in a sequence filmed on location.

Episode two, 'Limping Rabbit' (9 January 1962) also begins with a telecine sequence, one of thirteen such sequences in the episode which, according to Acting Drama Organiser Terence Cook, had a 'higher than average' budget, estimated at £4500, as a result of 'almost half' of it being shot on film.[7] With a cast list of twenty-one, plus four non-speaking parts, and thirty-nine scenes in its forty-five minute running time, 'Limping Rabbit' (originally titled 'Missing from Home' in earlier drafts) is typical of the narrative complexity of Kennedy Martin's scripts for *Z Cars*. The opening sequence of episode two also introduces an element of narrative continuity into the series when Janey Steele, the wife of PC Bob Steele, arrives home to find a brick has been thrown through her window, bearing out her husband's concern, expressed in episode one, that it is a 'rough area' for her to live in: 'They don't like policemen or policemen's wives round here.' In the first episode Janey had laughed off the black eye her husband had given her by telling him it would get her some respect from the neighbours. At the beginning of episode two, after returning home to discover the broken window, it seems that she has won the confidence of at least one of her neighbours when a woman calls in to tell her about a girl who is missing, knowing that Janey is the wife of a policeman who might be able to do something about it. In this manner the main story in episode two is introduced. Janey goes to the police station to report the missing girl. But this is only the beginning of a complicated narrative revolving around the enigma of a rabbit (hence the episode title) which, it transpires, is a toy rabbit belonging to a girl who has been kidnapped by a local villain, who is planning to ship her abroad to be sold into prostitution. The narrative enigma of a toy rabbit suggests a frivolous storyline but, while there is humour in the episode, especially in an early scene in a crowded betting office where Bert Lynch tries to sort out a dispute involving at least ten characters, the tone of the episode is quite dark. One of the incidental characters in the betting office has been asked by the kidnapper to collect the missing girl's toy rabbit in order to keep her quiet and it is the narrative enigma of the rabbit which proves crucial to the police tracking the girl down to a warehouse at the docks.

The final sequence at the docks was shot entirely on film, no doubt causing the escalation in the budget, and the narrative tempo increases as the hunt for the missing girl becomes more urgent as the police try to apprehend the villain before she is shipped abroad. The cutting between scenes in the final part of the episode is very fast for live television drama and it is the brisk pace of the narrative, together with the increased amount of telecine footage, which made *Z Cars* an exciting stylistic departure from previous British television drama. The dark nature of the storyline, with its implications of a white slave trade involving young girls operating out of a British port (the fictional Seaport), would have given added realism and seriousness to the episode.

After the first four episodes the running time of each *Z Cars* episode was increased to fifty minutes and in his next episode, 'Friday Night' (6 February 1962), Kennedy Martin introduced a far more complex narrative structure, interweaving several storylines instead of basing each episode around one main case. Twenty-six characters featured in the episode, with another fifteen non-speaking parts, and the mainly studio-based action took place on eight studio sets, with an additional nine tele-cine sequences. 'Friday Night' was well-received by viewers, according to the BBC Audience Research Report, gaining a reaction index rating of 69, higher than any of the previous episodes: 'Here was all the drama, tragedy, humour and sheer "slog" of routine police procedure, made all the more effective for being presented with commendable realism, and with never a suggestion of romanticism or mock heroics.'[8]

Although telerecordings exist of 'Four of a Kind', 'Limping Rabbit' and 'Friday Night' only one of the five other episodes credited to Kennedy Martin in the first series has survived. The 'missing' episodes include episode eight, 'Family Feud' (20 February 1962), the first episode in the series to list a script editor (John Hopkins), reflecting 'the necessary expansion of the initial small team to cope with the decision to extend the run from thirteen to thirty-one episodes' (Laing, 1991: 129–30). Kennedy Martin was unhappy with Elwyn Jones' appointment of John Hopkins as script editor, feeling it undermined his own role, which had essentially been that of an uncredited script editor on the series up to that point, and it marks the beginnings of his dissatisfaction with the series as it gradually changed from being a hard-hitting exposé of new policing methods to become a long-running series in which the police were to become the stars of the show.

In an article on *Z Cars* published in *Contrast* in the summer of 1962, but written before the first series had ended, Peter Lewis highlighted a change in the series as it moved from its radical beginnings to take up a position as a pillar of the BBC schedule:

> [T]he real danger to *Z Cars* is its sheer success. As soon as the BBC realized it was on a winner the run of the series was extended from the projected 13 episodes to 31. There is to be a second series after a six-week break. This was a hard-faced commercial decision and surely not a wise one. No writer can produce that many episodes on the run. There are now eight writers engaged on the series, which means that it is out of the control of its creator. There are already signs that the coinage of the writing is being debased for the sake of productivity. [...]
>
> [I]deally a series could have the development of a play spread out over its episodes. Its characters could grow as people grow in life. *Z Cars* began with plenty of strong, well-differentiated characters. It gave them the background and the elbow room to develop. But the development has not occurred. Could it?
>
> Troy Kennedy Martin thinks it should but doesn't think it will. 'It's like a meat factory,' he said. 'The organization isn't there to allow character development. You need a far more closely knit team of writers and

> directors bound together with a common attitude and enthusiasm. It calls for living together, living for the series, which is the sort of thing that has never happened in television. A series is a living thing, always twisting and turning. But if they insist on this sameness week after week then the characters tend to become caricatures of themselves. After a time you just get hollowness and nothing.' (Lewis, 1962: 314–15)

The extension of the series to thirty-one episodes exposed the differences between the small original team, differences that had initially proved constructive rather than destructive. With the necessary expansion of personnel as the series became established the original ambitions Kennedy Martin and McGrath had for *Z Cars* were eroded, to be replaced by the more formulaic 'sameness' of a long-running series, which is not to say that there was a decline in quality. With writers of the calibre of John Hopkins, Alan Plater and Allan Prior contributing episodes, and with David Rose still in charge, *Z Cars* continued to prosper for another three years, coming to an end in December 1965. At this point some of the original team, including Elwyn Jones, David Rose, Stratford Johns and Frank Windsor, went off to make *Softly, Softly* (BBC 1, 1966–70) while *Z Cars* was resurrected as a twice-weekly, half-hour series in March 1967, reverting in 1971 to a weekly fifty-minute format.

Of the other 'missing' Kennedy Martin episodes, the plot for episode eleven, 'Jail Break' (13 March 1962), was subsequently used, together with the plot for 'Four of a Kind', as the basis for a *Z Cars* novel, published in 1962.[9] Episode thirteen, 'Sudden Death' (27 March 1962), was the last of Kennedy Martin's six scripts for the original run of thirteen episodes, and episode twenty-seven, 'Teamwork' (3 July 1962), was transmitted after he had resigned from the series. The one other Kennedy Martin episode from the first series which has survived is episode sixteen, 'Invisible Enemy' (17 April 1962), which is notable for featuring Tony Garnett as Jack Nicholls, 'the tearaway with the thin lips', as PC Fancy Smith describes him. Set in a block of flats in Newtown, the plot revolves around the theft of money from a gas meter in a flat on the twelfth floor (a location which enables some remarkable shots looking down on the Z cars as they arrive at the building). Nicholls is suspected of the theft, but it is clear he is suspected mainly because of his appearance and his attitude towards the police. At the end it is revealed that a neighbour has broken into the flat and stolen from the meter in order to incriminate Nicholls, because she thinks he is part of 'the gang from across the park', who she fears.

John McGrath directed 'Invisible Enemy' and in a 1993 BBC documentary about television police series he was full of praise for Kennedy

Martin's writing: 'Troy's dialogue is wonderful. It's not at all natural-istic. It's formalised, it's a dance, it's a play with rhythms, it's a play with words that you wouldn't use normally but which Troy somehow manages to make believable in the mouths of people.'[10] The documen-tary used an extract from 'Invisible Enemy' to illustrate this, a scene in which Nicholls is being questioned by PC Jock Weir about why he was on the roof of the block of flats:

> *Weir*: What goes on up on the roof?
> *Nicholls*: Oh the washing gets dried and the kids make love.
> *Weir*: What takes you there?
> *Nicholls*: I like the fresh air copper. I like just an hour away from the smell of drying fat and stale beer and the diesel smoke. I like to get away from the sweat of the workers and the bad breath of the police.[11]

Forty-two years after delivering these lines, Tony Garnett reflected on Kennedy Martin's talent as a writer, especially his ability to write believable dialogue: 'Actors love his writing because it is not literary but it resonates at so many different levels, but at the top level it's play-able, and it's sayable, and that's unusual for a writer who hasn't been an actor.'[12]

There's also a lot of humour in Kennedy Martin's *Z Cars* episodes, a necessary ingredient which he felt was missing from the scripts of other writers. The humour takes different forms but it often arises out of the rhythms of the writing, something Kennedy Martin was particu-larly skilled at. One scene in 'Invisible Enemy' illustrates this very well. PC Fancy Smith is questioning Miss Sullivan, a nosey neighbour of the couple whose flat has been robbed, about some movement she saw in the flat when they were out:

> *Fancy Smith*: What kind of movement?
> *Miss Sullivan*: Shadows.
> *Fancy*: Shadows?
> *Miss S*: Aye, shadows.
> *Fancy*: What kind of shadows?
> *Miss S*: Shadows of the intruders, menacing.
> *Fancy*: What were they doing?
> *Miss S*: They were menacing, they menaced.
> *Fancy*: Well why didn't you do anything about it?
> *Miss S*: What, with those shadows menacing about? No.
> *Fancy*: But Ma Crawford's curtains were drawn weren't they?
> *Miss S*: Aye, so all I saw was shadows.
> *Fancy*: How many?
> *Miss S*: How can you count shadows? Two, three, four men.
> *Fancy*: Ah, this gang 'eh?
> *Miss S*: Aye! The gang from across the park.[13]

The scene continues in this manner, both amusing and gripping because of the intensity of the performances, emphasised by close-up camerawork and fast cutting, but also because of the rhythms of the speech. It is a distinctive feature of Kennedy Martin's writing for *Z Cars* and one of the ingredients which made the early episodes so enjoyable:

> John said my dialogue was really poetic rather than real, because I got in a lot of the rhythms of things ... I can remember one particular scene where they are looking for some guy in a bar and the fellow they are talking to is heaving the barrels up or down and he just says something like: 'Have you just seen so-and-so?' 'So-and-so?' 'Yes, so-and-so, has he been here?' 'You mean so-and-so?' Nothing happens but there's just this rhythm about the whole thing.[14]

'Invisible Enemy' becomes almost farcical when Barlow and Watt and yet more police arrive on the scene, with about eight policemen crowded into the flat to investigate a petty theft. Yet the story, as in most of Kennedy Martin's scripts, also has a dark undercurrent. Nicholls tells Fancy Smith that he comes up to the twelfth floor of the block of flats because his girlfriend used to live there, but she committed suicide. The suggestion is that she killed herself because someone told her Nicholls was going out with another woman. The gossip was the neighbour, Miss Sullivan, whose story was concocted again because of her fear of Nicholls as a member of 'the gang from across the park.' Superbly written and plotted, with some great characterisation and naturalistic performances that are well realised by John McGrath's sympathetic and imaginative direction, 'Invisible Enemy' is one of the best of the early *Z Cars* episodes, encapsulating what Kennedy Martin and McGrath were trying to achieve with the series.

There were to be only two more *Z Cars* episodes on which Kennedy Martin and McGrath collaborated: 'Teamwork' in July 1962 and the very last episode, 'Pressure' (BBC 1, 20 September 1978), for which they returned to the BBC sixteen years after leaving the series, reuniting with several of the original members of the cast who also returned for the final episode. 'Pressure' was filmed mainly on location in Liverpool, in colour and on video, using an Outside Broadcast unit. The opportunity to show parts of Liverpool that had been devastated by the recession of the 1970s was one of the reasons why Kennedy Martin and McGrath wanted to do the final episode. It gave them an opportunity to highlight the impact of rising unemployment on the Merseyside working class, a year before the election of Thatcher's Conservative government and four years before Alan Bleasdale's *Boys from the Blackstuff* presented a more celebrated portrait of the impact of mass unemployment on the area.

Like 'Friday Night', a much earlier episode on which Kennedy Martin and McGrath had worked together, 'Pressure' interweaves five different stories. The main one concerns Ferris (Tony Haygarth), who returns to Newtown at the beginning of the episode after an absence of several years working in Holland. As a returning exile, Ferris is the spokesman within the drama for the writer and director, themselves returning to Newtown after an absence of sixteen years. He arrives home, flaunting the money he's earned abroad, to find that all his mates are unemployed and the house he used to live in is now an empty shell. Ferris is a working-class poet, referred to as 'Rhymer' by his mates, and most of his dialogue is delivered in rhyming verse, sometimes as a voiceover – clearly a non-naturalistic technique for a mainstream series such as *Z Cars*. Towards the end of the episode he is stabbed by someone who has gone off with his wife and robbed of his hard-earned wages. This is the only moment of violence in the episode, in marked contrast to the violence in *Z Cars'* main competitor, *The Sweeney* (Thames, 1975–8), for which Kennedy Martin had written six episodes in the previous four years – his final episode, 'Hard Men', being screened just six days before 'Pressure'.

A second story in 'Pressure' concerns a young boy who turns up, hungry, at the police station. Bert Lynch (played once again by James Ellis), now an inspector, works with Maggie (Christine Hargreaves), a social worker, to discover that the boy has been abandoned by his mother and is living on his own in a rundown flat. The presence of the boy enables some comic business to take place, at the expense of the police, but the story also enables some serious concerns to be expressed about the pressures facing both the police and social services in contemporary Britain.

A third story is an internal investigation into corruption involving Detective Superintendent Boley (Alun Armstrong) who is being questioned by Detective Chief Superintendent Watt (Frank Windsor), back in Newtown especially to conduct the investigation (just as Frank Windsor was returning to the series for the first time since leaving for *Softly, Softly*).

A fourth story involves the installation of new steel shutters at the entrance to the police station, in anticipation of civil unrest as a result of the unemployment situation. This is also played for humour, to some extent, but again has a serious undercurrent, highlighting the way in which the police were becoming increasingly divorced from the public in the late 1970s, taking on a more coercive role as representatives of the State as the country approached the 'winter of discontent' which would culminate in the election of a Conservative government under the leadership of Margaret Thatcher.

The fifth story concerned a gas leak near the police station. Mainly played for comedy, this story enabled Kennedy Martin to have Brian Blessed, Joseph Brady, Jeremy Kemp and Colin Welland make cameo appearances as members of the public who wander in to the police station to report the smell of gas. It turns out that the odour is coming up through the drains and the leak is actually under a sewage plant, affording the opportunity for a joke about the prospect of there being 'a big brown cloud over the city for a week or two' if it blows up.

With the original Chief Constable (John Phillips) also putting in an appearance, the main original character missing from the final episode was Detective Chief Inspector Barlow (Stratford Johns). His absence may be significant. In his 1978 article, 'Four of a kind?', Kennedy Martin expressed concerns about the character of Barlow, who he felt had got 'out of control' following the original depiction of him as:

> ... a dreamer, a man who would never escape from the confines of Newtown, a passed-over Detective Chief Inspector whose ideas of promotion were to be forever thwarted, and indeed his motivation for the establishment of the Crime Patrol was yet another vain attempt to add to his stature.

> Although Stratford Johns' portrayal of the Inspector must have had something to do with the subsequent development of Barlow's character, one can't help feeling that a lot of other subconscious forces were at work. The avidity with which the press greeted the concept of Barlow as the stern face of authority, the vengeful father, surprised me; I felt it was a stereotype which would have been automatically resisted in the production office. After all, it seemed an amazingly old-fashioned concept. But this love affair with authority, this identification with power, the decision to go with the stream rather than check it, seemed to me to have undercurrents which had nothing to do with making a police series, but which reflected a certain atavism in English life and in the English character which I had thought dead. If there are psychological roots for British fascism – they are here. (Kennedy Martin, 1978: 125)

Had he read this it is possible that Johns may not have wished to participate in the final episode, even if invited, but it is also possible Kennedy Martin had no wish to resurrect a character who was partly responsible for *Z Cars* departing from its original concept, that of using the police as a vehicle for exploring people's lives and for finding out about contemporary society. To this extent 'Pressure' returned *Z Cars* to its origins. The episode attempted to explore the impact of social and political developments on people's lives in the late 1970s. It did this through its storylines about unemployment, about poverty and the disintegration of social welfare in contemporary Britain. It also commented on contemporary policing with its storylines about the fortification of the police station and corruption within the police force. It was fitting therefore that the episode ended with the new steel shutters being lowered, bringing down the curtain on *Z Cars* as a long-running series but also highlighting the barriers now existing between the police and the public they were there to serve. As a final coda, after the credits have rolled and the famous theme music ended, an explosion is heard, presumably that of the sewage plant going up as the gas explodes, a metaphorical portent of things to come in British society.

Redcap (1964–6)

After leaving *Z Cars*, and perhaps as a reaction to it, Kennedy Martin worked on experimental projects for the next two years, namely *Diary of a Young Man* and the unproduced *Macheath – Masterspy*, both six-part series. Towards the end of 1964, however, he returned to mainstream television with three scripts for the first series of ABC's *Redcap*, Kennedy Martin's first scripts for ITV. *Redcap* was about the Special Investigation Branch (SIB) of the Royal Military Police, the 'Redcaps' as they were commonly known. The series was devised by Jack Bell, a former navy man who was working as a journalist for the *Daily Mirror*. Bell introduced the series in an article in *TV World*, prior to the transmission of the first episode in the Midlands ITV region on 17 October 1964 (the series did not go out in the London region until May 1965):

> The SIB are the Army's detectives, their CID, if you like, and though there are little more than a hundred SIB men in the entire British Army, their 'beat' is the world. Malaya, Hongkong, Kenya, Aden, Berlin, Borneo – and Catterick. Wherever there is serious crime involving British troops or their families, the SIB are on the spot in a flash. (Bell, 1964: 22)

Given his background as a Second Lieutenant in the Gordon Highlanders, his war novel and previous television credits – two original plays about the army and a hard-hitting series about the British police – Kennedy Martin was a logical choice to write episodes for a series about a military policeman. In fact it was his younger brother, Ian, story editor on the first series of *Redcap*, who was responsible for getting Troy involved. The series gave the young John Thaw his first starring role in television, as the central character, Sergeant John Mann, whose task it is to investigate military misdemeanours in locations around the world. Although episodes were set in Aden, Borneo, Cyprus, Germany, Hong Kong and Malaysia, the furthest the cast ventured was Aldershot and most of the series was recorded in the ABC studios at Teddington.

'Corporal McCann's Private War' (ABC, 14 November 1964) was Kennedy Martin's first episode for the series. Recorded on videotape in Studio 2 at Teddington on 21 October 1964 the episode was transmitted in the Midlands region three weeks later as episode five in the series. When *Redcap* was eventually shown in London, six months later, 'Corporal McCann's Private War' was the first episode to be screened, suggesting it was considered the episode most likely to win viewers to the series against strong competition from the BBC, as Adrian Mitchell implied in his review in the *Sun*:

> It was a gala night for viewers. ITV marched in 'Redcap', a muscular new series which has already proved itself in the Midland, North and Southern regions. BBC1 countered with 'Not only .. but also.' …
>
> The first episode by Troy Kennedy Martin, of Z-cars, was set in Cyprus. It told of the search for a corporal absent without leave with three automatic rifles. There were several extraordinary moments. In one of them a door was opened during a search. There was a sudden pause and then came the whining sound of flies. You cannot judge a series by its first episode. But taking into account form and advance reports, 'Redcap' is something which must be watched. If I call it a global version of Z-cars, I mean it as a compliment. (Mitchell, 1965a)

It is perhaps not surprising Kennedy Martin should want to draw on his Cyprus experience for his first episode of *Redcap*. Nevertheless, 'Corporal McCann's Private War' has a complicated, and surprisingly 'political', plot for an episode of a popular ITV drama series. Corporal McCann (Ian MacNaughton) has gone missing with three guns in his possession. Mann discovers that McCann was arrested by Inspector Gregoriou (Warren Mitchell) after getting caught up in a brawl in a bar. After being released, McCann was abducted by Greek-Cypriot 'irregulars' who want his guns because they are planning an attack on the United Nations headquarters in Cyprus.

In the search for McCann, Sergeant Mann finds himself up against Lovelock, a Security Liaison officer who wants to get the guns back. Lovelock sees the incident as 'political', not an army matter. However it is Mann's more rational detective skills (Lovelock cynically refers to him as 'Sherlock') which triumph over Lovelock's speculation that McCann is in league with an 'extreme right wing group of Greeks'. In the denouement of what is a fast-moving, incident-packed episode, a wounded McCann is apprehended, the irregulars overcome and the guns retrieved.

In what was to become a trademark of Kennedy Martin's scripts (achieving its fullest expression twenty years later in *Edge of Darkness*) 'Corporal McCann's Private War' starts off with an apparently simple story about a missing soldier which opens out to embrace the tense international situation in Cyprus. The 'irregulars' who are planning to use McCann's guns in their attack on the UN building want to destabilise the political situation by threatening the delicate peace which the UN is trying to maintain. With the situation in Cyprus still tense in 1964, audiences would no doubt have recognised the real-life allusions in the story, giving this entertaining episode of a popular drama series a contemporary significance more often seen in serious plays or drama-documentaries.

Kennedy Martin also wrote episode seven of the first series: 'Night Watch' (ABC, 28 November 1964), in which Sergeant Mann investigates a 'ghost' that is haunting a regiment just back from Borneo. After Tony Garnett's appearance as 'Private Brown' in Kennedy Martin's first television play, *Incident at Echo Six*, this episode of *Redcap* features Hywel Bennett as 'Private Brown', the member of the regiment who first sees the ghost. Kennedy Martin also wrote the final episode of the first series, 'The Patrol' (ABC, 16 January 1965), in which Sergeant Mann investigates a murder in the Borneo jungle.

Between the first and second series of *Redcap* Kennedy Martin wrote plays for *The Wednesday Play*, *Out of the Unknown* and ITV's *Play of the Week* in 1965, returning in 1966 to write three more episodes for the second series. After the success of the first series, series two was networked to all ITV regions and Kennedy Martin's scripts formed three of the first four episodes to be shown. The opening episode, 'Crime Passionel' (ABC, 2 April 1966), was favourably received and Kennedy Martin's script praised by Peter Knight, writing in the *Daily Telegraph*:

> Crime series on television fall into such predictable patterns that anything which brings a fresh approach to the format comes as an unexpected but more than welcome bonus ... .
>
> The opening episode was set in the steamy jungles of Borneo, where a young misfit of a private goes berserk, killing a sergeant. A seemingly open and shut case of murder soon became enmeshed in an impenetrable web of lies and intrigue with the close-knit jungle unit closing its ranks to the outside investigation.
>
> Some of the cast were too clearly exposed at times as stock Army stage types. But Troy Kennedy Martin's script was written with a terseness of style that kept the action taut and tense ... . (Knight, 1966)

Episode three of the second series, 'The Killer' (ABC, 16 April 1966), set in Malaysia, also involved a plot in which members of a special Commando Unit are killed by their own side, while in episode four, 'Buckingham Palace' (ABC, 23 April 1966), Sergeant Mann 'investigates a murder in a blizzard and finds that Buckingham Palace and other

Stately Homes are being gambled away on a Cyprus mountaintop' (*TV World*, 21 April 1966).

Not only did *Redcap* allow Kennedy Martin to bring together two genres that had featured prominently in his previous scriptwriting – the military and the police – it also enabled him to further demonstrate his facility for writing successful popular television drama, for ITV as well as the BBC. In addition, the series gave him the opportunity to write for John Thaw as the central character, an experience he was able to replicate ten years later when he worked on another police series, *The Sweeney*.

Further adventures in ITV-land

Meanwhile, on a little-known 1966 television serial for which Troy Kennedy Martin wrote eleven episodes, under the pseudonym of Tony Marsh, he came into contact with the actor who was to star alongside John Thaw in *The Sweeney*. Dennis Waterman had a minor role as Will Akers in *Weavers Green* (Anglia, April–September 1966) a twice-weekly serial about a country veterinary practice, which was clearly trying to emulate BBC's radio serial *The Archers*:

> It's the sort of village townfolk dream of. Sleepy looking. Centuries old. A place where life revolves round the fields, the pig pens and the country markets. Now, twice weekly, you can meet the inhabitants. You'll find them easily enough, just follow the signpost to Weavers Green. Parish, village and railway station. East Anglia. 20 miles from Market Newton, Population: 813. (*TV World*, 1966: 4)

Weavers Green was created by Peter and Betty Lambda, who wrote the first twenty-nine episodes, and produced by John Jacobs. After three months the serial had become too much for the Lambdas to handle and Ian Kennedy Martin was brought in as the story editor and asked to recruit other writers:

> I was the story editor at Anglia and what happened was Anglia had the audacity to start a twice weekly soap and get it on to the network and Lew Grade was very angry about it, it was one of the meetings he missed and suddenly Anglia had a twice weekly soap about a vet living in this place called Weavers Green and we had a lot of fun with it, we really did. The most appalling things happened in this village. So what Lew Grade did in the end, because he got hold of the network, and he managed to get them to start changing the time slots, so the Monday slot which had been at 7 o'clock on ITV was suddenly changed to 6.30 and the Friday slot which was 7.00 on ITV went to 7.45 and then it moved from week to

week and so on ... Finally the network said, 'Look we can't go on with this because you know it's clear that some people are watching the Monday and missing the Friday completely and then watching the following Monday' ... Johnny Jacobs called me in and said 'Can you take this thing over because it's completely out of hand and anyhow it's finishing' ... So I said yes, but we needed to get a lot of scripts ... Troy was broke and I got in touch with him and said 'Do you want to do six of these quickly, you know, for £3,000', or whatever it was, and he said yes. So he became quite a regular.[15]

Troy decided to write under the name of Tony Marsh, a pseudonym he was to use again on two more series: 'Tony Marsh – I tried to think of the most dull and boring name I could think of and then people would forget – and then of course I forgot it myself.'[16] For a writer who had written a prize-winning television play, who was known as the creator of *Z Cars* and for the ground-breaking *Diary of a Young Man*, one can see why he did not want his name to be associated with a twice-weekly soap opera about country vets, but between episode thirty-three, transmitted on Thursday 28 July, and episode fifty, transmitted on Sunday 25 September, Troy Kennedy Martin wrote eleven episodes of *Weavers Green*, including the final three episodes. Although the serial was getting good ratings (according to Kennedy Martin the ratings rocketed after he introduced a witch to the serial[17]) Lew Grade finally succeeded in banishing it from the schedules, arguing that he needed the slot for ATV's *Emergency – Ward 10*.

Having written exclusively for the BBC until 1964, Kennedy Martin was beginning to diversify, with *Redcap* for ABC, and two *Plays of the Week*, plus episodes of *Weavers Green*, for Anglia. Then, in 1968, he wrote an episode for a series called *The Inquisitors*, commissioned by the new ITV company London Weekend Television (LWT) which took over the weekend franchise for London from ATV in August 1968. Seven scripts were written for *The Inquisitors*, by Roy Clarke (who wrote three), Trevor Preston, John Foster, James Mitchell and Kennedy Martin. Ken Wlaschen, whose *Tickets to Trieste* Kennedy Martin had adapted for *Storyboard* in 1961, was the script editor on the series. Three episodes were actually recorded, but the series was never transmitted, and it seems that the recordings that were made were subsequently wiped. The reasons why it was not shown are unclear, although it seems that the LWT board watched the episodes that had been made, did not like the results, and cancelled the series.[18]

Kennedy Martin's contribution to the series, 'The Binney Effect', was never produced, but the script suggests it was written as a studio drama, about a group of scientists at a science station, the Farnworth Radio

Telescope, who are investigating some mysterious signals that a scientist, Dr Binney, has picked up from outer space. Binney has committed suicide, possibly as a result of what he discovered from the signals, and the other scientists are trying to reconstruct his experiment. Kygor, a Russian scientist at Farnworth, tells one of the other scientists why he thinks Binney killed himself:

> I think he died of awe. He confronted the infinite power to the galaxy itself. He found what he called God in an exercise book. Not your God, or the God of the Muslim or the Hindu. The galactic essence. G.D. he called it in his letters. The Galactic Design. ... Unbalanced – he was mad. But perhaps one has to be mad to be great. His mind was too big for our world but too small to comprehend the galaxy. The reality he was confronting was of such proportions that it capsized him like a matchbox in a hurricane. Who can condemn him for taking the way out that he did?[19]

Kennedy Martin's script for *The Inquisitors* is similar in tone and subject matter – a polemical discourse on the quest for scientific knowledge – to his dramatisation of C. P. Snow's *The New Men*, written as an ITV *Play of the Week* two years before. Largely discursive, the script grapples with some fundamental theological issues, as this extract from the beginning of Part II, a recording of Binney talking about scientific and religious belief, indicates:

> You see the mistake they all make is going back to the beginning. What is the beginning. What does beginning mean. If God lives there all the time, then there is no beginning. You see some of them favour the Big Bang theory and then you're left with a picture of God, a detonator between his legs about to push the plunger, and then there's others that favour the pulsating universe as if God is continually switching on and off some giant galactic Hoover. It's all wrong. It's not just that we've got an anthropomophic [sic] view of god – we've got an anthropomophic view of Science.
>
> You know some clever feller sometime in the future is going to label these centuries as the Dark Ages. That'll put us in our place won't it. (HE LAUGHS AND THE LAUGH ECHOES AND ECHOES.)[20]

In 1969 Kennedy Martin had another strange encounter with an ITV company when he wrote five episodes for Yorkshire Television's rural police drama, *Parkin's Patch* (Yorkshire, September 1969–March 1970), writing once again under the pseudonym of Tony Marsh. After writing the screenplay for *The Italian Job* Kennedy Martin went to live in the south of France on the proceeds from the film and it was most likely in France, while he was writing *Kelly's Heroes*, that he wrote 'The Binney Effect' and the episodes of *Parkin's Patch*. His brother Ian also wrote episodes for the series: 'We sat in the south of France and just knocked out episodes of that. I took them back to England and got them right. It was just for the money really.' (Day-Lewis, 1998: 217)

Ostensibly there would seem to be less reason for the use of a pseudonym on *Parkin's Patch*. After all it was a police drama, albeit a softer representation of the police than *Z Cars*, and it attracted some good writers and directors: Elwyn Jones (who devised it), Robert Barr, Ian Kennedy Martin and Allan Prior all wrote episodes, while Michael Apted, Stephen Frears and Mike Newell were among the directors, all credited under their real names. Initially the series was in black and white with some episodes, such as Kennedy Martin's 'The Deserter' (31 October 1969), shot on film, on location, which may be why directors such as Frears, who directed 'The Deserter', were interested in working on the series, film enabling a variety of rural locations to be used, and a more cinematic *mise en scene* and cutting to be achieved. By the time of Kennedy Martin's second episode, 'The Birmingham Con' (28 November 1969), ITV had switched to colour, after which, presumably for reasons of cost, the series became mainly a studio drama, with only some exterior scenes being shot on film.[21]

Parkin's Patch was based around the character of PC Moss Parkin (John Flanagan) and dealt with an array of minor rural crimes. 'The Deserter' seemed to draw on a number of elements from Kennedy Martin's previous series with a story about a military sergeant, a 'Redcap', who pursues an army deserter to the village which is Parkin's 'patch', where Parkin assists him in tracking down the soldier, who has gone AWOL because his mother, who lives in the village, is dying. With its rural village setting and a police story involving a visiting military sergeant, 'The Deserter' seems to be an amalgam of elements from *Z Cars*, *Redcap* and *Weavers Green*!

Kennedy Martin's second episode, 'The Birmingham Con', took its title from a well-known con-trick which Parkin relates to a colleague when he finds that local villain Danny Shea (Jack MacGowran) has pulled a similar con at a furniture store in the village. For his third episode, 'The Manchester Passenger' (2 January 1970), Kennedy Martin wrote a Christmas ghost story, set on Boxing Day, about James Moggs (Wallas Eaton), a drunken Newcastle football supporter who is left behind in Fickley (the village where Parkin lives) when the coach taking him to a football match stops to get some beer. Parkin takes him and puts him to bed in the spare room, locking him in, but the man mysteriously appears in the kitchen. Parkin notices that Moggs has bottles of brown ale with a ten year-old label on them and Part One ends with another mysterious occurrence when Parkin, returning after leaving the room, finds that Moggs has disappeared and is nowhere in the house, even though the outside door was locked. Parkin goes to Leeds to check out Moggs' address and when, in the next scene, he arrives at the police station the sergeant has found a newspaper cutting for him about a Boxing Day accident fifteen years ago when fourteen Newcastle supporters were killed, one man surviving because he stopped to argue with a publican and missed the coach. The episode concludes with Parkin telling his boss of his discovery that Moggs had died in Leeds the previous evening, at 7.30 pm, an hour before Parkin had taken him in to his home in Fickley.

With each episode of *Parkin's Patch* lasting only twenty-five minutes there was not much scope for complicated plotting, but Kennedy Martin nevertheless managed to cram a lot of plot into the twenty-five minutes of 'The Manchester Passenger', contriving a suitably spooky Christmas ghost story for the series. Subsequent episodes by 'Tony Marsh' involved one in which the purchase of a large house by a famous pop star causes problems with the locals – 'Vickory' (23 January 1970) – and the final episode of the series, 'Two Gentlemen Standing' (20 March 1970), in which Parkin collaborates with an 'expert' from Scotland Yard to retrieve a stolen painting.

It seems odd that, having written screenplays for two major movies, Troy Kennedy Martin should spend time writing episodes for a weekly rural police drama, for Yorkshire Television. The pattern for many British writers, actors and directors, before and since, has been to start off writing for British television and then relocate to Hollywood when they get the chance. In fact, *Parkin's Patch* was transmitted between the UK release of *The Italian Job* and *Kelly's Heroes*, which probably explains why Kennedy Martin used a pseudonym for the series. It might have seemed very odd for a Hollywood screenwriter, which he had now become, to be seen to be writing episodes for a fairly nondescript British television series, which makes it all the more surprising that Kennedy Martin's next series for television, transmitted shortly after the release of *Kelly's Heroes*, was a situation comedy, written under his own name.

If It Moves, File It (1970)

If It Moves, File It (LWT, August–October 1970) was a six-part situation comedy for London Weekend Television, and clearly more to the company's liking than *The Inquisitors* had been. Kennedy Martin wrote eight scripts for the series, six of which were produced and transmitted, on Friday evenings at 8.25–9.00 pm. It was described in the *TV Times* as 'the first comedy series by Troy Kennedy Martin, but not his first comedy – he wrote *The Italian Job* ... ' (*TV Times*, 28 August 1970, p. 35). Following *The Italian Job*, which was hardly a 'comedy' but which contained some classic comic one-liners, Kennedy Martin developed *If It Moves, File It* as 'an exercise, to see could I write a situation comedy.'[22]

The series was based around two civil servants, Quick (John Bird) and Foster (Dudley Foster), who get caught up in a series of crazy situations while working for an anonymous government Ministry: 'Quick and Foster are the minions from the Ministry who would like to run the world but who are constantly on the run from Frogett (John Nettleton) the boss' (*TV Times*, 22–9 August 1970, p. 35). The series was directed by Derek Bennett who, until 1969, had been a director at Granada where, among many other productions, he had directed the first episodes of *Coronation Street*. Kennedy Martin was not too pleased with Bennett's work on the series: 'He did absolutely nothing with the first one and the first one worked out really well, but the others didn't really work as well as they could have done, and I put that all down to the director.'[23]

Episode one, 'Walled In' (28 August 1970), featured the inadvertent bricking-up of the hapless Quick and Foster in their own office, by builders working on the building. The situation is ripe for comedy, but the comedy takes on an absurdist slant as Quick and Foster try to summon the navy to rescue them, by tapping 'Mayday' on the office radiator. In fact the series seems to mark a return by Kennedy Martin to the surreal comedy that was evident in *The Long Spoon*, one of the *Story-board* adaptations from 1961. The original title for the series was *The Buck Stops Here*, a title Kennedy Martin preferred to *If It Moves, File It*:

> *The Buck Stops Here* was a much better idea of what it was about than *If It Moves, File It* ... it was about two people working in a nameless Ministry and it did have an unreal side to it ... like people come along to remodel the floor and they just brick in the wall and the window and they find themselves completely bricked in! So that's the sort of thing, and then you have the two of them arguing ... a bit sort of Laurel and Hardy ...
>
> There's another one where they get a new manager in and they both want to get off for the Derby, and they both come out with the same excuse that their grandmother's died, and one of their grandmother's has died, but the other one, who's always the one who gets the better of the big one, his grandmother hasn't died but he's got this coffin which is actually full of all the beer and sandwiches he's taking to the Derby! Then the coffin's get switched around ...
>
> I do think some of them are really, really stylish pieces ... It became more and more bizarre as it went on and they couldn't make those transitions. John Bird was one of the guys ... never remembered his lines ... People have said that some of them were really absolutely brilliant ... It

got more and more surreal towards the end until they finally rejected the last one which was just completely surreal, about people coming out of walls ... [24]

This element of absurdist fantasy in *If It Moves, File It* is evident in some of Kennedy Martin's other work, most famously in *Edge of Darkness* where his original script called for Ronnie Craven to turn into a tree at the end of the serial, a departure into surrealism which he was persuaded against by other members of the production team. What was unusual about *If It Moves, File It*, as a situation comedy, was that there was no canned laughter, an innovation Kennedy Martin did not entirely agree with: 'They made a decision ... to go without it and I think that really makes a difference. I think you really need the laughter.'[25] For at least two reviewers, however, the absence of a laughter track was a bonus:

> It took me about five minutes last night to realise that a small television miracle was happening with the first instalment of London Weekend's new comedy series *If It Moves, File It* (ITV), the latest invention of Troy Kennedy Martin.
>
> At first I wondered if there was some technical hitch; perhaps the laughter machine had broken or the audience had been given the wrong starting time and would presently clatter in shrieking with the hysteria that it is felt must accompany television comedy.
>
> Later, as the two principals began to deliver some rather clever lines, it occurred to me that maybe the audience was there all the time, but stunned into a total silence by the brilliance of the dialogue.
>
> Then at last it dawned. The producers – Humphrey Barker [sic], Derek Bennett, Andrew Vale, let their names be forever enshrined – had had the unprecedented courage to do without either a machine or an audience. For once the viewer was left to react in his own way and it was a blessed relief ... (Day-Lewis, 1970)

Martin Jackson, writing in the *Daily Express*, agreed: 'An added plus is the producer's wise decision to play the programme without aid of a studio audience. This means no contrived laughter to prop up the gags. A show as funny as this one doesn't need electronic aid to laughter.' He continued: 'I have been lucky enough to see some of the future episodes and the standard of last night's opening has been maintained. London Weekend can congratulate themselves, the BBC would have been proud of this situation comedy' (Jackson, 1970). Apparently LWT were not sufficiently proud of the series to preserve it and *If It Moves, File It* was subsequently wiped, going the way of many popular television drama and comedy series made during the 1960s and early 1970s.

Colditz (1974)

It was three years before Kennedy Martin's next television script, an episode of the popular BBC World War Two series *Colditz* (BBC 1, 1972–4). 'The Guests' (BBC 1, 28 January 1974) was not only Kennedy Martin's first script for the BBC for nine years, it reunited him with Gerald Glaister, who he had previously worked with fifteen years before on the Somerset Maugham adaptation, *The Traitor*. Glaister produced *Colditz*, a series he devised with Brian Degas. The first series ran from October 1972 to January 1973, returning for a second series in January 1974. 'The Guests' was the fourth episode in the second series.

Alongside the regular characters playing the British prisoners of war (including David McCallum, Jack Hedley and Christopher Neame) the series featured guest appearances, such as that of William Rushton who appeared in 'The Guests' as Major Trumpington. Trumpington is in charge of a small group of captured British commandoes who are taken to Colditz, where they are kept separate from the rest of the prisoners. These are the 'guests' of the episode title. (One of the captured prisoners, incidentally, is called Godbolt, a name Kennedy Martin had previously used for a character in *If It Moves, File It* and which he was to use again for one of the central characters in *Edge of Darkness*). The other Colditz prisoners try to help the commandoes escape, but the plan fails and the commandoes are transferred to Offlag 17. On route, however, they are collected by the Gestapo, who are seen digging a grave. The commandoes try to escape but are shot and killed, resulting in a surprisingly bleak ending to the episode, which closes with a shot of a grinning Gestapo officer.

Using a mixture of location filming and studio recording, 'The Guests' marked a return to the war genre for Kennedy Martin, though on rather a different scale to that of *Kelly's Heroes*. In spite of the bleak ending the episode has some moments of trademark Kennedy Martin humour, most noticeably in the shape of Willie Rushton's cartoonish Major Trumpington. Not everyone at the BBC thought this was good casting. According to BBC TV Weekly Programme Review Committee minutes: 'Shaun Sutton [Head of Drama] said that his view of William Rushton was that it was a mistake to include him in any programme. It had certainly been a grave mistake to cast him as a Scottish Commando officer in this story. Noble Wilson [Assistant Head of Features] agreed; it was not often that one sided with the Nazis in these adventures.'[26] Rather than write a typical *Colditz* episode Kennedy Martin decided to send it up a little, introducing some humour in the form of Major Trumpington and exploiting the 'evil Nazi' stereotype with a very downbeat ending:

I've always thought *Colditz* was all about writers trying to get out of the BBC, you know a big round building, escape to Hollywood, so that was the subtext ... But it was an interesting idea because it was about someone who was so objectionable – I based it on Randolph Churchill, who was in Yugoslavia during the war, just arrived in the middle of all these guys cosying up to Tito – so they decide to try and get him to escape, just get rid of the fucker! So that was really behind it and it's not really a *Colditz* idea, it's much more *Catch 22*.[27]

Fall of Eagles (1974)

Also in 1974, Kennedy Martin contributed an episode to the BBC historical drama, *Fall of Eagles* (BBC 1, March–June 1974), a thirteen-part series dramatising the collapse of three European dynasties in the late nineteenth and early twentieth centuries. A number of experienced writers contributed to the series, including Keith Dewhurst, Trevor Griffiths and Hugh Whitemore. Kennedy Martin wrote episode eight, 'The Appointment' (BBC 1, 3 May 1974), which deals with the appointment of a new chief of police by the Russian Czar Nicholas II (Charles Kay), following two tragic events: the massacre of 500 people in front of the Czar's palace in St Petersburg, on Bloody Sunday 1905, and the assassination of the Czar's uncle in Moscow. Nicholas appoints the ruthless Ratchkovsky (Michael Bryant) who creates 'Black Band' assassination squads in an attempt to forestall the revolution which is threatening – Trotsky having already set up an alternative government in St Petersburg. The real Trotsky is shown in archive footage in 'The Appointment' – in other episodes he is played by Michael Kitchen, with Patrick Stewart as Lenin.

Fall of Eagles, like *Colditz*, was screened on BBC 1, but *Fall of Eagles* was a more prestigious production, with lavish studio sets, an accomplished cast and location filming (at Harewood House and Lyme Park in 'The Appointment'). Like the other episodes, Kennedy Martin's 'The Appointment' was well researched, the historical context being conveyed through the use of archive footage, newspaper captions and voiceover narration. Although the *mise en scene* is lavish, it is the politics, rather than the décor, which is privileged, producer Stuart Burge wanting to present a serious historical drama, rather than a picturesque costume drama. Unlike 'The Guests', therefore, 'The Appointment' required a more serious approach and the research Kennedy Martin did for the episode was to prove useful when he came to write *Reilly – Ace of Spies*, which was set in the same period.

The Sweeney (1975–8)

Having worked together on *Redcap* (ABC), *Weavers Green* (Anglia) and *Parkin's Patch* (Yorkshire), the Kennedy Martin brothers were reunited in the mid-1970s on a fourth ITV series: Thames Television's *The Sweeney* (1975–8). Euston Films' popular police series grew out of a single drama called *Regan* (Thames, 4 June 1974) which was written by Ian Kennedy Martin and shown as part of a series of filmed dramas called *Armchair Cinema*. This short series of six dramas succeeded *Armchair Theatre*, the long-running anthology series which Thames acquired in 1968 when the company was formed out of a merger between ABC and Associated-Rediffusion. Taking over Associated-Rediffusion's London weekday franchise, Thames produced another six series of *Armchair Theatre* from 1968–74, but the establishment by Thames of Euston Films in 1971, to make filmed dramas for the ITV network, represented a significant shift in policy, away from the production of studio-based plays towards location-based, filmed drama.

Initially, Euston Films took over production of *Special Branch* (Thames, 1969–74), a series about an elite Scotland Yard division investigating international crime and espionage, two series of which had been made, on videotape, in 1969–70. According to Lloyd Shirley, the Controller of Drama at Thames who helped to set up Euston Films: 'The original brief was to do a 13–part one hour series and we opted for *Special Branch* plus some singles which would go out under the title of *Armchair Cinema*. A fairly obvious title but a logical one to the management of those days because of the long-running *Armchair Theatre*' (Alvarado and Stewart, 1985: 43). Euston made two filmed series of *Special Branch* that were transmitted in 1973–4. Towards the end of the second series (for which Ian Kennedy Martin wrote one episode), production began on the films for *Armchair Cinema*, the second of which, *Regan*, became the pilot for *The Sweeney*. So confident was Euston of *Regan*'s series potential that the first series of *The Sweeney* went into production before *Regan* had been transmitted. Their confidence was justified. The *Armchair Cinema* films proved to be very successful, with the first one, *The Prison* (28 May 1974), topping the ratings, while *Regan* was joint third, being seen in seven million homes.[28]

The Sweeney was conceived as a replacement for *Special Branch*. Ian Kennedy Martin wanted to address the changes that were happening within Scotland Yard at the time, with the new Chief Commissioner, Robert Mark, creating a new management structure and introducing measures designed to tackle police corruption. Ian Kennedy Martin decided to base the series around the Flying Squad, a special CID unit otherwise known as 'The Sweeney' (short for 'Sweeney Todd', cockney rhyming slang for the Flying Squad), with Detective Inspector Jack Regan (John Thaw) as the central character, a maverick detective not dissimilar in his methods and attitude to the 'rogue' detectives who emerged in American cinema in the late 1960s and early 1970s, most famously epitomised by 'Dirty' Harry Callaghan (Clint Eastwood) in the *Dirty Harry* films. Ian Kennedy Martin always had John Thaw in mind for Regan, having worked with him on *Redcap*, and Dennis Waterman was brought in to play Regan's sidekick, Detective Sergeant George Carter.

Given his background on *Z Cars*, his recent involvement with Hollywood action movies, and his awareness, through Gordon Newman, of corruption in the Metropolitan Police, not to mention the fact that *The Sweeney* was created by his brother, Troy Kennedy Martin was an obvious choice as one of the main scriptwriters for the series:

> *The Sweeney* was about the Flying Squad. It was a notion of my brother, Ian Kennedy Martin, who took it to Euston in the form of a ninety minute pilot. To paraphrase G. F. Newman's Inspector Pyle, *Softly, Softly* was 'well overdue', and Ian couldn't help reflecting that its continuance on the screen owed less to its popularity than to a loss of nerve at the BBC. That is that if they took it off, they would have to replace it with something with a contemporary edge. And the controversy over the original *Z Cars* was still somehow lodged in its collective subconscious.
>
> However, Euston had no such qualms. They took it on the assumption they were making an extension of *Special Branch*. Ian had other ideas. He requested that I should be taken on as part of the package and insisted that John Thaw should play Regan. The whole thing was to be built round Thaw.
>
> I was in two minds about the project. It had been fifteen years since I had written for a police series – *Z Cars* – except for a stint with *Redcap* – again a John Thaw vehicle. I was also divorced and broke.
>
> In the previous year I had co-written with Gordon Newman a film for Tony Garnett. This was to be the quintessential police film. It never got off the ground, but from Gordon Newman I had picked up a great deal of information about Metropolitan CID – their language and style. This was to be of immense use in *The Sweeney*. (Kennedy Martin, 1978: 130–1)

Having developed the idea and written the pilot, Ian Kennedy Martin then had a major disagreement with Ted Childs, the producer of *Regan* who went on to produce all the *Sweeney* series. Childs had strong ideas about the format for the series, which Ian Kennedy Martin could not agree with, so he decided to leave before the series had even started. Troy decided to remain involved however, a decision which Childs was very pleased with: 'I think Troy was the definitive *Sweeney* writer because it was a logical development from the things he and John McGrath were doing on *Z Cars* before' (Alvarado and Stewart, 1985: 57). Troy Kennedy Martin was also glad that he remained involved: 'I soldiered on, and I'm glad I did so. I think the scripts that I wrote were better than the ones for *Z Cars* – and contributed to the success of the series' (Kennedy Martin, 1978: 132). Troy Kennedy Martin wrote three episodes for the first series of *The Sweeney*, although he is only credited for two. Episode two, 'Jackpot' (9 January 1975), was credited to Tony Marsh because Kennedy Martin had a disagreement with producer Ted Childs and director Tom Clegg about cuts they wanted to make:

> They made certain cuts in the script which they said had to be made for financial reasons ... I said I'd take my name off it if they did that and they didn't believe me and I took my name off it. It was just part of the war that you have to do ... there was always this fight, because they were made on an absolute budget shoestring ... but the only threats you have are taking your name off them, so I did ... I think 'Jackpot' was almost the first one I did.[29]

The first draft of 'Jackpot', which had working titles of 'The Last of The Big Spenders' and 'Biggleswade's Run', is dated October 1973 and a second draft dated April 1974,[30] showing that Kennedy Martin was working on scripts for *The Sweeney* before his episodes for *Colditz* and *Fall of Eagles* were transmitted, before *Regan* was screened and at least fifteen months before the first *Sweeney* episode, 'Ringer', written by Trevor Preston, launched the series on 2 January 1975.

Regardless of the dispute about cuts, 'Jackpot' is an interesting episode, beginning with the Flying Squad violently apprehending a gang which has just carried out a robbery, an incident which might have come at the end of a more conventional crime episode. An enigma is established when it is discovered that a bag of money, containing £35,000, has disappeared and the remainder of the episode is concerned with solving this enigma, with accusations being made that one of Regan's squad may have been involved. Having started with the catching of the villains, much of the episode is concerned with reconstructing the events leading up to the robbery, including the analysis of film shot by the police when they caught the gang, to see if they can ascertain what happened to the missing bag of money. In a resolution not untypical of Kennedy Martin's *Sweeney* episodes the police discover what happened to the money but fail to get it back. It transpires that the young daughter of the gang leader, Biggleswade, is dying of cancer and is being looked after by his sister, Irene. Biggleswade had contrived to get the money to Irene via her boyfriend, but the boyfriend has made off with it: 'He won't surface again till that money's spent', says Regan at the end of the episode. While not lacking in violence – several members of the Flying

Squad, including Regan and Carter, sport cuts and bruises following the apprehension of the gang – there is an element of dry humour in 'Jackpot' that was to become a distinctive feature of Kennedy Martin's episodes for *The Sweeney*. By including humour he wanted:

> to take the edge off them in a way that other people like Trevor Preston didn't. He did go for a gut-wrenching and a psychological drama and he's really good at that. So the mix was very good on *The Sweeney* ... a lot of my *Sweeney*'s were tongue in cheek and I do think that I probably gave the John Thaw character, or the John and Dennis characters, a more comedic twist than the series would have allowed.[31]

Episode three, 'Thin Ice' (16 January 1975) was the first one to go out with Troy Kennedy Martin's name on it and, with Alfred Marks, Brian Glover and Bill Dean all in the cast, this episode also contained a good deal of humour. With Tom Clegg again directing, 'Thin Ice' is about Regan's attempt to arrest Bishop (Alfred Marks), a gang boss he has been after for some while, but his efforts are frustrated by Pringle (Peter Jeffrey) of the Fraud Squad, whose pursuit of Bishop causes him to go abroad. Unusually for *The Sweeney* a black and white flashback sequence is used to show Regan's previous attempts to arrest Bishop being thwarted by Pringle – an attempt by Kennedy Martin to introduce an element of 'back story'. As in 'Jackpot', Kennedy Martin was keen to depart from the conventional narrative development of most police dramas and his scripts were often quite unusual in terms of plot development, a characteristic that made them more interesting according to Dennis Waterman, who thought they were 'quite quirky and difficult to work out, and a bit jaundiced – which was nice' (Fairclough and Kenwood, 2002: 79)

The other reason for Kennedy Martin introducing humour into his episodes was to salve his conscience at writing for a series which could be said to be glorifying the Flying Squad, a specialist police unit which, in real life, had a reputation for ruthlessness and corruption. In the sociopolitical context of the 1970s, which became known as the 'law and order decade' because of a steep increase in crime and a breakdown in the political consensus of the postwar years, the Flying Squad, and the police generally, operated as the coercive arm of the State. The activities of the Flying Squad represented a significant change in policing in the 1970s, towards a more authoritarian and aggressive force where the violent and often illegal methods of the Flying Squad were sanctioned as legitimate because of the social 'breakdown' in law and order. The introduction of a degree of comedy into his *Sweeney* scripts was, therefore, Kennedy Martin's way of deflating the macho image of the Flying Squad:

> The reason I was writing from this more comedic way was I was really concerned about the Flying Squad at that time, which was fairly corrupt

... and so I had a conscience, saying why was I writing – apart from the money! – a detective series which was glorifying the Flying Squad at that particular time? So the idea, in order to clear my conscience, was to try to use these as exercises in this kind of action-comedy. You couldn't have written a whole series based on that comedy.[32]

In this respect Kennedy Martin's *Sweeney* episodes have something in common with *The Italian Job*, which parodied the heist movie and used humour to make the robbery self-consciously comic. In his *Sweeney* episodes there is often a tension between the realism of the plots, a realism which is enhanced by location filming, and the comedy, which serves to puncture the seriousness of the plots, giving his episodes a different quality to those of Trevor Preston and the other writers. The difference is suggested in Dennis Waterman's description of Kennedy Martin's episodes as 'quite quirky and difficult to work out, and a bit jaundiced'.

As previously noted, there is often an unconventional approach to plot development in Kennedy Martin's scripts, evident in 'Jackpot' as well as subsequent episodes written under his own name, together with a tendency to juxtapose violence and comedy in ways that are sometimes unsettling, but which can also enhance the realism of a situation:

Humour really helps realism. It's the actual humour of something that actually brings out the realism, as much as a piece of scenery or a set design. Reality has this humour in it, particularly the more ghastly it is, and that's often excised, or not even thought of, as a component when you want to write the kind of serious or tragic piece.[33]

Kennedy Martin's scripts also tend to highlight Regan's cynical attitude towards authority, allowing him to resolve his internal conflict about writing for a series which could be seen to be glorifying the Flying Squad by having Regan take up an ambiguous position: against the villains, but also against what Regan sees as the petty bureaucracy and unnecessary interference of his superior officers.

Kennedy Martin's writing for John Thaw as Jack Regan was particularly well considered in his third episode, 'Night Out' (6 February 1975), when Regan is given an assignment requiring him to be holed up with an ex-girlfriend in a room above a pub, next to a bank where a robbery is taking place. Sergeant Carter is marginal to this episode in which Regan is very much the central character, required to do the dirty work for his superiors, including in this case shooting three villains in a rare *Sweeney* gunfight, while his boss takes all the credit at the end. Chris Dunkley's *Financial Times* review praised the episode, especially the manner in which Kennedy Martin conveyed Regan's sarcastic attitude towards his superiors, noting also how comedy was used to heighten the realism of the situation:

> As is often the case, the best series drama of the week came in one of the police epics, this time Thames' *The Sweeney* with an episode called 'Night Out' by Troy Kennedy Martin. The plot appeared to have been inspired by the 'radio controlled' bank raid which was carried out a few years ago and involved Jack Regan (played by John Thaw) in spending the night with an old flame since she lived in the room above the pub which stood next door to the bank.
>
> We have had plenty of independent minded, stubborn cops before of course, but none quite so scornful of his superiors as Regan and none with quite such a searing line in sarcasm. The nice thing about the character is that irritating, banal things happen to him: he shins up a ladder to the bank roof in the dark, his specially issued revolver clutched in his fist, and falls flat on his face in a puddle. Two of the armed robbers later creep across the roof and burst in on the detective (who has, realistically, just told his old friend 'I'm not hysterical, I'm terrified') and shortly after he has dealt with them his HQ rings to warn him that they have intercepted a radio message and two of the villains are coming in across the roof ... (Dunkley, 1975)

It was nearly eighteen months before Kennedy Martin's next *Sweeney* episode, 'Selected Target' (6 September 1976), which was the opening episode in the third series. Despite not contributing to the second series Kennedy Martin adeptly demonstrated his familiarity with the series in an early scene in which Regan is searching in his boss's office for an appraisal report his boss has written about him. After watching Regan go through the desk, filing cabinet and safe Carter tells Regan that the report is in the typing pool and he quotes from a section he has memorised: 'Detective Inspector Regan continues to get results but undoes much of this goodwill by continually questioning the decision of superior officers', a scene which, as James Murray wrote in his *Daily Express* review, 'amusingly re-established the nature of the series within minutes' (Murray, 1976). Reviewers complimented the quality of the script and the use of humour in 'Selected Target', with Nancy Banks-Smith particularly enjoying the names given by Kennedy Martin to the two villains and Ronald Fraser's performance as one of them, Titus Oates, the partner in crime to Colley Kibber (Lee Montague):

> Oates (Ronald Fraser enjoying himself as much as I enjoyed him) sank his teeth into phrases rich as brandy-pickled peaches, 'So often creatures with no backbones have the harder shells.' ... 'Poor Horace, he's been primed, rehearsed and wound up like a clockwork rabbit' ... (and representing himself pathetically as 'fleeing from refuge to refuge while Kibber's wrath rages.') (Banks-Smith, 1976)

Lacking the narrative dexterity of his scripts for the first series, 'Selected Target' is nevertheless notable for the fact that Colley Kibber gets away with the crime, an example of Kennedy Martin continuing a tradition he had established in *Z Cars* of showing that the police do not always solve the crime and capture the villains. Unlike other police series, the realism of *The Sweeney* occasionally extended to showing 'a massive defeat for the forces of law and order', as Sergeant Carter says at the end of the episode, as if quoting a newspaper headline.

Kennedy Martin also wrote episode three in the third series, 'Visiting Fireman' (20 September 1976), a title he was to use again in 1983 for an episode of *Reilly – Ace of Spies*:

> I can't remember what 'visiting fireman' really means now but it's something to do with a stranger coming into your midst ... in this one it's about a Turkish policeman who comes to London and who knows Jack Regan and who's here following up plutonium or something that's been shipped out of the middle-east by some truckers who are actually working for a shady branch of the intelligence service ... It's one of my favourites ... Jack thinks he's being followed by the guy behind, who's looking really guilty, so he reverses back towards him and the guy sees this car coming and he reverses back, so you get this reverse chase down the street and the other guy crashes into a car at a crossroads ... so it's full of little things like that ... it does go a bit too far but it has quite a good story about the smuggling of radioactive material because the guy who's smuggling it gets ill and they don't know why and it's because he's got this stuff in the back ... [34]

'Visiting Fireman' actually has two distinct plots, another departure for *The Sweeney* which usually contained just one storyline per episode. In fact the plotting of 'Visiting Fireman' is perhaps too ambitious for a fifty minute episode, stretching the *Sweeney* format beyond its limitations. The inclusion of a story about the international smuggling of plutonium was a distinct departure for the series, perhaps illustrating Kennedy Martin's desire to move beyond generic crime series, anticipating the larger-scale global narratives of his 1980s serials, especially *Edge of Darkness*. Kennedy Martin was also considered to have transgressed the boundaries of good taste in this episode when he included a final scene in which Helga, a German barmaid, is seen in Regan's apartment, half undressed and wearing a German steel helmet, which she complains Regan has made her wear. The scene was cut when the episode was repeated, but Kennedy Martin resurrected it in his next *Sweeney* episode when he included a scene in which Regan calls at Helga's flat to collect the steel helmet, only to end up in bed with Helga's flatmate, who is also seen wearing the helmet.

Between the third and fourth series of *The Sweeney*, Kennedy Martin wrote the script for the second *Sweeney* feature film, *Sweeney 2* (UK, 1978), which was filmed in November–December 1977 and released in the UK in April 1978. The plot involves the Flying Squad trying to catch a gang which is carrying out a series of bank robberies, designed to finance their life of luxury in Malta. Eventually the gang is caught after doing one last job and, in a violent denouement, Regan is spattered with blood when the gang leader shoots himself after killing the woman who had led the Flying Squad to the gang's hideout. Taking advantage of the possibility of including more violence and bad language than was possible in the television series, *Sweeney 2* is noticeably darker in tone, while still containing much of Kennedy Martin's trademark humour: 'It was really written like a Cowboys and Indians film, people coming over the edge of the hill and hitting banks. Again there was a lot of humour in it, but they all wanted to go and have a holiday in Malta so I had to write in all these Malta scenes, which really ruined the thing.'[35]

Kennedy Martin's final *Sweeney* episode was 'Hard Men' (14 September 1978), for the fourth and final series. This episode featured Detective Sergeant Freeth (James Cosmo) from Strathclyde CID, who travels down to London in pursuit of three Scottish villains (the 'hard men' of the title), where he is joined by Regan and Carter in trying to capture them. This provides Regan and Carter with the opportunity for a number of jokes at the expense of the Scots (an opportunity Kennedy Martin would have delighted in given his own Scottish upbringing). Once again, Regan and Carter are really pawns in the plot, unaware that Freeth has done a deal with a Glasgow gang leader to arrest one of the villains while the gang leader has the other surviving villain killed, as retribution for trying to kidnap his daughter.

Together with Trevor Preston, who wrote eleven *Sweeney* episodes, Troy Kennedy Martin helped to establish *The Sweeney* as something more than a run-of-the-mill crime series. Not only did it quickly become established as one of ITV's most popular programmes, rivalling and often surpassing *Coronation Street* in the ratings, *The Sweeney* was acclaimed by critics and even subjected to rigorous academic analysis when an issue of the journal *Screen Education* was devoted to the series in 1976.[36] On the DVD commentary to 'Night Out' Troy Kennedy Martin describes to Ted Childs the perplexed response of the *Sweeney* writers to the intellectual scrutiny given to the series by *Screen Education*:

> The BFI did this pamphlet and I got all the writers round to my place and showed them and it was really about what *The Sweeney* was all about – this was a *petit bourgeois* series which had these deep semiotic undertones – and it was full of long words which none of us could under-

stand, but I took great pleasure in distributing to the six writers that were present this thing and they all looked at it, hoping it was going to not only mention their names but actually be something they could understand, and there was this stunned silence for about ten minutes as they tried to plough their way through![37]

In 1978, speaking on *Crimewriters: Police Story* (BBC 1, 3 December 1978), a BBC programme about television police series, Kennedy Martin described his *Sweeney* stories as a form of 'high fiction', involving a heightened, exaggerated drama, as opposed to the realist approach adopted by G. F. Newman in *Law and Order* (1978), a series Newman developed from the script he and Kennedy Martin collaborated on a few years before:

> I've tried to go for a higher fiction simply because I think that to confront the corruption would be too bald, so one's gone for broader characters, bigger than life stories, a strong element of humour and the kind of action you can get with film cameras rather than with television cameras in a studio.[38]

The distinction between Kennedy Martin's penchant for a 'higher fiction', as opposed to the documentary realism of *Law and Order*, is a useful one in describing his approach not only to *The Sweeney* but to screenwriting generally. While the stories may often seem 'bigger than life', the characterisation 'broad' and the narratives spiced with action and humour, there is usually a subtext, often of a socio-political nature, which elevates his scripts, raising them above the average fare for popular, generic television drama.

The six episodes Troy Kennedy Martin wrote for *The Sweeney*, plus the final *Z Cars* episode which was transmitted six days after 'Hard Men', were to be his final contributions to television drama series. After 1978 he turned his attention to serials, or mini-series, which occupied him for the next few years. With *Z Cars* and *The Sweeney* beginning and ending a sixteen year period of writing for popular drama series, Kennedy Martin had undoubtedly made a major contribution to the police genre with scripts that were often complex, quirky and humorous. Having spent the late 1960s and early 1970s pursuing a career as a Hollywood screenwriter, Kennedy Martin found, on his return to British television, that writing episodes of *The Sweeney* could, if anything, be a more creative and satisfying experience than writing screenplays for Hollywood movies:

> I really was proud of *The Sweeney* and particularly in those days when I really thought of myself as a Hollywood scriptwriter. It was sort of slumming in a way to do it, although I desperately needed the cash, but in fact I enjoyed it far more and felt it was much more creative than anything I was doing, or ever did, out there.[39]

Notes

1 Troy Kennedy Martin, interviewed by the author, 25 September 1998.
2 David Rose, interviewed by the author, 26 February 2003.
3 BFI, TKM Collection, Item 19, *Z Cars*, memo from David Rose to Robert Barr, Elwyn Jones, Troy Kennedy Martin, Norman Rutherford and Mavis Johnson, 25 September 1961.
4 BFI, TKM Collection, Item 19, *Z Cars*, memo from David Rose to Robert Barr and Troy Kennedy Martin, regarding deadlines for episodes 14–26, 29 January 1962.
5 BBC WAC, T5/2,444/1, Audience Research Report, *Z Cars: Four of a Kind*, 30 January 1962.
6 John McGrath, interviewed by the author, 27 April 2000.
7 BBC WAC, T5/2,445/1, memo from Terence Cook to the Senior Assistant Programme Planning, BBC Television, 30 April 1962.
8 BBC WAC, T5/2,449/1, Audience Research Report, *Z Cars: Friday Night*, 28 February 1962.
9 Troy Kennedy Martin, *Z Cars*, London: Trust Books, 1962.
10 John McGrath, *Barlow, Regan, Pyall and Fancy*, BBC 2, 31 May 1993.
11 Ibid.
12 Tony Garnett, interviewed by the author, 18 March 2004.
13 *Z Cars: Invisible Enemy*, BBC, 17 April 1962, National Film and Television Archive.
14 Troy Kennedy Martin, interviewed by the author, 25 September 1998.
15 Ian Kennedy Martin, interviewed by the author, 19 March 2004.
16 Troy Kennedy Martin, interviewed by the author, 17 April 2003.
17 Telephone conversation with the author, 1 February 2005.
18 I am grateful to Dick Fiddy for passing on correspondence with Richard Fitzgerald, who was investigating the fate of *The Inquisitors* in 2001–2.
19 Troy Kennedy Martin, *The Inquisitors: The Binney Effect*, BFI Library, pp. 16–17.
20 Ibid, p. 19.
21 Episode transmission dates varied in different ITV regions. The dates given here are from the Southern editions of the *TV Times*.
22 Troy Kennedy Martin, interviewed by the author, 27 March 1986.
23 Troy Kennedy Martin, interviewed by the author, 25 September 1998.
24 Ibid.
25 Ibid.
26 BBC WAC, TV Weekly Programme Review Committee Minutes: *Colditz: The Guests*, 30 January 1974, p. 12.
27 Troy Kennedy Martin, interviewed by the author, 4 April 2003. Kennedy Martin was very familiar with *Catch 22*, having adapted an extract from it as a BBC Television Training Exercise at the end of 1965, the last thing, in fact, he did for the BBC until the episode of *Colditz* in 1974.
28 Before 1977 audiences were measured in terms of homes rather than individual viewers. Seven million homes would have been equivalent to about fourteen million viewers. The average audience for the first series of *The Sweeney* in 1975 was nearly seven and a half million homes. By the time of the fourth series, when audiences were being measured by individual viewers, the average audience was just under fifteen million.
29 Troy Kennedy Martin, interviewed by the author, 27 March 1986.
30 BFI, TKM Collection, Item 38, *The Sweeney: Jackpot*.
31 Troy Kennedy Martin, interviewed by the author, 17 April 2003.
32 Troy Kennedy Martin, from the DVD audio commentary to 'Thin Ice', *The Sweeney: The Complete Series 1 (1975)*, FremantleMedia, 2003.

33 Troy Kennedy Martin, from the DVD audio commentary to 'Night Out', *The Sweeney: The Complete Series 1 (1975)*, FremantleMedia, 2003.
34 Troy Kennedy Martin, interviewed by the author, 17 April 2003.
35 Troy Kennedy Martin, interviewed by the author, 27 March 1986.
36 *Screen Education*, No. 20, Autumn 1976.
37 Troy Kennedy Martin, from the DVD audio commentary to 'Night Out'.
38 Troy Kennedy Martin, quoted in *Crimewriters: Police Story* (BBC 1, 3 December 1978)
39 Troy Kennedy Martin, interviewed by the author, 17 April 2003.

Drama serials 5

With the decline of the single play on British television during the 1970s and 1980s, authored television drama increasingly took the form of the serial, or mini-series, a development that was mainly the result of increasing financial pressures as British television entered a more 'cost-effective' era (Gardner and Wyver, 1980). Series and serial drama provided an opportunity to spread the costs of production, while building and retaining audiences. The single play, on the other hand, was not only expensive to produce, it could not guarantee audiences in the way that series and serials could. Anthology play series, such as ITV's *Armchair Theatre*, *Playhouse*, *Saturday Night Theatre*, *Sunday Night Theatre* and *The Sunday Drama* all ended during the 1970s, while the BBC's *Play for Today*, *Playhouse*, *Play of the Month*, *Play of the Week* and *Premiere* were phased out in the late 1970s and early 1980s.

Dennis Potter showed the potential of the original drama serial with *Pennies from Heaven* (BBC 1, 1978), which followed his seven-part adaptation of Thomas Hardy's *The Mayor of Casterbridge* (BBC 2, 1978) and his earlier six-part *Casanova* (BBC2, 1971). Multi-part dramatisations of novels had been present on British television since the early 1950s but, apart from Nigle Kneale's trailblazing 1950s *Quatermass* serials, the original drama serial was less evident until writers such as Potter, John Finch, Trevor Griffiths, Alan Plater, Trevor Preston and Troy Kennedy Martin began producing long-form drama in the 1970s and 1980s. Such serials usually comprised six episodes but could be longer, with John Finch's *Sam* (Granada, 1973–5) extending to an exceptional thirty-nine episodes.

Fear of God (1980)

Troy Kennedy Martin had experimented with the drama serial in the early 1960s with *Diary of a Young Man* and the unproduced *Macheath*

– *Masterspy*, both of which were in six parts, but it was not until the end of the 1970s that he returned to the multi-part serial, initially with a four-part adaptation of a novel by Derry Quinn. *Fear of God* (Thames, February–March 1980) was produced in 1979 as part of Thames Television's *Armchair Thriller* series: eleven short drama serials shown in two series in 1978 and 1980 (two of the six serials in the second series were produced by Southern TV). Of the eleven serials, five were six-parters while the remaining six had four episodes. As each episode was only half an hour (twenty-five minutes plus a commercial break) these serials were barely more than feature length, but the episodic structure (accommodating commercial breaks) did require a different narrative strategy to that required for the single play.

This is evident in Kennedy Martin's four-part adaptation of Derry Quinn's novel. Episode one, 'A Question of Gravity' (26 February 1980), begins with the death of a young woman, Rosamund Clay, a neighbour of journalist Paul Marriot (Bryan Marshall). Having fallen from the roof of the building there is an immediate enigma about whether she jumped or was pushed. Before the police arrive – two seedy detectives including Alun Armstrong as the Regan-like DI Trahearne – Marriot looks over the young woman's flat, finding the kettle boiling, music playing, and a diary. As Marriot reads the diary, Rosamund Clay's words are heard in voiceover: 'I am a member of the Regiment of God and when I am taken to the room it is for my own good.' Immediately prior to the first commercial break, therefore, the implication is that the young woman's death is somehow connected to the mysterious religious cult, the Regiment of God. Sensing a sensational story, Marriot begins to dig further, finding out that Rosamund Clay had been missing for two years. An enigma emerges about a 'music room' which she writes about in her diary, but after receiving a visit from 'someone from Whitehall' Marriot's newspaper censors his story. On the verge of giving it up, Marriot hears a noise in Clay's flat but, while he is investigating, someone gets into his own flat and sets light to Clay's diary, bringing the first episode to a close.

Episode two, 'The Noise' (28 February 1980), begins with a recap of the events of the first episode, an obligatory convention for the drama serial. Marriot attends Rosamund Clay's funeral, where the 'spiritual advisor' of the Regiment of God, an American, insists on speaking at the service. Marriot discovers more about the Regiment of God, which is apparently interested in sound weapons technology, and the episode ends with a mysterious aural force breaking all the crockery in Marriot's flat while something, or somebody, attempts to break in.

Episode three, 'The Music Room' (4 March 1980), begins with Marriot having his ears checked by his doctor, to whom he recounts the story of the 'noise attack'. His doctor thinks Marriot is having a breakdown, following the break-up of his marriage, but when Marriot plays him a recording of the noise the doctor takes him more seriously. With Rosamund's younger sister Nicola (Madeline Church), Marriot goes to the Regiment of God's military-style headquarters, where they find their way to the Music Room. Marriot discovers that the Regiment of God is in possession of sound equipment developed by the US Army, which they plan to use to brainwash young people. Episode three ends with Marriot and Nicola being subjected to another attack by sound waves in his flat.

At the beginning of episode four, 'Bang!' (6 March 1980), Marriot and Nicola Clay are taken to the London HQ of the Regiment of God where General Stapleton (Robert Austin), its founder, tells them he believes America and Britain face a common enemy: 'atheistic communism'. Stapleton lets them go, on the understanding they return with Rosamund's ashes. Nicola returns with the casket, but it contains a bomb she has concocted with friends in the school chemistry lab! Having been tipped off they are about to be raided, Stapleton is preparing to leave the HQ, which they have booby-trapped with dynamite. The serial ends apocalyptically when Nicola's bomb goes off, triggering further explosions. A comic coda back at Marriot's flat sees him, Nicola and the two detectives toasting their success with his home brew and the serial finishes on a light-hearted note when Marriot's bottles of booze all pop their corks and erupt.

With a mixture of studio scenes recorded on video and exteriors shot on film, *Fear of God* was clearly not a Euston Films production, although its two detectives seemed to be parodying Regan and Carter from *The Sweeney*. Derry Quinn's source novel allowed Kennedy Martin little scope for humour but one can see how he might have been attracted by the subject matter of a religious cult planning to use military sound technology to brainwash young people. Unfortunately the low-budget production values undermined the serial's potential as a serious issue-based drama and the limitations of the 4 x 25 minute episode format worked against any sustained elaboration of its themes, inhibiting character development and the building of narrative tension. With each episode needing to recap on previous events the story might have worked better as a self-contained single drama. Ultimately, however, the source material was probably too insubstantial to sustain a four-part serial.

Produced in 1979 and transmitted in 1980, *Fear of God* can be seen as a transitional drama in the Troy Kennedy Martin oeuvre, bridging the gap between his contributions to drama series in the 1970s and the more sustained drama serials of the 1980s. As a contemporary thriller however, dealing with potentially interesting issues of right-wing religious cults brainwashing young people, using sound weapons technology developed by the military, *Fear of God* did provide Kennedy Martin with the opportunity to explore some contemporary concerns, within a drama serial format. This interest in contemporary social and political issues would, however, be developed with more success in his two subsequent BBC serials.

Reilly – Ace of Spies (1983)

Although it was produced by the same ITV company as *Fear of God*, the twelve-part *Reilly – Ace of Spies* (Thames, September–November 1983) was an altogether different project, a lavish production shot entirely on film, with a budget of £4.5 million, the most expensive Euston Films production since the formation of the company in the early 1970s. After developing a reputation for London-based crime dramas, Euston began to branch out in the 1980s, first with *The Flame Trees of Thika* (1981), a seven-part adaptation of Elspeth Huxley's autobiographical novel, filmed on location in Kenya, followed by *Reilly – Ace of Spies*, an international espionage drama set in Russia, Persia, Manchuria, London and New York, although the serial was mostly filmed at Elstree Studios with some location filming in London, Paris and Malta.

Reilly – Ace of Spies had a long gestation and Troy Kennedy Martin's involvement with it dated back to the early 1970s. The serial was inspired by Robin Bruce Lockhart's book about the Russian-born Sigmund Rosenblum, who became a British spy under the adopted name of Sidney Reilly and was active for nearly three decades in the early twentieth century. Lockhart's book, *Ace of Spies: Sidney Reilly*, was first published in 1967 and the television producer Stella Richman acquired the rights to it when she was Controller of Programmes at London Weekend Television. When Richman set up as an independent producer she offered it to LWT, with Kennedy Martin as part of the package, in 1974, but LWT could not afford to produce it. Several other companies also subsequently rejected it, including the BBC.[1] Eventually, when Richman's rights to the property expired, Kennedy Martin took it to Verity Lambert, Chief Executive of Euston Films. Lambert was very keen to do it and spent three years trying to organise co-production deals in order to raise the money for what was going to be by far Euston's most expensive project.

Verity Lambert asked Chris Burt, who had worked on *The Sweeney* and other Euston series as a film editor, to produce the serial. Burt remembered Kennedy Martin mentioning *Reilly* when they were editing *Sweeney 2*, at the beginning of 1978, when the rights to the property were still held by Stella Richman, giving some indication of the protracted gestation of the project. Lambert eventually arranged several sales deals, pre-selling the serial 'to Mobil in the States and to Australia, French-speaking Canada and Dutch TV' (Alvarado and Stewart, 1985: 110). While this enabled filming to go ahead there were still considerable production constraints, according to Chris Burt:

> We couldn't afford to go to Dundee or Glasgow which we knew was perfect for Russian scenes and we had to shoot it within the limits of people going backwards and forwards from their homes every night – although we did go to Malta of course to shoot the battle sequences and the Port Arthur sequences, and to France to shoot bits of Paris, but that was as much as we had. We had the money to go away for four weeks and that was it. And the Kremlin and all the rest we couldn't afford to go and do. (Alvarado and Stewart, 1985: 113)

Despite this the international dimension of *Reilly – Ace of Spies* was established from the outset. The extended first episode (75 minutes instead of 52) – 'An Affair With a Married Woman' (5 September 1983) – begins with Sigmund Rosenblum, having not yet assumed the name of Sidney Reilly, travelling to Odessa on his first mission for the British Secret Service. The year is 1901 and the episode opens with a steam train travelling through the Russian countryside (Malta doubling for Russia) on its way to Odessa, when it is halted by Russian Cossacks on horseback. Rosenblum is detained, along with two English travellers, the Reverend Thomas and his young wife Margaret. This 'cinematic' opening sequence was clearly intended as a visual statement designed to grab the attention of the television audience. Much of the subsequent action in the first episode takes place on studio sets, with some location filming in Malta for the Russian exterior scenes and some in London.

While detained in the southern Russian town of Baku, Rosenblum persuades Margaret, who is treated badly by her husband, to help him escape so he can complete his mission, inviting her to stay with him overnight in order to provide him with cover, which she is only too pleased to do. Rosenblum carries out his mission but we see nothing of it, only learning he was successful in a meeting back in London between members of the government and the Secret Service. Margaret, meanwhile, is imprisoned by the Russians for helping Rosenblum escape. When she is finally freed and allowed to return to London she finds herself at the centre of a scandal, as a result of her 'affair' with Rosenblum. Needless to say, Margaret and Rosenblum are eventually reconciled and, following the death of her elderly husband, they marry at the end of the first episode, Rosenblum assuming the name of Sidney Reilly prior to sailing with Margaret to Port Arthur in Manchuria, where he is to undertake his next mission.

Like all Euston productions, *Reilly – Ace of Spies* was filmed on 16mm, rather than the more expensive 35mm film stock used for feature films, yet the production values were high, with the early twentieth-century setting evoked in meticulous detail by the design team:

> With Malta doubling quite convincingly for Russia, Persia and Manchuria the thing looks wonderful, and in Sam Neill – a sort of short order Sean Connery – the serial has the kind of star who gets his picture pinned underneath schoolgirls' desks ... Between the scripts and Euston's camera-work (film, of course) *Reilly* has a marvellously authentic Edwardian patina and an authority which lifts it ever so slightly out of the costume-soap bracket. (Stoddart, 1983: 21)

Unlike other contemporary costume dramas, such as *Brideshead Revisited* (Granada, 1981) which displayed the hallmarks of the kind of 'heritage' drama (a nostalgic view of history) that was to become popular on British television in the 1980s and 1990s, *Reilly – Ace of Spies* attempted a serious approach to history, albeit with a veneer of glamour and romance, sufficient to attract a popular audience. Sam Neill may have been a star 'who gets his picture pinned underneath schoolgirls' desks' but he played Reilly with an icy detachment that was entirely suited to an occupation requiring duplicity and ruthlessness, and Kennedy Martin reinforced the mystery surrounding Reilly by withholding information about him in the early part of the serial, letting the audience know little about his background until episode four, when Reilly's step-sister Anna is introduced.

Striving to achieve a balance between the serious dramatisation of real historical events, action-adventure and romance, *Reilly* proved to be a popular success, its first two episodes attracting nearly ten million viewers, while the serial averaged over eight million. In fact *Reilly* was not a conventional serial, in the sense of having a continuing storyline, such as *Fear of God*, *The Old Men at the Zoo* and *Edge of Darkness*. There was no need to recap the story at the beginning of each new episode because episodes were largely self-contained narratives, although some stories did run over two episodes, such as the one about the re-equipping of the Russian fleet in episodes five and six, when Reilly operates as a double agent, working with the Germans to gain the contract in order to pass the details on to the British. In this case the connection between the episodes is made clear in the titles, episode five, 'Dreadnoughts and Crosses' (28 September 1983), being followed by 'Dreadnoughts and Doublecrosses' (5 October 1983).

The story of Reilly's involvement in an attempt to overthrow the Bolsheviks in 1918 is also told over two episodes, with episode seven, 'Gambit' (12 October 1983) and episode eight, 'Endgame' (19 October 1983), dealing with the complicated and confused situation in Russia following the revolution, when Reilly led an attempt to oust Lenin and install a new government. This story, in fact, is continued in episode nine, 'After Moscow' (26 October 1983), when Reilly escapes to London after the failure of the plot, only to find that he now has a price on his head. The Bolshevik episodes cover a turbulent period in Russian history and the intricacies of the narrative in this middle portion of the serial foreground the chaos and complex politics of the situation, ensuring that *Reilly* cannot be seen simply as a nostalgic costume drama about the romantic exploits of a British spy. Throughout the serial Kennedy Martin wanted to demystify rather than glamorise the real historical events he was dramatising and the complicated political aftermath of the Russian Revolution, described in episodes seven and eight, provides a good illustration of his approach:

> I hope we convey that Lenin wasn't the father-figure he later became. I wanted to show that he cracked jokes, felt he wouldn't last 60 days, was every day confronting a new situation and wondering if he was going to be in power at the end of it. If one can get across the anarchy and confusion of the time, then Reilly's attempts to de-stablilize the Revolution become dramatically feasible. (Kennedy Martin quoted in Billington, 1984)

Apart from the political narratives which continue over two or three episodes there are some other elements of serialisation, mainly involving Reilly's love affairs. Reilly's relationship with Margaret, for example, was an ongoing storyline through the first few episodes and she reappears in the final episode, by which time Reilly has married twice more after contriving a story about Margaret being killed in an accident in Bulgaria. Her reappearance, and the news that they have never been divorced, is an indication of Reilly's duplicity – he is by no means an unblemished romantic hero.

In order to provide a context for each episode, a narrational voiceover is used from episode two onwards, providing the audience with historical information and ensuring Reilly's activities are seen within a wider political context. The narration serves to emphasise the historical authenticity of the serial, Michael Bryant's matter-of-fact voiceover functioning in marked contrast to the nostalgic narration provided by Jeremy Irons in *Brideshead Revisited*. At the beginning of episode two, 'Prelude to War' (7 September 1983), for example, the narrator relates how:

In the spring of 1904, Reilly found himself in the ancient Chinese province of Manchuria, a land so rich that both the Russians and the Japanese were greedy to possess it. From his vantage point as a shipping agent in Port Arthur, which was the headquarters of the Russian Pacific fleet, Reilly came to realise that the Russians were ill-prepared for war. As the crisis developed, Reilly pleaded in his dispatches to Cummings in London, that the British do something to avert the catastrophe that would follow a Japanese attack, but the British and Japanese had recently become allies and Cummings was loath to interfere. Instead he instructed Reilly to place himself at the disposal of the Japanese navy, thereby ensuring his reluctant participation in the coming war.

The second episode clearly illustrates the difficulties and dilemmas of Reilly's task as he finds himself having to carry out orders to assist the Japanese in their preparations for war with Russia, Reilly's mother country. In contrast to the more romantic exploits of the fictional James Bond, Reilly often found himself caught in these moral dilemmas, and Kennedy Martin used this to explore the role of the spy in wartime:

> In the second episode, set in Port Arthur in 1904, I posit the idea that Reilly believes he can right the world by being an agent, that he can warn the British that the Japanese are preparing to invade Russia, that there is going to be an almighty war and that no good can come of it. He warns the Secret Service that the Russians are not going to be able to win, that the balance of world power will be affected and that Far Eastern nations will take over. He feeds all the information back to London and gets little response. So, one is left asking certain questions. What is the nature of spying? How is information evaluated? What happens when ideas are ignored? (Kennedy Martin quoted in Billington, 1984)

Sam Neill did a reasonably good job in conveying these dilemmas, but one of the problems of the casting of this New Zealand actor as Reilly was that his Russian origins were not readily apparent. Neill convincingly played the English gentleman spy, making it easy to think of him as 'British', when in reality his allegiance was as much to Russia as it was to Britain. This meant it was possible, in episode two, to overlook Reilly's dilemma in Manchuria. While Sam Neill's emotionless detachment was, on occasions, entirely believable, there were other occasions when it would have been useful to be reminded that he was, in fact, Russian. In short, Sam Neill was more convincing as Sidney Reilly than he was as Sigmund Rosenblum.

While *Reilly – Ace of Spies* may have been based on real historical events it was undoubtedly a drama, as the casting constantly reminded us. With Sam Neill as Reilly, Kenneth Cranham as Lenin, David Burke as Stalin, and with Leo McKern, Norman Rodway, Peter Egan, Jeananne

Crowley, David Suchet, Bill Nighy, Tom Bell, Hugh Fraser, Ian Charleson, Clive Merrison, Anthony Higgins, Lindsay Duncan, Warren Clarke and Michael Angelis all appearing in the serial, *Reilly* could claim to represent 'the best of British acting', one of the criteria for 'quality drama' identified by Charlotte Brunsdon (1990: 85).

As far as Kennedy Martin was concerned, *Reilly* was not a drama-documentary but a work of popular dramatic fiction which could, nevertheless, engage with real historical events and issues in a serious way:

> The audience is watching fiction, albeit fiction with a background of history. What I was trying to do was something like E. L. Doctorow in 'Ragtime': that is, to weave a piece of high fiction out of real people and historical events. I wasn't simply trying to adapt Bruce Lockhart's book for TV. I was hoping to create something that would bear comparison with Somerset Maugham's Ashenden spy stories or the Graham Greene of 'Stamboul Train.'
>
> I was also keen to use the stories to highlight greater truths, to prove that mainstream television could incorporate ideas. Take, for example, the episode where Reilly is in St. Petersburg acting as agent for a German shipping company while sending the naval designs back to the Admiralty in London. I wasn't interested in the mechanics of that, which is Plot C from the 'Espionage Writers Handbook.' What fascinated me was that Reilly was, above all, a businessman making money out of espionage rather than a prototype James Bond whose sole job was being employed by the British government. In that episode, the greater truth I was after was that the British Navy was prepared to sell its own shipyard workers down the river at a time of high unemployment in order to get its hands on the rival German plans. (Kennedy Martin quoted in Billington, 1984)

The reference to Somerset Maugham is a reminder that *Reilly – Ace of Spies* was not the first time Kennedy Martin had written an espionage drama. In the late 1950s he had adapted Maugham's *The Traitor*, an espionage drama set in Europe in 1916, as a forty-five minute television play, while the theme of spying was also central to the unproduced *The Little Goat*, which he had also worked on around the same time. The reference to *Reilly* as 'high fiction' is also significant given that this is how he described his approach to *The Sweeney*, an altogether different piece of popular television fiction. The connection highlights a fundamental quality of Kennedy Martin's approach to screenwriting, which is his concern to work in the popular mainstream of television drama without sacrificing an interest in history, politics and ideas. While he has often dramatised real events and real people he has generally done so by eschewing naturalism, realism and documentary-drama, choosing to work instead in the realm of 'high fiction' in order to aspire towards a 'greater truth.'

For Kennedy Martin, *Reilly – Ace of Spies* was a vehicle for exploring history, politics and ideas within a mainstream drama format, and Sidney Reilly was a suitably complex and ambiguous figure to place at the centre of the drama. A heroic fantasy figure such as James Bond, whose allegiance was unambiguously towards the British government, would not have allowed for the searching examination of moral and political ambivalences that Kennedy Martin found in the subject of Sidney Reilly:

> My attitude is that Reilly was courageous, daring, radical in his views, a Social Democrat up to a point and that he was defeated in the end by an anti-Semitic, right-wing British Establishment that didn't have any sympathy with what he was up to. But my basic point is that he was definitely a political creature, as well as a buccaneering businessman. (Kennedy Martin quoted in Billington, 1984)

In some respects the production constraints on *Reilly* worked in favour of Kennedy Martin's aim to focus on the politics and the moral ambiguities of Reilly's situation, denying the possibility of the serial being given a lavish 'heritage' treatment in which the past is 'de-historicised' (Cooke, 2003: 168). In other ways, however, the higher production values which the bigger budget enabled for this Euston production compromised the harder, bleaker vision Kennedy Martin originally had of the world in which Reilly operated:

> I thought it was really softened ... It was a management problem ... Jim Goddard was okay, the directors were fine, Martin [Campbell – who shared the direction with Goddard] was fine. It was just that the producers really were trying to throw their weight around ... What one wanted to do was to produce something like *Shanghai* [*Express*] or one of those thirties Von Sternberg things, very cold, very brittle, icy, very stylised, black and white ... The scripts could have done it. Sammy wasn't bad. They just softened it up, told him to smile, got involved with the plots, it was the wrong decision. It was never meant to be taken out and big sets built at Ealing or wherever it was. So everyone got into building big sets and having what they thought was film, which was essentially shooting everything on a stage.[2]

Notwithstanding Kennedy Martin's reservations, *Reilly* was far more cinematic than anything Euston had done before and demonstrated his skill in writing cinematic scenes. While there was a need, in some scenes, for a considerable amount of dialogue to convey the political complexity of some of the episodes, there were many scenes where the plot could be communicated with little or no dialogue. Kennedy Martin gives an example of a scene, in episode ten, which he originally wrote without dialogue but which was changed, partly for reasons of cost but also because the scene may have shown a side of Reilly's character which it was felt would lose audience sympathy for him. The original conception of the scene provides a good illustration of cinematic writing:

> In *Reilly* an example would be – which we weren't allowed to do – where he shoots the woman he's sleeping with, who's working for the Russians, and he finds out when they ambush his car. He's coming back to her – the only way they could have known the route is because he leaves a letter by the mantelshelf in one of the rooms in case he's late back so she can check it out. So when he gets back after the ambush he just goes into the darkened house and there's the letter and it's open, it's been read. Then he goes up to the room and she's asleep and it's just the looks between them, she knows that he knows that she knows, and then he gets into bed with her and makes love with her, and then in the morning he takes her down to the seashore – he took her to a lake in the series because they couldn't afford a seashore – and he makes her take her clothes off and then swim out to sea. So you then have the whole business of sea being death and all that sort of stuff and he makes her go further and further out and he stands there with the gun and you wonder, is she going to drown or what? And then he shoots her and then you see the hands go down into the sea and you cut away and her clothes are hanging on a secondhand stall somewhere in Brooklyn. So the whole thing is done without any dialogue.[3]

In the scene as filmed, however, there is dialogue. Eugenie (Eleanor David) hears Reilly returning to the house, gets out of bed and waits until he enters the bedroom, when he tells her his potential assassin is dead and holds up the opened letter, saying: 'You tried to kill me', a fact that is fairly obvious from what has gone before. There is no scene in which they get into bed and make love. Instead there is a straight cut to a scene in the woods as they walk to the lake, Reilly walking behind Eugenie who is wearing a silk robe over her nightdress. There is early morning mist and the sound of crows but no dialogue until Reilly tells her to stop by the side of the lake. An exchange of looks precedes Eugenie removing her robe and her necklace, but not her nightdress, before she walks into the lake, up to her waist in water before Reilly shoots her in the back. Instead of a cut to her clothes hanging on a stall in Brooklyn there is a fade to the next scene in Berlin.

While the sequence is fairly faithful to the writer's original intention, the inclusion of dialogue was an unnecessary concession to expositional clarity. The cutting of the love-making scene slightly diminishes Reilly's cold-hearted killing of Eugenie, although his shooting of her in the back is still a shock, and the changes made to the location prevent the association of the sea and death that Kennedy Martin had originally intended. The sequence is still a powerful one, illustrating Reilly's ruthlessness, but the changes made in the passage from script to screen illustrate how the original intentions of a writer can be undermined during production.

Totalling nearly eleven hours in screen time, *Reilly – Ace of Spies* was a major achievement for one writer. Although based on the Robin Bruce Lockhart book there was a lot of work involved in turning the bare facts of Reilly's life into a twelve-episode serial and Kennedy Martin reckoned he wrote 'a million words and 80 revisions of scripts' over a four-year period before *Reilly* finally got to the screen (Billington, 1984). While he felt his original concept had been 'softened' the serial was a serious work of historical fiction that was both a popular and critical success: 'Euston's best foray into historical mode was 1983's *Reilly – Ace of Spies*, blessed with superb scripts by Troy Kennedy Martin ... ' (Cornell, Day and Topping, 1996: 358). Verity Lambert also recognised that the success of *Reilly* had much to do with the quality of Kennedy Martin's scripts: 'I just thought it was a wonderful, extraordinary story and Troy's scripts were just superb ... '[4]

While *Reilly* may have been overshadowed as a spy drama by the BBC's John Le Carre adaptations – *Tinker, Tailor, Soldier, Spy* (1979) and *Smiley's People* (1982) – and as a historical drama by Granada's two major costume dramas of the 1980s – *Brideshead Revisited* (1981) and *The Jewel in the Crown* (1984) – both of which were subsequently held up as beacons of 'quality' television drama, *Reilly – Ace of Spies* was nevertheless a major achievement for Euston Films, an entertaining drama about British politics, international affairs and espionage in the early years of the twentieth century. *Reilly* also marked a new stage in Troy Kennedy Martin's screenwriting career as he made a successful transition from writing single plays, feature films and series episodes to the longer form of the drama serial, representing a highpoint in his oeuvre to rank alongside *Z Cars, Diary of a Young Man, The Italian Job, Kelly's Heroes, The Sweeney* and *Edge of Darkness*.

The Old Men at the Zoo (1983)

While *Reilly – Ace of Spies* was a major production requiring a huge investment of Kennedy Martin's time in the early 1980s, it was not the only serial he was working on. The five-part adaptation of Angus Wilson's allegorical novel *The Old Men at the Zoo* (BBC 2, September– October 1983) was in development at the same time as *Reilly* and for five weeks in September–October 1983 the two serials were being shown in parallel, transmitted on Wednesday and Thursday evenings.

Whereas with previous adaptations of novels Kennedy Martin had been required to conform to the length of a single play (even the four-part adaptation of *Fear of God* was in total no longer than a single drama), with *The Old Men at the Zoo* he had the luxury of five episodes and 250 minutes of screen time to play with. The length was necessary because Wilson's novel was ambitious: a futuristic plot (written at the end of the 1950s but set in the 1970s) about an isolated Britain facing a nuclear conflict with a fascist European state. Wilson set his novel within the enclosed world of London Zoo, which he used as a metaphor for the antagonisms, rivalries and political manoeuvring taking place in the wider world:

> Fictional dystopias, it is often said, reflect the age in which the author is writing rather than the future in which the book is set. Orwell's *Nineteen Eighty-Four* is really about 1948. And Angus Wilson's *The Old Men at the Zoo*, first published in 1961 but set in a slump-ridden Seventies, is about the late Fifties. In the book, tension between Britain and a United Europe quickly escalates into full-scale atomic warfare. In reality, de Gaulle was cold-shouldering Britain out of the Common Market while CND was reaching the first peak of its popularity. To point to these parallels isn't to suggest that Wilson's imagination was limited, but to emphasise the complex political and social satire which is at the heart of the novel. (Craig, 1983)

In adapting the novel Kennedy Martin was faced with the immediate problem that Wilson's future was now in the recent past and he was forced to make a number of changes to update it, setting the drama in the late 1980s, instead of the 1970s, and making the country with which Britain was on the verge of war not a United Europe but an Arab state, the conflict in Kennedy Martin's version being about oil. Kennedy Martin was writing, of course, with knowledge of the oil crisis in the early 1970s which Angus Wilson had not foreseen, a crisis which had affected global power relations significantly and cast a long shadow that powerful Western nations were still coming to terms with in the 1980s. The opportunity to adapt Wilson's novel for television enabled Kennedy Martin to address this global economic development and to postulate on the growing possibility of nuclear warfare, which was once again back on the agenda with pro-nuclear right-wing governments in power in Britain and America.

The opening credits make it clear that this is not a literal adaptation of the Angus Wilson novel but 'a version for television by Troy Kennedy Martin'. The animated graphics of the title sequence highlight the key ingredients of the serial, opening with a view of the planet to suggest the global significance of the drama, followed by a series of sketches of zoo animals – giraffes, a panda and a lion – the latter portrayed with a crown on its head. The lion then becomes the crowning feature on a Coat of Arms depicting a lion and unicorn, set against a background of the Union Jack. As the title music changes to become more ominous in tone the image fragments to reveal the silhouettes of five figures emerging against a Union Jack skyline, both the Union Jack and the figures dissolving and disappearing as the title of the drama appears onscreen.

Episode one, 'A Tall Story … ' (15 September 1983), begins with the arrival at the zoo of Simon Carter (Stuart Wilson) to take up his post as the new Secretary of the Zoological Gardens. He arrives amidst a scene of panic and confusion following an incident in the giraffe house in which Filson, a young keeper, has been mortally injured by a giraffe. Through this incident Carter is immediately alerted to the shortcomings in the zoo's health and safety procedures, the incident serving to highlight the general malaise at the zoo which Carter, as a 'new broom', will endeavour to rectify. Like the novel, much of the first episode is concerned with establishing the rivalries between the 'old men' of the zoo: the curators of the different animal houses, the director, Dr Leacock (Maurice Denham) and the zoo's president, Lord Godmanchester (Robert Morley), whose personal wealth is indicated by his chauffeur-driven Rolls Royce (registration number: A1 GOD) which he uses despite the petrol shortage arising from the oil crisis. As he tells Carter at their first meeting: 'We still rely on the Arab commission for our petrol, which is why only the police and my own chauffeur drive motor cars.'

When Carter arrives at Godmanchester's office, having been summoned to see him, there is a news item on television reporting that the Minister of Defence has ordered Britain's Trident missiles be realigned from their previous targets beyond the Iron Curtain following 'the widening breach between Europe and the Arab world.' Kennedy Martin would adopt a similar tactic in *Edge of Darkness* of using television news reports to communicate wider political events and give a political 'reality' to the drama. In the earlier episodes of *The Old Men at the Zoo* these global developments generally provide a backdrop to the drama at the zoo, alluded to only occasionally in conversation or by having characters like Carter watching or listening to news reports, but as the serial proceeds world events increasingly encroach on the otherwise insulated world of the zoo.

When Carter tells Godmanchester the people running the zoo are in 'a frightful muddle', Godmanchester replies: 'Chaos is the word I prefer, ever since the money run out in '84.' By such means it is made clear that the drama is taking place sometime in the future – there is not much in the way of visual iconography to indicate this, apart from a slightly futuristic-looking ambulance at the beginning – but also that Britain in this near future is an impoverished nation. The tone adopted is light-hearted, almost casual, as the following exchange between Godmanchester and Carter illustrates:

> *Godmanchester* (handing Carter a cup of tea in a delicate china cup): You know we're going to have a war. We're all likely to get blown up.
> *Carter*: Thank you. Is it that bad?
> *Godmanchester*: The Arabs won't back down and the Europeans ... well you know what the French are like, the chances of them blowing each other to smithereens are very high, and of course once they're in, we are. How do you feel about that?
> *Carter*: Well I don't like the idea of my wife and two children dying in a nuclear firestorm ...
> *Godmanchester*: Sugar?
> *Carter*: Er, no.
> *Godmanchester*: Well it's on the cards you know, sometime in the autumn.

In the novel, the first meeting between Carter and Godmanchester does not take place until Chapter two and it is Godmanchester who visits Carter, rather than vice versa. There is no conversation about the fuel crisis or an impending war with 'the Arabs' in the novel. Kennedy Martin elevates Godmanchester in his version, dispensing with Carter's first-person narration, which clearly makes him the central character in the novel, through whom all of the events are channeled. In the television version the significance of the developing world crisis is made clear early in the first episode, yet in such a manner that the satirical tone of the novel is retained.

Godmanchester is anticipating being recalled to government to help out with the national crisis and he informs Carter that, contrary to what the Americans think, 'the Arabs have the bomb and are able to deliver it.' He tells Carter he wants him to activate Dr Leacock's plan for a national zoo in the country, in order to move the animals out of London. This is not simply to save the animals in the event of nuclear attack but because he needs 'some sort of metaphor, to alert the nation to the danger it's in. I don't want anything so violent that they panic and the bottom drops out of sterling. I want something that only the English understand and the only thing they understand is animals.' Godmanchester's proposal is to move the animals to Wales, most of which he bought up 'during the great land slump of 1984.'

There are many ways in which Kennedy Martin updates and augments Wilson's novel, contriving as he does so to inject some characteristic humour into the story. The first meeting between Carter and Godmanchester is a prime example, especially when Godmanchester tells Carter about his purchase of Wales:

> You may not be aware of it Carter, but during the great land slump of 1984, I bought up most of Wales. I don't mean the smelly bits with the people in it, I'm talking of the mountains and the fells. Of course I was aided by the wholesale burning down of holiday homes by owners desperate to collect the insurance and the unflagging enthusiasm of a band of Welsh-speaking incendiaries. I don't mind admitting I'd made these acquisitions from the basest of motives, but now that I've suffered my second coronary all thought of profit has deserted me. I'm planning to leave Wales to the nation, as some sort of national wildlife reserve.

The casting and performance of Robert Morley as Lord Godmanchester was crucial to the realisation of a satirical tone in the serial and Kennedy Martin clearly enjoyed writing the part. He did, however, feel the central characters, including the 'old men', should have been cast younger than they were:

> I liked the performances of the old men but I would have preferred it if they had been much younger, in their late forties and early fifties, and the young men would be really young. I think that it's a reflection of our time that they think a young man is thirty-five, whereas a young man is twenty-five. If the hero had been twenty-five then the old men would have been in their forties.[5]

Kennedy Martin felt this was 'a problem in the mind of the director. He wanted to play the old men as old because he didn't want to think of himself as an old man.'[6] The director, Stuart Burge, was sixty-five when he directed *The Old Men at the Zoo*. While Burge had been directing for television since the early 1960s he was best known as a theatre director. His work for television tended towards the naturalistic and he was not, therefore, the ideal choice for a drama requiring a satirical approach. Burge's attitude towards the ages of the 'old men' may have been different to Kennedy Martin's but his contacts and casting skills did result in *The Old Men at the Zoo* boasting an impressive cast. In addition to Robert Morley as Lord Godmanchester and Stuart Wilson as Carter, the cast included Maurice Denham as Edwin Leacock, the zoo's director, plus Robert Urquhart, Marius Goring, Andrew Cruickshank, John Phillips and Richard Wordsworth as the zoo's curators. There was, however, a 'staginess' about some of the acting, possibly as a result of Burge's direction, which detracted from the satirical comedy Kennedy Martin was aiming for in his adaptation. Some scenes are sluggish when they needed to be more dynamic to release the satirical wit contained in the script. That the serial was shot on video may have contributed to this sluggishness, video giving the drama the look and pace of a low-budget production, whereas film would have enabled a more stylish *mise en scene* and faster cutting.

The highpoint of the second episode, 'Godmanchester's Plan' (22 September 1983), was Leacock's Attenborough Lecture, which he uses to promote the idea of a national reserve. Anticipating the fragmentation of British television into specialist channels, more than ten years before it occurred, Kennedy Martin has BBC 3 covering the lecture. He also took the opportunity to send up such television events by having Leacock begin his lecture by singing 'Home on the Range', dressed in a cowboy hat, much to the dismay and embarrassment of Carter and the zoo's curators, most of whom were opposed to the idea of a national reserve. Anticipating the trend towards 'infotainment' in serious television programming Kennedy Martin has the producer of the BBC 3 programme come up with the idea for the song in order to present Leacock not, as Carter assumes, as a modern-day Noah but 'like the Lone Ranger.'

Meanwhile, with the possibility of conflict between Britain and the Arab state, Bilad al Hawa, escalating, Carter finds the relationship between himself and his American wife deteriorating as a result of their respective country's responsibility for the impending conflict. Among Kennedy Martin's additions here is the irony, not without contemporary foundation, that Britain was responsible for supplying Bilad al Hawa with the bomb as a nuclear deterrent, which may now be used against it; and in a clear allusion to Britain's involvment in the 1981 Falklands conflict, Martha Carter tells her husband: 'The days are gone when you can send a gunboat without reference to the rest of the world, it's too goddamn dangerous.'

Episode three, 'Exodus' (29 September 1983), sees the evacuation of the zoo animals to a national reserve in Wales. Godmanchester wants the move to happen speedily and he gets the board to agree to an immediate evacuation, which takes place despite the objections of some of the curators. The evacuation has the desired effect, encouraging a similar exodus among the population of London, including the departure of Carter's wife and children to America. However, the lack of forward planning becomes apparent when animals start escaping from the reserve, and when Leacock's daughter is killed there the project is deemed a failure, much to the delight of Robert Falcon, whose opposition to the project preceded his departure to the Amazon jungle.

At the beginning of episode four, 'Armageddon' (6 October 1983), Falcon returns to take over from Leacock as the director and immediately implements a plan to reintroduce 'Victorian virtues' to the zoo by holding an 'Empire Day': 'Something to remind the chaps of how things once were. We shall transform the zoo back to 1890, a giant Noah's Ark where man and beast lay down together under the Pax Britannica … Certain moral texts will be displayed about the cages reflecting the Victorian virtues of piety, industry and social responsibility.' The allusion to Margaret Thatcher's much-publicised advocacy of a return to 'Victorian values' in British society in the early 1980s was unmistakable, Angus Wilson's 'British Day' taking on a new meaning in the context of Thatcherism.

Given the limitations of the budget the nuclear firestorm at the end of episode four is dealt with quite well, with electronically generated special effects simulating the strike on London, and the escaped eagles from the zoo circling against a backdrop of a huge mushroom cloud. Immediately prior to the attack the army arrives at the zoo to shoot the most dangerous animals and when Carter is visited by Emile Englander (Marius Goring) in hospital, apparently two years after the event, he is told that the animals were eaten when the food ran out. Englander, the new director of the zoo, is dressed in the uniform of the fascist organisation One Europe and when Carter asks him why he is wearing it Englander replies: 'Because we're in charge now old boy. We've taken over.'

The final episode, 'The Year of the Yeti' (13 October 1983), begins, unusually, with Carter's voiceover, the only occasion when Kennedy Martin retains the first-person narration of the novel. On returning to the zoo, Carter expresses his surprise at how little London was damaged. Nevertheless, as he narrates: 'some seven million people were killed by the three warheads that fell over the Midlands and Wales. There was strict Marshall law and the zoo was under tight security like a government research establishment.' In the post-apocalyptic aftermath of the nuclear attack the zoo is being used by One Europe as a political weapon to reinforce its rule. When Carter returns the zoo's stuffed yeti is being removed because 'it has become the symbol of national liberation' by those opposed to the fascist regime of One Europe. The vision of a fascist regime coming to power following the nuclear attack is brought out much more forcefully in Kennedy Martin's version of *The Old Men at the Zoo* than it was in Wilson's novel. As Richard Last wrote in the *Daily Telegraph* after the final episode had been screened:

Faced with the absence of the ending they thought Angus Wilson ought to have written, but didn't, Jonathan Powell and his adaptor Troy Kennedy Martin proceeded to invent it. Wilson's brief, half-hearted evocation of

Fascist terror became a full-blown Nazi death camp. The symbolism the author shrank from, or perhaps never envisaged – putting humans who had once supervised captive animals into cages of their own – was spelt out in grisly detail. (Last, 1983)

Sanderson (Andrew Cruickshank) is caught distributing leaflets for the Yeti resistance movement and when Martha Carter, who has also shown her support for the movement, is taken away Carter goes off in search of her, only to end up in one of the cages in which One Europe is keeping members of the resistance. Eventually the prison where Carter and Sanderson are held is liberated by members of the resistance movement and One Europe is overthrown. At the end of the episode Carter makes it known he intends to stand for election as the new director of the zoo.

Kennedy Martin's version of *The Old Men at the Zoo* was generally well-received by reviewers and his updating of Wilson's novel for a Thatcherite Britain of the early 1980s was seen to have enriched it:

Troy Kennedy Martin's script has been cunningly loaded with additional dialogue – linguistic nods and winks in the direction of Britain as we know her today. The update has been achieved with masterly if chilling effect, almost as if Angus Wilson's fantasy of 1961 has indeed become the reality of 1983. (Davidson, 1983: 6)

Few writers of any calibre would have the wit or cunning to write a 'costume drama' set in the future. Fewer still would turn the opportunity to present such a trenchant and contemporary analysis, while at the same time taking such a clear delight in the possibilities of television … From the opening sequence with its chilling pun between the ambulance klaxon, the cascade of zoo animal whoops and the screams of the dying zoo-keeper to the Quantel pyrotechnics as The Bomb goes up, the series revels in fun and wit as much as in ideas. (Craig, 1983)

Where *Reilly – Ace of Spies* enabled Kennedy Martin to explore major international events from the early years of the twentieth century, through the real-life character of Sidney Reilly, *The Old Men at the Zoo* enabled him to address contemporary political concerns, through an assortment of characters who provide plenty of scope for the realisation of Kennedy Martin's brand of witty, linguistic humour. Where *Reilly* did not afford much scope for humour, Angus Wilson's allegorical novel certainly did and Kennedy Martin took full advantage of this in his adaptation. While lacking the production values of *Reilly* and *Edge of Darkness*, *The Old Men at the Zoo* nevertheless provided Kennedy Martin with the opportunity to give some serious issues a satirical treatment. If the combination of satire and nuclear warfare in the serial is sometimes awkward, Kennedy

Martin's engagement with these issues was an important rehearsal of themes that were to receive a more sustained examination in his next serial, the contemporary nuclear thriller *Edge of Darkness*.

Edge of Darkness (1985)

The six-part serial *Edge of Darkness* (BBC 2, November–December 1985) is Troy Kennedy Martin's magnum opus. Like *Reilly – Ace of Spies* it had a long gestation, which in many ways enriched the drama, enabling its complicated plot to be fully elaborated, with new layers of complexity being added as real-life events unfolded during the early 1980s. By the time of its transmission, towards the end of 1985, *Edge of Darkness* had a contemporary political relevance which considerably enhanced its impact. This was not just a highly entertaining thriller but an original drama serial which skilfully tapped into the zeitgeist of the mid 1980s, just as Alan Bleasdale's *Boys from the Blackstuff* (BBC 2, October-November 1982) had summed up the state of the nation in the early 1980s.

The origins of *Edge of Darkness* date back to the mid–late 1970s when Kennedy Martin was also trying to get *Reilly – Ace of Spies* off the ground. This was a time when he was finding it difficult to get worked produced, especially at the BBC: 'I would have liked to have worked then but I didn't think that there was the remotest chance that I could.'[7] During the four-year period from 1976–9 his only screen credits were for one episode of *The Sweeney*, the second *Sweeney* feature film and the final episode of *Z Cars*, the latter being his only BBC credit in the ten years between 1974 and 1983. It was a relatively fallow period:

> In the mid-late seventies I found myself really without anyone that I could work for and so I began to just develop ideas for myself and I reached a stage where I was telling other people like Paula Milne and Fay Weldon and Trevor [Preston] and Gordon Newman – we all knew each other quite well – that the only thing about the television play, it was never going to be produced, or the series, and you just had to go in there and write for yourself and so I was writing all this stuff on the understanding that it would never be done.[8]

Thanks to Verity Lambert at Thames *Reilly* did get done and it was as a result of the support of Jonathan Powell at the BBC that both *The Old Men at the Zoo* and *Edge of Darkness* were commissioned. Powell produced a number of 'quality' drama serials at the BBC in the late 1970s and early 1980s, including adaptations of literary classics such as Dennis Potter's seven-part dramatisation of Thomas Hardy's *The Mayor of Casterbridge* (BBC 2, 1978) and Fay Weldon's five-part adaptation of Jane Austen's *Pride and Prejudice* (BBC 2, 1980). He also produced the John Le Carre espionage serials, *Tinker, Tailor, Soldier, Spy* (BBC 2, 1979) and *Smiley's People* (BBC 2, 1982), followed by *The Old Men at the Zoo*, after which he was appointed Head of Series and Serials at the BBC. Having had very little work produced at the BBC since the early 1960s, Kennedy Martin suddenly found there was someone in a position of power at the Corporation who was sympathetic to the kind of drama he wanted to write: 'Absolutely – and very enthusiastic about it, since he'd just done *Tinker, Tailor* ... and some of the other things. Also he came over with a classics series so he actually believed in strong storytelling and good quality work.'[9]

The support of first Verity Lambert and then Jonathan Powell illustrates how important it is for a writer to have a patron, especially in the more competitive era of the 1980s when it was becoming increasingly difficult for writers to get work commissioned, especially if that work was in any way critical of the dominant ideology. Kennedy Martin acknowledged that the Le Carre serials had been important in paving the way for an ambitious drama serial like *Edge of Darkness*:

> The advent of Le Carre's work on the BBC really enabled *Edge of Darkness* to be done. First of all it set up a precedent that this sort of work was popular and would gain audiences and secondly the producer, Jonathan Powell, was going to go on and become the Head of BBC Serials and he was the person who encouraged me to produce the scripts for *Edge of Darkness*.[10]

Having decided to commission the serial, Jonathan Powell asked Michael Wearing if he was interested in producing it. In the late 1970s and early 1980s Wearing had been working for BBC English Regions Drama at Birmingham, where he produced *The History Man* and *Boys from the Blackstuff* before going to London to work on what would be the final season of *Play for Today*:

> After the *Play for Today* season, when they finally said that's it, we're not doing any more plays, Jonathan asked me down to the Serials Department ... and he said, 'How would you like to do *Blott on the Landscape?*', the Tom Sharpe thing which Malcolm Bradbury had adapted. So I thought well, yes, possibly, and then he said 'I've got this altogether more problematic piece ... ' (laughs) ... Troy had been researching this, as I soon found out, for years and years and years, it was a real labour of love and he was working out how on earth to do it, even then. Jonathan said 'I want to do this but I don't know how, what do you think?' So of course I read it and instantly said this is very extraordinary, what there was, even then. So I said alright I'll do it, or I'll attempt to do it!'[11]

Wearing brought in Martin Campbell, who directed five episodes of *Reilly – Ace of Spies*, and they spent many weeks working with Kennedy Martin to get the scripts into shape. At this stage the drama was called *Magnox*[12] and, unusually for a project where the scripts were not yet finished, production was scheduled from 25 June to 19 October 1984, so they were working to a deadline. The collaboration between Kennedy Martin, Campbell and Wearing in developing the serial throws into question the whole issue of authorship in television drama. Traditionally, especially with the single play, the writer was always considered the author of the piece, but with *Edge of Darkness* Wearing and Campbell worked very closely with Kennedy Martin in pulling the project together, although Wearing finally acknowledged 'he wrote it really, of course he did':

> What I found out was that he had all this stuff, really big set-piece stuff, and they were hours down the story. That whole thing down the mine, the break-in, he'd written that before he'd written episode three or four. So there were these big stepping stones in a rather difficult river to cross, with no way of jumping from one stone to the next ... The job was to suggest how we joined it all together and it got to the point where Martin Campbell and I were actually writing scenes and showing them to Troy, saying what about this, and he used to read them and give us six out of ten or something! But we sat there night after night after night, going steadily crazy. Because the thing was – this is why it could never happen now – because it wasn't totally finished, by any means ... it had nevertheless been green lit for production, because Jonathan could do that as Head of the Department in those days, so it was pencilled in to go shooting six months down the line, so we were working to a deadline.[13]

Even before Wearing and Campbell became involved, during the period when Kennedy Martin was first developing the storyline, a number of influences, ideas and events were combining to shape the serial, most of which can be detected in the completed work. Kennedy Martin's previous work on police series clearly informed the portrayal of the central character, Ronnie Craven (Bob Peck), a dour Yorkshire police detective who finds himself at the centre of an increasingly complex political web. The character of Craven is cut from the same mould as the stony-faced Detective Chief Inspector Frank Barlow in *Z Cars*, a gruff, no-nonsense character who occasionally reveals a wry sense of humour. Kennedy Martin's Sidney Reilly also shares some of the same qualities of a cool, contained character whose severe expression masks inner emotions which sometimes break through to the surface. This melancholy figure is a recurrent Kennedy Martin character type, informed, perhaps, by his recollected feelings of loss at the death of his mother when he was a teenager, or even, at a deeper level, by the sense of loss that has been the historical experience of generations of Irish emigrants.[14]

Craven is initially investigating allegations of ballot rigging within a miners' union and the miners' strike of 1984–5 was to become part of the backdrop to the events that unfold in *Edge of Darkness*. According to Kennedy Martin this narrative strand was originally going to be the political element in the serial, before being superseded by the nuclear story which became central to the drama:

> I was determined it would have a real political element and at the beginning I thought that the miners' strike might provide me with one. Unfortunately that didn't work out. So I became more interested in the nuclear option and the nuclear state, on which there were half a dozen books, but that didn't really take off until I'd found the 'Star Wars' speech of Reagan.[15]

Given that the miners' strike did not start until March 1984 and that President Reagan's 'Star Wars' speech was delivered on 24 March 1983, it seems likely that Kennedy Martin was drawing on the experience of the 1973–4 miners' strike in earlier drafts of the serial, while anticipating the outbreak of the miners' strike of 1984 at least a year before it occurred. Certainly the Thatcher government's advocacy of the use of nuclear power and nuclear weapons as a form of defence, together with its hostility towards the miners, was already apparent when Kennedy Martin was developing the serial:

> The bitterly fought Inquiry into Sizewell B and the continued problems at Sellafield contributed to the feeling of a country moving remorselessly towards a nuclear state, with all that meant for the loss of civil liberties. There was no hint of the privatization of the CEGB as yet, but with a battle with the miners looming, it was obvious that nuclear power was becoming a more attractive option, and a permanent way of crushing them. (Kennedy Martin, 1990: viii)

What is clear is that President Reagan's 'Star Wars' speech, in which he proposed the building of a Strategic Defence Initiative to protect America against nuclear attack, was the catalyst for Kennedy Martin developing the story as a global political narrative, rather than a domestic political thriller.

Yet there are other layers that add narrative complexity to the serial, of which the ecological theme and the issue of environmental politics are the most significant. The ecological theme was heavily influenced by the theories of the British scientist James Lovelock, whose book, *Gaia: A New Look at Life on Earth*, was published in 1979. Lovelock's thesis is that the Earth is a self-regulating and self-sustaining organism, capable of looking after itself and resisting any disasters which might threaten its existence, including nuclear fall-out. Kennedy Martin had read Lovelock's book and he adapted the thesis to form part of the developing narrative of *Edge of Darkness*. In Greek mythology Gaia is the name of the Earth Goddess and in the serial this is the name Kennedy Martin gives to the ecological organisation with which Emma, Craven's daughter, is involved. After her death, early in the first episode, Emma (Joanne Whalley) metaphorically assumes the role of the Earth Goddess as she returns to instruct Craven on the ability of the planet to look after itself.

Craven undertakes a journey of enlightenment and politicisation during the course of the serial, a conservative police detective who comes to occupy a far more sceptical, anti-establishment position by the end. Through his investigation into Emma's death he learns about her involvement with Gaia and the environmental politics with which she was involved. While she metaphorically represents the Earth Goddess, Craven comes to assume the role of the Celtic Green Man, taking up Emma's environmental mantle and assuming an ideological position in support of the planet and its ability to 'look after itself.' Kennedy Martin wanted to take this as far as having Craven turn into an oak tree at the end of the serial, a transformation he described in an earlier version of the script, but other members of the production team, including Bob Peck, were concerned about this daringly non-naturalistic ending and Kennedy Martin was persuaded against it. Consequently a more 'realistic' and technically feasible ending was produced, although the idea of Craven as the metaphorical equivalent of the Green Man was retained.

In addition to the primary narrative of Craven's investigation into Emma's death and the 'back story' which explores the ecological and nuclear issues behind her death there is 'a third story' which operates at a deeper structural level. This is an allegorical strand in which Darius Jedburgh (Joe Don Baker), the renegade CIA agent, is a Teutonic Knight struggling against the Dark Forces, whose chief representative in the serial is Jerry Grogan (Kenneth Nelson), President of the Fusion Corporation of Kansas, a modern-day Knight Templar obsessed with the power of plutonium, the 'holy grail' which will power an escape from the planet:

> Thus this aspect of the 'back story' read something like this: descendants of the Templars, disestablished and unaware of their past, act in concert to bring the human race to the point of departure from the planet. By the human race they mean, of course, a small band of privileged soldier-scholars whose mission will be to conquer the galaxy by fire and by sword.

> The funds for their galactic ambitions come from the mutual fear the
> two great empires, Russia and America, have for each other. This fear
> allows them access on both sides to unaccountable resources with which
> to pursue their goal. (Kennedy Martin, 1990: xii)

Kennedy Martin acknowledged that this deeper structural narrative
was 'obscure' and unlikely to be picked up by viewers, but it highlights
the many levels on which the serial operates: as a detective story, as a
nuclear thriller and as an allegorical narrative invoking deeper myths.
An awareness of these mythical elements is not essential for enjoying
the detective story, or to appreciate the ideological themes of the nuclear
thriller but, as Kennedy Martin pointed out, the mythical elements were
'rather like yeast in the making of bread, they were an essential element
in developing the characters' (Kennedy Martin, 1990: xii).

Edge of Darkness was first screened on BBC 2, in six episodes, from
4 November to 9 December 1985. It received a huge response and was,
unusually for a drama serial at the time, repeated on BBC 1 just ten days
after the final episode had been shown on BBC 2. For its BBC 1 repeat
it was shown in three parts on consecutive nights and the average audience of four million which it had on BBC 2 doubled to eight million
for the BBC 1 repeat. The complexity of the unfolding narrative meant
it was difficult to join the serial after episode one, unlike *Reilly – Ace
of Spies* where it was possible to watch most episodes without having
followed the serial from the beginning, so the early repeat was welcome
for viewers who had not seen the serial on BBC 2. For many viewers,
however, the repeat offered a second opportunity to participate in the
hermeneutic pleasure of unravelling a labyrinthine narrative in the
more concentrated form of a three-part version shown on consecutive
nights, rather than a six-episode version screened over six weeks.

As a thriller with a complex narrative structure *Edge of Darkness* is
extremely well suited to the serial format. It exemplifies the kind of
long-form drama the television serial is particularly suited to and which
Kennedy Martin feels he does best:

> I've come out of a literary rather than a theatre tradition and my bent
> is towards the long form. Long-form drama is really what I do best and
> I do think the writer still has a major role to play in it. I think it's one
> of the few areas where naturalism or realism still has a role to play. It
> links up with the nineteenth-century novel, it's a development of that.
> That's its heritage, not Terence Rattigan or the 1930s stage and not really
> cinema. So it's a kind of literary form, long convoluted stories and lots
> of characters.[16]

The complexity of the narrative, and the way in which the various ingredients and influences are incorporated into the story, is best described

through an analysis of how the plot develops over its six episodes.

Episode one, 'Compassionate Leave' (4 November 1985), opens with shots of nuclear waste containers being transported by train, followed by a scene in which Craven is shown reluctantly agreeing to postpone his investigation into alleged ballot rigging at a miners' union. The opening sequences take place at night in the pouring rain and it is still pouring when Craven goes to collect Emma from a student meeting that is being addressed by the Labour MP Michael Meacher – one of several examples where the drama used real-life characters and events to lend a veneer of realism to the story, serving to authenticate the fictional narrative.

As Craven and Emma arrive home they are confronted in the rain by a hooded gunman who blasts them with a shotgun, killing Emma when she runs forward in front of her father. The death of Emma provides the initial disruption which motivates the rest of the narrative. Who killed her and why? And was it really Craven, rather than Emma, who was the intended target? Craven subsequently adopts the mantle of the classic *film noir* detective, psychologically scarred because of the killing of his daughter (his wife has previously died from cancer and he has brought Emma up on his own since she was ten years old), alienated from the political manoeuvring of those around him and, in typical *noir* fashion, a detective increasingly at odds with his superiors as he undertakes his own investigation.

The narrative disruption caused by the killing of the protagonist's daughter early in the story, motivating his quest, is a familiar narrative strategy, typical of many Hollywood thrillers. Its narrative function of course is to hook the audience, even more important in television where there is not a captive audience, as in the cinema, and where a drama has to compete with the programmes on offer on other channels. The epic scale of *Edge of Darkness* however, three times longer than the average feature film, enabled not only a greater complexity than is often achieved in a feature film but also the playing out of some scenes at greater length than one might normally expect.

Such is the case with Craven's reaction to the death of his daughter, which hangs heavy over the remainder of the first episode. Shortly after she is killed Craven goes into her bedroom, a scene described at length in the published script, occupying five minutes of screen time. This is how Kennedy Martin describes the last part of the scene:

> He crosses to the bed. It is still blowing outside; still raining hard. Craven hears the gate creak and swing. He crosses to get the shotgun. He puts it beside the art nouveau bedside table and sits down again. He pulls open a drawer and takes out a Kleenex box first and then a cheque book, a passport and a wallet. He opens the wallet. It has some French francs

in it; he puts it to one side, uninterested. He opens the passport, hoping to get one more glimpse of Emma. It is Emma's face all right. In the second drawer is a vibrator. He looks down at it, then kisses it gently. He puts it away with the other things. The third drawer is empty except for an automatic pistol. He takes it out. It is a 9mm Hungarian Firebird. He is completely taken aback by its presence. He lies back on the bed, gun in one hand and the battered old teddy in the other. Above him is the round orb of the earth, with a string of Mexican beads attached to one side. (Kennedy Martin, 1990: 16)

What is established in the first episode, and underlined in subsequent episodes, is the near-incestuous relationship between Craven and Emma, which this scene makes explicit. The scene, and the closeness of the relationship, is dwelt on at great length in order to emotionally involve the viewer in Craven's grief, while the gun, maps and Geiger counter he discovers in Emma's room provide the narrative enigmas which engage the viewer intellectually. Not only does Emma's death motivate Craven's narrative quest, it provides the human basis on which a drama of global significance is to unfold. Michael Wearing describes how the drama starts on a human scale before opening out to encompass global issues:

> In simplistic terms, the story opens with the most sustained evocation of individual grief in bereavement that I can readily recall, and pushes outwards through these characters on a steadily widening canvas to a graphic recognition that, with the spectre of nuclear destruction hovering over contemporary life, the survival of our planet is at stake. (Lane, 1985: 4)

For Kennedy Martin this was a deliberate strategy, facilitated by the serial form: 'The art is to start with a familiar idea and take the audience with you on a plane, so that when they look down they are thousands of miles above the Earth' (Summers, 1985: 38). The ingredients which anticipate this widening of the narrative scale are all present in the scene in Emma's bedroom, from the personal possessions which are all that Craven now has to remember her by, to the Geiger counter, maps, gun and the NASA poster of the Earth which hangs on Emma's wall (included in the original script but not in the scene as filmed).

Emma's death activates Craven's memories of the death of his wife from cancer ten years earlier. Before Craven goes into Emma's bedroom there are flashbacks to his wife's funeral, followed by the young Emma telling her father that he should sleep with her now that Mummy isn't there (the first hint of the incest theme). The extremely close relationship Craven had with Emma helps to explain why he subsequently 'resurrects' her after her death, initially hearing her voice, then holding conversations with her until, finally, she reappears for him. He literally cannot let her go. The original idea, apparently, was for Emma's voice to be heard after her death, conveying the idea that she continued to exist in Craven's mind, but the flashbacks to Emma as a child prompted the idea of having the adult Emma appear, for Craven only, as a material being who would suddenly appear as if from nowhere and then disappear again.

While clearly a departure from naturalism Emma's appearances and disappearances are handled 'realistically', being introduced gradually and discreetly so that it seems 'natural' Emma should reappear and have a continuing role in the story because of the close relationship between Craven and herself that has already been established. The key scene in this gradual process occurs in the first episode when Craven is driving down to London, with the young Emma in the back of the car. However this is not a flashback. Craven makes the journey to London because he thinks it is where her killer will be. While driving he 'talks' to Emma about two previous trips to London, when he received a medal from the Queen and when Emma's mother was having an operation to remove a tumour from her breast. On this occasion, however, the young Emma appears in the back of the car, in the narrative present with Craven. Kennedy Martin describes how this manifestation of Emma as a 'ghost' was arrived at:

> We'd come to an agreement that Emma would be a projection of Craven's imagination, he would be talking because he was in denial ... We had her as a young girl in the back of the car, going to London, and the scene should have been shot with two separate shots, one of Craven and then he would talk to her and you'd see one of her, and then you'd go back to Craven. But Martin [Campbell] shot it as a two-shot with Emma in the back of the car, leaning over at Craven's shoulders, so at that point she became a ghost, because if Craven was real then this Emma was real, it wasn't just something that he had invented, and Martin became immediately aware of that and said 'Is that alright, playing it this way?' and without any hesitation I said 'Sure, it's fine.' ... This was actually a quantum leap in portraying Emma and completely changed this strand in the story.[7]

Once again, this illustrates the collaborative manner in which *Edge of Darkness* was developed, even during the course of filming. Kennedy Martin had not originally envisaged Emma appearing as a ghost in the serial until Martin Campbell shot the scene this way, but when he did, this opened up all sorts of narrative possibilities. The 'quantum leap' was the departure from naturalism and a tacit acknowledgment that the mythical theme of Emma as the Earth Goddess would be an important part of the story and that she would continue to have an active role to play in the narrative after her death. In subsequent episodes she would appear to Craven not as a child but as the adult Emma, actively participating in the story by advising Craven about the ability of the planet to 'look after itself'.

By the end of the first episode Craven has become aware that Emma was involved in as yet undisclosed activities of which he, apparently, had no knowledge, hence his bemused and increasingly perplexed response to the discovery of the Geiger counter, the gun and the International Irradiated Fuels (IIF) radiation symbol that he finds in her clothes. From the simple revenge theory held by his superior the story opens out to involve the British government, in the shape of Guy Pendleton (Charles Kay) who contacts Craven shortly after his arrival in London to tell him that Emma was 'some sort of terrorist' and that there is a file on her. Pendleton is a shady figure, attached to the Prime Minister's office, who is 'looking after' the Prime Minister on the night Craven meets him. The PM is at the BBC being interviewed by Robin Day about Britain's nuclear deterrent and Craven hears part of the programme in his hotel room before going to meet Pendleton.

Prior to this, in fact before Craven leaves Yorkshire to travel to London, there is a scene in which the American CIA agent Darius Jedburgh is introduced when he brings Pendleton satellite photographs of Northmoor, a nuclear waste disposal plant in Yorkshire. Jedburgh's appearance is the first suggestion of American involvement in the narrative. This scene is not in Kennedy Martin's original script for episode one, but when the American company Lionheart Television International became involved as co-producers of the serial they requested that Jedburgh, played by the American film star Joe Don Baker, be introduced before episode two, when Kennedy Martin intended to introduce him. Apart from this one request, Michael Wearing described Lionheart as a 'model of non-interference' (Henry, 1985: 30). By the end of the first episode the story has opened out from a murder mystery – who killed Emma and why? – to become a story involving nuclear waste and the British government, with a suggestion the American government may also be involved in some way.

In episode two, 'Into the Shadows' (11 November 1985), more is revealed about Emma's involvement with the ecological organisation Gaia and its expedition into Northmoor to try to find out if International Irradiated Fuels is engaged in the illegal manufacture of plutonium. It is also revealed, by Henry Harcourt (Ian McNeice), a city businessman who has been 'drafted' by the government to find out what is going on in Northmoor, that James Godbolt (Jack Watson), the miners' union leader

Craven was investigating, has a 'close relationship' with the Northmoor management and that IIF may well have been involved in rigging the union ballot, to ensure that 'their man' was re-elected. Northmoor thus emerges as a major enigma to be explored.

Jedburgh's role as a flamboyant CIA agent who drives a white Rolls Royce and wears a Stetson hat is developed: 'with Reagan in the White House we get to keep a higher profile.' The larger-than-life character of Jedburgh provides an opportunity for some typical Kennedy Martin humour to be introduced. On their first meeting Jedburgh tells Craven he is from Dallas: 'Have you been to Dallas, Craven? ... It's where we shoot our Presidents. The Jews have their Calvary, but we got Dealey Plaza.' Jedburgh has been instructed by Harcourt – a confirmation of collaboration between the British and American governments – to let Craven see the CIA file on Emma, who has been classified as a terrorist after leading the expedition into Northmoor.

The episode ends with Craven's voiceover as he reads from the file, in which he learns about an inquiry, chaired by Dr Anthony Marsh, into abnormal radioactivity levels at the Corrie Reservoir, near Craigmills in Yorkshire, Craven's home patch. Northmoor was the suspected source of the radiation and Emma had led a team of scientists associated with Gaia into the mine: 'Since all those connected with this adventure are now dead or have disappeared, it is difficult to discover what their mission was, or whether it was successful.' This prompts Craven's flashback to a scene in a laboratory at Emma's college when she tells him: 'Tony Marsh is dead. Car accident on the motorway.'[18] This flashback reveals that Craven knew Emma was following the inquiry and also that he warned her against any idea of going into Northmoor to find out if IIF was operating a reprocessing plant.

Meanwhile the police have been continuing their pursuit of Emma's killer. In episode three, 'Burden of Proof' (18 November 1985), their investigations enable Craven to identify a gunman named McCroon (Sean Caffrey), an ex-Provisional IRA man recruited by Craven as an informer in Northern Ireland eight years earlier. Emma's boyfriend, Terry Shields (Tim McInnerny), is found dead shortly after he has told Craven that Emma discovered a 'hot cell' in Northmoor. Jerry Grogan, President of the Fusion Corporation of Kansas, is introduced and a parliamentary inquiry into Grogan's proposed takeover of IIF commences. Grogan is greeted at the airport by Robert Bennett (Hugh Fraser), managing director of IIF, who briefs him about the 'situation' at Northmoor where 'the chamber's still too hot' to get in. Clemmy (Zoe Wanamaker), an associate of Pendleton's, tells Craven how she met Jedburgh in Nicaragua during the revolution when she was working as a 'liaison officer' for the Sandinistas, and that Jedburgh helped to found Gaia in 1977. The episode draws to a close with Emma's funeral, followed by a scene in which Assistant Chief Constable Ross (John Woodvine), Craven's boss, agrees to Craven's request to take the watch off his house in return for Craven agreeing to see a doctor (Ross thinks Craven is cracking up – a suspicion which Craven's report on what he has learnt in London only serves to confirm, as far as Ross is concerned). The final shot in the episode is of McCroon, outside Craven's house.

In episode four, 'Breakthrough' (25 November 1985), the *noir*-ish iconography of episode one returns as McCroon confronts Craven, inside his house, with a shotgun. Just as Craven is on the verge of getting him to say who he is working for a police marksman kills McCroon. The police close the case. Craven has a breakdown and is taken into hospital. Returning home he discovers a spring has appeared in the garden near where Emma was killed (a trace of the mythical theme – the spring representing Gaia, the Earth Goddess). Craven re-establishes contact with Emma who provides him with a vital clue, a list of stations on the London underground which, as Craven discovers when he breaks into the MI5 computer, is a guide to the IIF facilities at Northmoor. The computer also confirms that McCroon killed Emma on orders from Northmoor security.

Jedburgh, returning from a trip to El Salvador, tells Craven he helped set up Gaia as an ecological pressure group when President Carter was trying to stop the worldwide spread of nuclear weapons, which meant stopping the manufacture of plutonium, of which Britain was the largest producer. Subsequently American government policy was reversed, but by then Gaia had its own momentum and Jedburgh was no longer able to control the organisation. James Godbolt, the miners' union leader, tells Craven he got involved with Northmoor when the Ministry of Defence took over the mine in the 1960s, before it was sold to IIF. He also says that IIF thought Craven had led the Gaia team into Northmoor because, as an 'old caver', Craven knew the shafts and vents of the old pits. However, Godbolt says IIF made a mistake, because he took the Gaia team into Northmoor to show that, despite being compromised by his involvment with IIF, he 'hadn't completely sold out.' Craven tells Emma he plans to go into Northmoor. He teams up with Jedburgh, who has received orders from the White House to 'get into the ball park and steal the ball.'

In episode five, 'Northmoor' (2 December 1985), Grogan learns through his Washington contacts that Craven and Jedburgh plan to go into Northmoor. He informs Bennett, who alerts Northmoor security in advance of the incursion. It becomes apparent that Harcourt and

Pendleton are using Craven, hoping he will get evidence that plutonium is being manufactured illegally at Northmoor. After being led through the disused mineshafts by Godbolt, and discovering a nuclear bunker ('a doomsday equivalent of Harrods'), Craven and Jedburgh come upon the remaining bodies of the Gaia team as they make their way to the hot cell: 'There's been a hell of an accident here ... Gaia – they must have blown the whole cell.'

As the serial reaches its dramatic highpoint there is less need for exposition. Instead, much of episode five is taken up with the expedition into Northmoor, interspersed with cutaways to the inquiry taking place at the House of Commons. As Craven and Jedburgh make their way to the metaphorical 'heart of darkness' where the plutonium is being stored the importance of location filming, 'in and around a gold mine in Wales' (Kennedy Martin, 1990: 130), was clearly essential in order to realise the nightmarish, subterranean atmosphere of Northmoor. One need only compare this to Kennedy Martin's 1966 adaptation of *The New Men* – where the accident exposing one of the scientists to a lethal dose of radiation was enacted in the television studio – to realise how important Andrew Dunn's photography and Martin Campbell's direction was to the visual impact of *Edge of Darkness*.

Episode five has a classic cliffhanger ending. Craven is trapped in a seemingly hopeless situation in a dismantled MOD office as the IIF security guards close in. Desperately trying all the telephones in the office he finds one which is still connected to a basement office in Downing Street. When it is eventually answered he shouts 'Get me Pendleton!' down the line, as gas is pumped into the room in which he is trapped. However, as Kennedy Martin points out in the published script, the justification for demanding Pendleton – Craven's knowledge that Pendleton is employed by the Cabinet Office – was unfortunately lost when the words 'Downing Street' were 'accidentally omitted' during filming when the Duty Officer answers the telephone (Kennedy Martin, 1990: 151). Nevertheless, the episode still has a dramatic cliffhanger ending, at least in the original six-part version. When the serial was re-edited into three parts for the BBC 1 repeat this scene was immediately followed by one in which Pendleton visits Craven in hospital, somewhat undermining the dramatic impact of the previous sequence, with no explanation as to how Craven's predicament was resolved. The re-edited version illustrates the problem of screening serials in anything other than their original episodic form.

As the serial draws to a close in the final episode, 'Fusion' (9 December 1985), a number of narrative strands are drawn together and most of the enigmas are resolved. A British government minister tells Harcourt he knows about the production of plutonium at Northmoor – Harcourt's involvement, it transpires, was part of a plan to deceive the Americans into thinking the British government did not know what was going on. While Grogan wants to acquire IIF for its plutonium, which he needs for his company's Strategic Defence Initiative research, he is afraid the Commons inquiry might block the takeover, so he uses his Washington contacts to have Darius Jedburgh ordered to go into Northmoor to steal the plutonium. Jedburgh, it is revealed, escaped from Northmoor with the plutonium (carrying it in a Harrods shopping bag), but when he discovers on whose behalf he has stolen it he turns renegade, killing four CIA agents who try to apprehend him, before hiding the plutonium in a Scottish loch, in 'an explosive configuration.'

The nuclear narrative moves to its climax with a NATO conference on Directed Energy Weapons at the Gleneagles Hotel. Jedburgh debunks Grogan's messianic speech by saying that, when you read between the lines, what he is advocating is 'not democracy but a despotism ... an absolute state where authority will derive not from the people but from the possession of plutonium.' At this point Jedburgh produces two bars of the plutonium stolen from Northmoor and irradiates Grogan.

Meanwhile Emma tells Craven, who, like Jedburgh, is now dying of radiation sickness, that 'the planet will protect itself' and she explains the significance of the 'black flowers' which will grow to cover the planet in the wake of a nuclear apocalypse, enabling life to evolve again. In a final shoot-out, Jedburgh is killed, but Craven is spared because, as he is told, 'you're on our side.' He insists he is not. (It was because Craven was 'on their side' that Emma did not tell him about the Gaia expedition into Northmoor.)

Some final loose ends are tied up in a concluding voiceover, delivered by Harcourt in the form of a letter to Clemmy (who had slept with Craven when she was assigned to 'look after him'), while Grogan supervises the retrieval of the plutonium from Loch Lednock. Craven is seen standing on the ridge of a hill overlooking the loch. Two dissolves across deserted landscapes indicate the passage of time, perhaps to a post-apocalyptic age, and in the final image Emma's black flowers are seen growing in the snow on a mountainside.

This summary of the plot indicates the narrative complexity of the serial, moving from a detective *film noir* to a political thriller with international implications to a nuclear thriller with implications of global apocalypse. Ronnie Craven's 'personal tragedy' becomes a quest on behalf of the future of the planet. Clearly Craven bears the hermeneutic code for much of the serial – we gain knowledge as he does. At the beginning he is clearly right-wing in his political views, indicated by the conversation with the young Emma in the car when he derides 'communists', reactionary where Emma is progressive. The same can be said of Darius Jedburgh, who does, after all, work for the CIA. Both Craven and Jedburgh, however, move to the left politically as the narrative progresses and their understanding of the political subterfuge of those around them grows. At the end they are on 'the same side' and it is not the side of those from whom they had previously taken orders. Jedburgh refuses to hand over the plutonium he has been ordered to steal, realising it will go to Grogan, and Craven tells Clemmy he wants the report he has written to go to Gaia, not to the Chief Constable.

However, there is a crucial difference between their positions at the end. Craven has moved towards Emma's position and ends up 'on the side of the planet'. Jedburgh, on the other hand, while insisting he is 'on the side of the angels', opposed to the 'dark forces who would rule our planet', believes man will always win against nature, implying he does not believe in Gaia and its ecological determinism. To all intents and purposes Kennedy Martin leaves the audience with this choice of ideological positions at the end of the serial. There is little doubt Craven and Jedburgh are the two main characters with whom the audience is encouraged to identify and there is no encouragement to identify with any of the authority figures who are politically to the right of the positions the two protagonists come to adopt. Any sympathy for Harcourt and Pendleton is undermined when they are seen dining with 'the enemy' – Grogan, Bennett and the Cabinet Minister – at the end.

The fact that Jedburgh is killed, leaving attention to be centred on Craven in the final scene, may privilege the latter's position. The final image, in particular, focusing on the black flowers growing in the snow, suggests an affirmation of the Gaia thesis Craven has come to support, namely that 'the planet will look after itself.' This resolution in favour of an ideology where the ultimate fate of humankind is beyond human intervention could be seen as reactionary, detracting perhaps from the more progressive aspects of the serial, which are bound up with the narrative trajectories of both Craven and Jedburgh. However, 'progressive' and 'reactionary' are relative concepts. What is progressive at one historical moment may seem reactionary at another, depending on the political position adopted by the viewer.

Edge of Darkness was produced in a far more reactionary political climate than the previous generation of BBC 'social issue' dramas. The debate about progressive television drama in the context of Thatcherism was not so much about how socialism could be achieved, as it had been in the previous two decades, but about how a total hegemony of right-wing ideology could be averted. Progressive cultural producers, whether they be writers, film-makers or television producers, were being squeezed in the 1980s. In such a climate oppositional voices have to speak louder in order to be heard, or they have to find other means. The political thriller, feeding on conspiracy and paranoia, was one vehicle progressive dramatists and film-makers turned to in the 1980s. It also had the advantage of being a popular genre and the authors of *Edge of Darkness* – Kennedy Martin, Martin Campbell and Michael Wearing – utilised the genre with great skill. In the course of telling an epic story they tapped into a number of contemporary concerns: government secrecy, collusion between the British and American governments, and the threat to the environment and the future of the planet posed by nuclear energy and, especially, nuclear weapons. Events in the real world – Chernobyl, Sellafield, Trident and the Strategic Defence Initiative – all contributed to a growing concern about nuclear issues during the 1980s. *Edge of Darkness* dramatised these concerns in a highly effective way.

Without doubt *Edge of Darkness* is a work of 'high drama.' It is also an extremely erudite piece of fiction. In his annotations to the published script Kennedy Martin cites the Book of Kells, E. M. Forster, Ho Chi Minh, Adlerian psychoanalysis, Vladimir Propp's *Morphology of the Folk Tale*, 'New Age' philosophy, Zen Buddhism, Shakespeare's *Hamlet*, Plato's *The Republic*, Sherlock Holmes and John Buchan – for whom 'the Scottish locations were originally included as a homage' (Kennedy Martin, 1990: 156). All of these were ingredients in, or influences on, the script, usually alluded to implicitly rather than explicitly. Many of the references are extremely subtle and may well have been missed by the majority of viewers. For example, when Pendleton describes Harcourt to Craven: 'Double First at Cambridge and an authority on E. M. Forster, he tells me, but a complete twat, I think when it comes to making connections', only keen Forsterites are likely to have picked up the reference to Forster's famous phrase: 'Only connect.'

Pendleton continues, in an aside Kennedy Martin modestly prefers not to annotate: 'I myself favour an Irish education. Anyone who has examined the Book of Kells cannot but be impressed by the labyrinthine coils of the Celtic imagination' (Kennedy Martin, 1990: 45). The Book of Kells, of course, is housed at Trinity College, Dublin, where Kennedy Martin was a student at the beginning of the 1950s, receiving an Irish education. More than thirty years later it seems only fitting that his Celtic imagination should dream up a story as labyrinthine, and as politically pertinent, as *Edge of Darkness*. Without doubt it is one of the great works of television drama.

Notes

1 BBC WAC, T48/351/1, memo from Colin Tucker, Producer, BBC Drama Serials, to Head of Serials, re 'Ace of Spies – Troy Kennedy Martin': 'I'm not terribly enthusiastic either, there's something missing, some element of involvement in Reilly and in – by extension – the whole idea … Reilly, remains a lay-figure, a functional character only, just not interesting enough, nor weighty enough to carry a serial … '

2 Troy Kennedy Martin, interviewed by the author, 27 March 1986.

3 Ibid.

4 Verity Lambert, speaking at a symposium on 'Producing Popular Television Drama' at the University of Reading, 16 October 2004.

5 Troy Kennedy Martin, interviewed by the author, 27 March 1986.

6 Ibid.

7 Ibid.

8 Ibid. Documentation in the BBC Written Archives Centre shows that Kennedy Martin received a number of commissions from the BBC in the mid–late 1970s but the only one he actually completed was the script for the final episode of *Z Cars*. On 21 April 1975 he received a commission for 'The Seven Sleepers', a ninety-minute all-film episode for a series called *Officers and Gentlemen*; on 9 August 1977 he received a commission to write a fifty-minute episode called 'Security' for a series called *1990* (BBC 2, 1977–8), but his contract for this was cancelled on 28 September 1977; on 23 January 1979 he was commissioned to provide a 'breakdown' of Olivia Manning's 'Balkan Trilogy' with a view to writing the scripts for an eight-part serial, but on 19 September 1979 he asked to be released from this commitment (the serial was subsequently dramatised by Alan Plater as *Fortunes of War*); and on 8 November 1979 he was commissioned to write a *Play for Today* on the subject of the Corrie Bill, for which he received a fee on 22 November 1979, but nothing seems to have come of this and Kennedy Martin has no recollection of it. (At the time of writing access to BBC Written Archives Centre papers is restricted after 1979 so it has not been possible to check to see if this contract was subsequently cancelled).

9 Ibid.

10 Troy Kennedy Martin, interviewed for *Political Thrillers: Plays of State*, BBC 4, 22 June 2003.

11 Michael Wearing, interviewed by the author, 2 June 2005.

12 The title was changed to *Edge of Darkness* because Magnox was the trade name for the alloy used to contain nuclear reactor fuel and the BBC feared trouble from British Nuclear Fuels and the Central Electricity Generating Board if they used it (see Patterson, 1985: 8).

13 Michael Wearing, interviewed by the author, 2 June 2005.

14 A suggestion made by Troy Kennedy Martin himself during a lunchtime conversation with the author on 15 April 2005.

15 Troy Kennedy Martin, interviewed for *Magnox – The Secrets of Edge of Darkness*, Special Feature on the DVD release of *Edge of Darkness*, BBC Worldwide, 2003.

16 Troy Kennedy Martin, interviewed by the author, 27 March 1986.

17 Troy Kennedy Martin, interviewed for *Magnox – The Secrets of Edge of Darkness*.

18 Tony Marsh, Kennedy Martin's pseudonym, is used in *Edge of Darkness* as the name for one of the incidental characters in the serial, someone who has been killed off before the story has even begun!

The hostile waters of British television in a deregulated age

Since *Edge of Darkness* Troy Kennedy Martin has had relatively little work produced. In the twenty years since that award-winning serial he has been credited for just four screenplays, two of which were scripts where he helped out with re-writing or made a minor contribution, and one was an adaptation. Yet in this period he has worked on at least fifteen other projects, some screenplays, some television drama serials and single dramas. The ratio of work written to work produced in this period reveals much about the circumstances in which writers now work. Although, as previous chapters have shown, Kennedy Martin has always had some projects which have not come to fruition the ratio of produced to unproduced work was far greater from 1958–85 than it has been since. In that period, for every one script not produced there were five that were. Since 1985, however, the ratio has swung the other way and for each project that has made it to the screen there are at least another three that have not.

It is no coincidence that this turnaround occurred as British television entered a new deregulated era, with greater competition resulting from an increase in the number of channels and a shift from a writer-led television drama to a consumer-led culture where the main concern is to maximise and retain audiences. In this new broadcasting environment the contribution of the writer has been devalued. Television executives now set the agenda for the type of drama produced and power has shifted from the writer and the producer to channel controllers. Increasingly, in this more competitive environment, the tendency has been to go for the safe option, the tried and tested formula, and the 1990s saw a steep increase in the production of soap opera and generic drama, especially police, medical and costume drama.

In this new deregulated environment original, authored drama gradually disappeared from the schedules and the opportunities for writers, whether new or established, to get original, non-generic drama commissioned declined. This development has caused many commentators to look back, longingly, to a so-called 'golden age' in the 1960s and 1970s when writers had the freedom to produce original, innovative drama without the pressure of achieving high ratings. While regretting the narrowing of choice that has come with the shift towards a television culture in which potential ratings success dominates decision-making, Kennedy Martin nevertheless cautions against the idea that the 1960s and 1970s represented a 'golden age' for television drama:

> It was never as 'golden' as people make it out to be. I think one's got to be careful of romanticising one's youth, as it were. Certainly there was an awful lot of dross, but there was a lot more freedom, so you got that with the good things. Nowadays I think they've gone too far the other way and it's too much demographics and it's too controlled and it's run from above. There was a great deal of freedom handed down to people then and I think that's the way that you should work with artists, to give them as much freedom as you can, whereas now it goes the other way. I remember in 1985 someone in America saying 'Did the Director General read the scripts of *Edge of Darkness*?' and I thought, that's a question that could never possibly be asked on this side of the ocean, but now I'm not so sure! Certainly the Controllers say that they read everything that's going to go out, or read a lot of material and make the choices. There was a time when producers did that, and then it was Heads of Departments did that, and now it's the Controllers. So I think that this must narrow the choices, and when most of it's now about audience ratings, particularly BBC 1 and ITV 1, there's no real room for anything other than tabloid drama and series, long-running series, the soaps. ... I think that it's far too managed, it's over-managed, and a lot of imagination is held back because people are frightened of taking chances.[1]

The other significant factor in this period, as far as Kennedy Martin's work is concerned, is that screenplays for feature films and television films far outnumber the drama serials he has worked on since *Edge of Darkness*. The four produced scripts have all been screenplays, one being a Hollywood feature film and the other three being television films. In addition, he has written, or partly written, another seven screenplays since the late 1980s, none of which have been produced.

After *Edge of Darkness* Kennedy Martin spent some time in Australia, where he worked on a serial for Australian television called *The Warming*, which started life as a story about an Indonesian invasion of Australia before developing into a story about climate change. In the wake of *Edge of Darkness* Kennedy Martin was still exploring environmental issues but, while in Australia, he developed the theme in relation to global warming, conducting research for this project in Australia and Indonesia. *The Warming* was partly written, but Kennedy Martin was unable to complete it, the ending, as on previous occasions, proving an obstacle.[2]

Around the same time, also in Australia, he worked on a screenplay for a film called *Troppo* which was bought by Warner Brothers and had Martin Campbell lined up to direct at one stage. *Troppo* – an Australian term for people going crazy when the sun gets to them – also had an environmental theme and was described by Kennedy Martin as 'an *African Queen*-type scenario involving nuclear waste.'[3] But the project ran aground, as so many scripts do in Hollywood:

> It was an expensive movie and it was a sea movie and although it was contemporary and it had a kind of environmental element to it you have to be able to get the top stars. Then the Warner's people asked for it to be rewritten this way and that way and it never really got back its old magic. They papered the town with scripts – it was just not the way you actually put together a movie ... it was green-lit by the management and all they had to do was to find a Harrison Ford or someone who would do it and of course these guys don't really want to go to the Philippines or somewhere and be in hurricanes when they can shoot something in Los Angeles or nearby.[4]

Spending time in America as well as Australia in the late 1980s Kennedy Martin had his second flirtation with Hollywood, after an absence of more than a decade. His one Hollywood screenwriting credit in this period was a joint credit with Harry Kleiner and Walter Hill on the latter's *Red Heat* (USA, 1988), a post-Cold War thriller featuring Arnold Schwarzenegger as Ivan Denko, a Russian law enforcer pursuing a Georgian drug dealer to America, who reluctantly teams up with US detective Art Ridzik (James Belushi) in an oddball partnership. According to Kennedy Martin 'Just the opening sequence was mine and the rest was Walter's. The opening sequence was the only good thing in it really ... '[5] Yet there was a lot of humour in the partnership between Belushi and Schwarzenegger, with more than a hint of Darius Jedburgh in the Belushi character, suggesting Kennedy Martin's input may have been significant. Ivan Denko, however, was a long way removed from Sidney Reilly!

Another screenplay Kennedy Martin wrote in the mid–late 1980s was *Open Cut*, an adaptation of a novel by J. M. O'Neill. Following the success of *Edge of Darkness* Michael Wearing was interested in working with Kennedy Martin again: 'We wanted to do another one called *Open Cut*, which he wrote a great script for. *Open Cut* was a bank robbery story ... about an IRA bank raid. While they're waiting for the safe to open one of the robbers gives the bank staff a lecture in Irish history, it was wonderful!'[6] Kennedy Martin made the bank robbers ex-IRA men who had been on a blanket protest while in prison, but the novelist apparently objected to this and the project was subsequently dropped by Thames TV, who had commissioned it:

> It's a really good *film noir* piece and what actually happens is that the novelist baulked at the idea of these two people being IRA people ... he felt that his own life would be threatened if it came out that these guys were members of the IRA ... So rather like the Maschwitz thing it just disappeared off the schedules, I mean they just said 'We can't do this because the novelist objects to it.' ... What scuppered it was that and the political thing and the whole business about the blanket [protest] ... I think this guy [J. M. O'Neill] was worried about the IRA but I think Thames and Ted [Childs] were worried about crossing a political line with the government, so between them they scuppered what was a very good script.[7]

The 'Maschwitz thing' is a reference to *The Little Goat*, the story by Eric Maschwitz that Kennedy Martin was asked to adapt in 1959 which was subsequently dropped by the BBC for political reasons (see the section on unproduced work in Chapter two). Kennedy Martin's experience with *Open Cut* suggests that little had changed, as far as the sensitivity of television companies to political issues was concerned, thirty years later.

There were also two unfinished screenplays in this period: *Broken Light*, described by Kennedy Martin as a post-*Edge of Darkness* thriller written in the style of a *Thin Man*-type comedy,[8] and *Blinder*, an original science-fiction story about children taking over the world, which also remains to be completed:

> I didn't know where to go in the second half, but it's got a really good opening. It's about a Russian space laboratory and it crash lands and releases this toxin which covers the Earth which only affects adults and so the entire adult population of the area, if they don't want to go into a coma, have to go underground, leaving only the children in charge! And of course it's about the frantic hunt to find the bits of the lab that still survive the trip and see if they can find some way of finding out what it is that happens to these ... But before it happens they've got some time before it begins to take hold and so the kids are trained to run everything. So it's a really great wish-fulfilment thing for kids, they fly the aeroplanes and things like that, and as time goes on the disease, or whatever it is, affects the older kids, so eventually it's the very young kids that are the only ones left, everyone else is carted off to the subways or whatever. ... That was another big idea, like *The Other Side* ... a big metaphor.[9]

The Other Side was another television project Kennedy Martin was working on with Michael Wearing in the late 1980s and early 1990s, a Philip K. Dick-style science-fiction drama commissioned by the BBC as a six-part serial:

It's about people who can move from one world to another, it's parallel universes really, and the other one's exactly like this but it's a completely different world. So it just exposes what this world is like by showing what the other one is. ... It's really a kind of satire about the bureaucracy involved ... well about American corporations really. But now what's happened is that whole corporate thing has just landed at the BBC and they're ten times worse than the Americans! Well they aren't, but they're on a level with them.[10]

Given the potential scale of this project and the BBC's emphasis on 'accountability', at the expense of creativity, in the 1990s it is perhaps not surprising *The Other Side* was not produced. Like many other writers and creative personnel who felt ostracised by the new corporate ethos at the BBC, Kennedy Martin was highly critical of Director-General John Birt and his 'efficiency drive'. In a newspaper article complaining about the axing of BBC 2's *Moving Pictures* programme, for which he was the presenter, screenwriter Howard Schuman recalled a meeting at the BBC in which a small group of writers met with Birt and BBC executive Will Wyatt:

> We were each asked to make a short opening statement about what we felt was wrong with BBC drama. The great Troy Kennedy Martin was the last to speak. 'Well, you see John, actually you're a Leninist. You've replaced a rigid and uncreative bureaucracy with an even more rigid and even less creative bureaucracy.' At which point, John Birt began ferociously to write something on his yellow legal pad. Later, Troy asked me what I thought Birt was writing. I reckoned he was writing 'Never invite Troy Kennedy Martin up here again.' (Schuman, 1996: 11)

Hostile Waters (1997)

Kennedy Martin did eventually get a screenplay produced at the BBC, perhaps largely due to the fact that it was independently produced by Tony Garnett's World Productions company, in a BBC co-production with the American channel, HBO. *Hostile Waters* (BBC 1, 26 July 1997) was a dramatisation of a real-life incident which took place in 1986 when a Russian submarine collided with an American submarine off the east coast of America, an accident that left the Russian sub seriously damaged and which threatened to cause a major nuclear incident. The collision, which was not made public at the time, happened just before a nuclear summit in Reykjavik between Presidents Reagan and Gorbachev. The potential seriousness of the incident threatened the success of the summit and it was hushed up, but when details of what had actually happened were eventually revealed it became clear that not only was this one of the most potentially serious incidents of the Cold War, it was also a story which would make a great drama:

> The sixteen missiles carried by the Russian ship *K219* were locked on to targets from Florida to New York, and 'fail-safe' mechanisms were set to trigger their launch in the aftermath of the collision. An Eastern seaboard nuclear disaster (not to speak of the inevitable rewriting of subsequent political history) was narrowly avoided because of the heroic actions of two ordinary sailors from the 'evil empire'. (Paget, 1998: 9)

Kennedy Martin chose to tell the story largely from the point of view of the Russian submariners and, under the leadership of Captain Britanov (Rutger Hauer), they were sympathetically portrayed. The efforts of the submariners to extinguish a serious fire caused by the accident, and to prevent a nuclear meltdown of the *K219*'s reactor, with one of the youngest crew members dying in the process, were presented as heroic by the film's director, David Drury. Rutger Hauer, as Derek Paget notes in his book, *No other way to tell it: dramadoc/docudrama on television*, was attracted to the project 'both because of "the size of its Chernobyl-like subject" and because it was "a good adventure too"' (Paget, 1998: 33). The enclosed nature of the drama, largely confined to the submarines with occasional cutaways to meetings in rooms in American and Russian naval bases, could easily have leant itself to an old-fashioned television studio drama, but Paget goes on to discuss how Kennedy Martin's script was by no means simply a dialogue-led 'talking heads' drama but one where the dramatic impact would reside as much in what characters did as what they said:

> The acting challenge in portraying Britanov lay precisely in the lack of words and the emphasis on actions and expressions in the script. Hauer observed: 'The script is structured as a series of commands – there's no room for overt characterisation ... Character is not in how they talk, but in what they do.' The synergy with film drama could hardly be more evident. (Paget, 1998: 33)

As a television film *Hostile Waters* did not have the budget of a comparable Hollywood movie like *The Hunt for Red October* (USA, 1990), also a submarine drama, but *Hostile Waters* was nevertheless very successful in generating tension. In addition, the involvement of HBO enabled actors like Rutger Hauer, Martin Sheen (as the captain of the American submarine) and Max Von Sydow (as an admiral in the Russian navy) to be recruited for the film, ensuring it would not appear parochial, as British television films often do. Kennedy Martin later revealed: 'I really wanted to do *The Hunt for Red October* and I went up for it – it's one of the few things that I've ever put myself forward for – and didn't get the job, so when this came up I thought I'll try and do something better than *The Hunt for Red October*.'[11]

When *Hostile Waters* was transmitted, as part of the BBC *Screen One* series, Kennedy Martin was typically modest about his screenplay, suggesting all the work had been done by the people who had been researching the event, but it is easy to see why he was interested in writing it, given that his last BBC production was also a nuclear thriller:

> One of the things that attracted me to the project was that, like *Edge of Darkness*, the story starts off small but then develops into something that has huge repercussions. Of course, I've taken some dramatic licence. Not everything you see on the screen actually happened, but I'd say that three quarters of it did. Documentary-maker William Cran, who researched the incident with the help of the *Panorama* reporter Tom Mangold, presented me with 200 pages of detailed notes. Everyone had done a fantastic job. I just had to adapt the stuff. (Clarke, 1997: 6)

According to producer Tony Garnett, it was because Kennedy Martin had written the script that World Productions got involved with *Hostile Waters*, which was a rather different project to drama series such as *Cardiac Arrest* and *This Life* that World was producing at the time:

> I only got involved with *Hostile Waters* because it was Troy. It was an HBO/BBC production and I knew it was going to be aggravation. I'm very wary of these 'A True Story' things because it is difficult to keep faith with the audience on those things. I won't say I will never do them but I am very wary of them, but I only did it because Troy wrote it, and it was a brilliant screenplay. He brought a whole lot of research material to life and made you feel that you were living it and in addition he's now so accomplished a screenwriter, which he's earned, not in British television, but through being beaten up year after year after year by people in Hollywood, but the best of them do know their craft. He really understands the structure of screen fiction and he can write things now that actually work structurally like a Swiss watch but don't feel as though they are anything but things inevitably happening to people because of the premise. I mean he really is head and shoulders above most people writing in Britain, isn't he?[12]

On the evidence of the number of unproduced scripts and screenplays Kennedy Martin has written since 1985 not everyone shares Garnett's opinion of Kennedy Martin's qualities as a screenwriter. While working on *Hostile Waters* he was also writing a screenplay for what would have been a big-budget Hollywood film, had it been made. Kennedy Martin had originally been asked to write a script about the Italian racing car magnate, Enzo Ferrari, by the Hollywood producer Sydney Pollack back in 1990. The director Michael Mann then got involved and was developing the project with Robert De Niro lined up to play the lead.[13] Kennedy Martin was still working on drafts of the screenplay in 1996–7, in the hope it would still get made, only for it to become yet another unrealised Hollywood movie.[14]

Another screenplay he was working on in the late 1990s was *Watson's Chalk*, about the events at Mogadishu in Somalia in 1993 when a unit of US Army Rangers attempted to capture two top lieutenants of a renegade warlord, only to get caught up in a fierce gun battle with Somali gunmen, during which two American Black Hawk helicopters were destroyed. Kennedy Martin was working on this in 1998, but the project was superseded by Ridley Scott's film of the same subject, *Black Hawk Down* (USA, 2001).

Two more television projects also came to nothing in the late 1990s. *Pizza* was developed for Channel Four as 'a counter-*This Life*' drama series, about a group of young people working in a pizzeria in Leeds.[15] Kennedy Martin wrote treatments for six episodes and scripts for two, with the assistance of his daughter Sophie: 'It's all about twenty-eight year olds, which I know nothing about, but she knows a lot.'[16] The central characters in *Pizza* were to be working-class, rather than the middle-class characters of *This Life* (hence the 'counter-*This Life*' description), and Kennedy Martin wanted to include an element of magic realism in some of the storylines. He also wanted the drama to have the energy of something like *Queer As Folk*, which Channel Four decided to produce instead of *Pizza*.

Another unproduced project from the late 1990s was *The Angel Tapes*, an adaptation of a novel by David M. Kiely which Kennedy Martin was developing for Michael Wearing, who was then working for an independent production company called Irish Screen. *The Angel Tapes* was written as a two-part drama, with a plot hinging on the threat of bombs exploding in Dublin. Set on the eve of the millennium, the bombs had been planted by Irish Loyalists in the 1980s but were expected to explode as a consequence of the 'Millennium Bug', a phenomenon predicted to cause widespread chaos when clocks returned to zero at the dawn of the new millennium. An ingenious idea, the project went the way of other unproduced work when the actual event at the heart of the drama – the transition from one millennium to another – came and went, making the premise on which the drama was based redundant.

Bravo Two Zero (1999)

One film which did see the light of day before the end of the millennium, on which Kennedy Martin collaborated with Andy McNab, was

Bravo Two Zero (BBC 1, 3–4 January 1999). Directed by *Sweeney* director Tom Clegg, *Bravo Two Zero* was based on McNab's book about his experience during the first Gulf War, when he led an SAS unit on a special mission behind enemy lines to cut an Iraqi communication link and prevent SCUD missiles being launched towards Israel. Produced in 1998 as a feature-length film, *Bravo Two Zero* was screened on BBC 1 in two parts, on consecutive nights, at the beginning of January 1999 and was subsequently repeated as a single drama, the initial two-part screening seemingly being a scheduling decision.

While the subject of an elite army unit operating behind enemy lines, whose members are captured and subjected to brutal interrogation techniques by the Iraqi army, is thematically similar to some of Kennedy Martin's early television plays, there is little in terms of characterisation, humour or politics which might identify *Bravo Two Zero* as a Kennedy Martin screenplay. Rather, it is clear from the start this is Andy McNab's story, emphasised by the first-person narration delivered throughout by Sean Bean, playing McNab. Given his previous experience with war scenarios, from *Incident at Echo Six* to *Kelly's Heroes*, it seems likely Kennedy Martin was brought in to assist McNab in dramatising his Gulf War experience and perhaps to spice up the dialogue a little. If so, he was not too successful.

One of the problems with the film, as drama, is that McNab's SAS mission accomplished nothing and the story is all about the unit fighting their way back to the border. This turns *Bravo Two Zero* into an action movie, with plenty of heavy duty gunfights which mostly take place at long range, giving little scope for characterisation or any kind of subtext. When the opportunity for a little human interaction does arise the cast is not really up to it, lacking both the quality and the charisma of actors like Clint Eastwood and Donald Sutherland in *Kelly's Heroes*, or Rutger Hauer and Martin Sheen in *Hostile Waters*. The protracted interrogation sequences, which take up most of the second half of the film, are little more than an exercise in sadism – they may have been realistic but they do not make the film, dramatically, any more interesting.

The chief problem with *Bravo Two Zero* is the source material. This is clearly a story by Andy McNab about his SAS adventure in Iraq, told from his point of view. Had Troy Kennedy Martin been given free rein to adapt McNab's book this may have turned out differently – at least the characterisation and the dialogue may have been a little more engaging.

Red Dust (2005)

The new millennium saw little change in Troy Kennedy Martin's fortunes as far as getting work produced was concerned. At the beginning
of the decade he adapted an H. E. Bates short story called *The Cruise of
the Breadwinner* for Carlton TV, only to see the project abandoned when
John Thaw, who was lined up to play the central role, fell ill and died.
Kennedy Martin was also involved with a project for the BBC about
a terrorist attack on London involving the use of a 'dirty bomb'. This
was a topical subject in the wake of the terrorist attacks in America in
September 2001 but Kennedy Martin disagreed with the director about
how to approach the subject. Kennedy Martin wanted to explore the
events leading up to the attack, as Ronan Bennett did in his script for
Hamburg Cell (Channel 4, 2 September 2004), a drama-documentary
about the preparations for the attacks on the World Trade Centre and the
Pentagon, whereas the director was more interested in dramatising the
attack itself and its aftermath, highlighting the problems such an attack
would cause for the emergency services. Consequently Kennedy Martin
withdrew from the project, which was eventually screened as *Dirty War*
(BBC 1, 26 September 2004).

Following this Kennedy Martin was involved with another project
concerning a contemporary political issue when he worked, for a while,
with director Peter Kosminsky on a screenplay about the events leading
up to the Hutton Inquiry into the death of the government weapons
inspector, David Kelly. Their collaboration on the project was announced
in *Broadcast* in August 2003:

> It has filled newspapers and news bulletins for months – now the Iraq
> dossier row and subsequent death of government scientist Dr David
> Kelly is to be made into a docu-drama for Channel 4 ... Film-maker Peter
> Kosminsky, who made the hard-hitting New Labour drama *The Project*,
> has teamed up with Troy Kennedy Martin, writer of *Edge of Darkness* and
> *The Italian Job*, to bring the scandal to the screen. The feature-length
> piece, working titled *The Truth Game*, will have a 'broad focus' – unlike
> that of Lord Hutton's inquiry into Kelly's death – and will attempt to
> cover all the key individuals and events in the crisis, including the way it
> has been covered by the media. (Holmwood, 2003: 1)

Kennedy Martin was particularly interested in exploring the relationship between the government and the BBC, whose broadcast suggesting
the government's case for supporting the American-led invasion of
Iraq had been 'sexed-up' was at the heart of the controversy. It became
apparent, however, that Kosminsky wanted to concentrate on David
Kelly's involvement, eschewing the 'broad focus' mentioned in *Broadcast*. While Kennedy Martin produced a draft screenplay for *The Truth*

Game, Kosminsky decided to develop his own script, focusing on David Kelly and renaming it *The Government Inspector* (Channel 4, 17 March 2005).

Before either of these projects, however, Kennedy Martin was commissioned by BBC Films to write a screenplay based on Gillian Slovo's novel about the Truth and Reconciliation Commission in post-apartheid South Africa. Kennedy Martin's screenplay for *Red Dust* (BBC 2, 9 July 2005) is a sensitive and skilful adaptation of Slovo's novel, in which Sarah Barcant (Hilary Swank), a white South African lawyer, returns to South Africa, on the request of her mentor Ben Hoffman (Marius Weyers), to represent ex-ANC activist turned politician Alex Mpondo (Chiwetel Ejiofor) at a Truth and Reconciliation hearing where ex-policeman Dirk Hendricks (Jamie Bartlett) is requesting amnesty for crimes committed under the apartheid regime. Under the terms of the Truth and Reconciliation Commission, if Hendricks tells the truth about the interrogation and torture of Mpondo in the mid 1980s Hendricks will be granted amnesty and freed from the prison sentence he is currently serving. Ben Hoffman has another motive, however, for persuading Sarah to represent Alex. He hopes she will be able to discover the fate of Steve Sizela, another ANC activist who was tortured at the same time as Mpondo. Sizela's father, James (Mawongo Dominic Tyawa), has never rested in his attempt to find out what happened to his son, who disappeared following his arrest. The other central character involved in the disappearance of Steve Sizela is Piet Muller (Ian Roberts), Hendricks' superior officer, who will be revealed as the person responsible for torturing Sizela to death.

In writing the novel Gillian Slovo drew on her own experience of growing up in South Africa, one of three daughters born to Joe Slovo, who set up the armed wing of the ANC with Nelson Mandela, and Ruth First, a campaigner against apartheid who was murdered by South African security forces in 1982. In 1998 Gillian Slovo participated in a Truth and Reconciliation hearing when the men responsible for her mother's death were granted amnesty under the scheme. This experience informed the writing of *Red Dust*, in which she constructs a fictional narrative to describe the process of the Truth and Reconciliation Commission, telling the story from the different viewpoints of the main characters involved. One of Troy Kennedy Martin's first decisions in adapting the novel was to abandon this multiple viewpoint and make Sarah the leading character:

> I've taken it as read that the lead character in the story is Sarah. This is *the* starring role, for which, possibly, a top of the line star will be sought.
>
> This is not the case in Gillian's book where the story veers from Sarah

to the moral plight of Alex, and his duel with Hendricks, the torturer, and similar parallel situation, James Sizela and Muller. But this power-play threatens to marginalize Sarah if her story is to become the main one. To put it more clearly – this is not a re-run of *Death and the Maiden*. The female protagonist in *Red Dust* is not the person who has been tortured and now confronts the torturer. She is the lawyer of the person who has been tortured – so is one step removed from the inciting incident (to use a McKee-ism).

It is therefore inadvisable to construct a story which follows Gillian's narrative. In Gillian's book, a multi-viewpoint is possible (she looks at the story from six apparent P. O. V.'s.) The new narrative should favour the story being seen through the eyes of one character – Sarah.[17]

As Kennedy Martin indicates, making Sarah Barcant the central character was not only important dramatically, it meant the role might then seem more attractive to a 'top of the line star', whose participation was likely to be crucial if the film was to attract the funding necessary to film on location in South Africa, and it was a sign of the quality of his script that the Oscar-winning actress Hilary Swank agreed to take the part. Swank had won the Best Actress Oscar for *Boys Don't Cry* in 1999 and, following the completion of *Red Dust*, she won the award for a second time in 2005 for her role in Clint Eastwood's *Million Dollar Baby*. Chiwetel Ejiofor was also becoming well-known for his roles in films such as *Dirty Pretty Things*, *Love Actually* and *Melinda and Melinda* and, with these two actors on board, it is surprising *Red Dust* did not secure a cinema release. The film is visually stunning, shot in widescreen with a cinema release in mind. This meant that some scenes had to be 'panned and scanned' for its television screening to accommodate the 4:3 format of the conventional television screen. The small typeface of the opening credits and the minuscule size of the closing credits on the television screen was another indication that the film had been made with a larger screen in mind.

Abandoning the multiple viewpoint of the novel and making Sarah the central character was only the first of several changes Kennedy Martin made to the novel, which contained a great deal of description and interior reflection: 'Again, in Gillian's book, there is a whole lot of interior thought and description. This is not possible in the screenplay. The story has to be externalized and a new locus found which brings into foreground the relationship of Sarah and Alex. To keep this, a new character has also been created, the Truth Commission itself.'[18]

Kennedy Martin wanted there to be more about the members of the Truth and Reconciliation Committee than appeared in the final cut of the film and he was disappointed that some of the scenes that took place at the hotel, where Sarah and the members of the committee were staying, were omitted from the final cut. Kennedy Martin felt these scenes gave character to the committee and introduced an element of humour:

> The humour I definitely wanted in and in fact what happened, there was a centre section and it's interesting that when they excised it they excised out I think the element which would've given it a cinematic release, because the hotel in which she stays and the hotel manager and their relationship with the two ex-policemen, who were all Boers, and also the background of the people who were adjudicating the hearing, that all took place in and around the hotel. So there were some scenes there which were kind of funny and for some reason or other, although they'd built the hotel and they'd shot the scenes, they decided to cut the whole thing out … the humour was in there.[19]

The Truth and Reconciliation hearing is central to the film and it is here that both Alex and Sarah question Hendricks about his version of the interrogation and torture of Alex and Steve Sizela in 1986. While Kennedy Martin wanted Sarah Barcant to be the central character, the story of Alex Mpondo's torture, and Steve Sizela's death, is clearly at the heart of the film and Kennedy Martin introduced flashbacks, from Mpondo's POV, in order to reveal what happened during his interrogation and, eventually, what happened to Steve Sizela:

> The flashbacks had to be such that would help you with the story … but on the other hand they aren't to be so obvious that the audience can guess in ten minutes or a half an hour … So I got three things that he had flashbacks about that couldn't be worked out. One was he felt when he was interrogated that there was a fire going on, and then there were other things, there was a hard floor, you know a mud floor, not lino or something, that was in the book, and the third thing was the drip of the water in the tap, and I'm not sure whether that was in the book or not, but certainly the use of the drip and the use of the fire gave you these instant flashback indicators that you could pick up in a micro-second, very quickly.[20]

Early on in the film, when Sarah is preparing to represent Alex, an anomaly in Alex's statement is revealed when he refers to the earth floor of the cell and to a bush fire burning outside the building in which he was interrogated. Both of these are inconsistent with Hendricks' version of the story, that Alex was interrogated in the police station in the small South African town of Smitsrivier. The breakthrough in the hearing comes when Sarah gets Hendricks to admit that Alex and Steve were taken elsewhere, to a farm outside the town, where they could be interrogated, and tortured, without anyone finding out. Kennedy Martin wanted to use these 'flashback indicators' as enigmas through which the truth would gradually be revealed. In addition to the floor and the fire he wanted there to be a third indicator, a dripping tap, which would be the first thing Alex hears when he and Sarah enter the farm building later that evening, after Hendricks has admitted to its existence. The dripping tap was to be an aural indicator, confirming for Alex that this is the place where he was tortured, and where Steve Sizela was killed:

> The drip I didn't get through. In the end the director stopped the drip and he [Alex] comes in, you're wondering about this drip which this guy's hearing ... what Hilary Swank does in the film is that she gets the bad guy to admit that these things were happening, that there was a place to get water, there was a fire outside and then that brings the exposition that he was being tortured not where he thought he was being tortured but somewhere else. So the whole plot rests on these flashbacks and the drip I thought was important. ... It's at night that he visits the original place that he'd been tortured and it's dark and he's got a torch and eventually he finds that there's a tap there, but there's no aural reference, and the aural references always precede visual references in film, you always start any movie or a scene with 'fade-up sound, fade-up vision', so you need that sound in there and he [the director, Tom Hooper] decided, in a kind of hyper-critical way, which I think just to a certain extent reflected on the analysis of the script all the way through, 'Well we can do without the drip', but if, coming to that dark place, he'd just heard the drip then the audience would have been aware before he found the tap ... I went to see the Hilary Swank film, *Million Dollar Baby*, which Clint Eastwood had directed, and I just thought, coming out of that, Clint Eastwood would have kept the drip in! He wouldn't have hesitated for one second, and that to me is the difference between real storytelling ... where you go for that obvious thing, the drip, the fire ... [21]

Troy Kennedy Martin's explanation of the need for 'the drip' may seem incidental but it illustrates, once again, how a writer is often at the mercy of directorial decisions. In this case Kennedy Martin believed the dripping tap was dramatically important and he felt BBC Films should have supported him in this instance because the script had already been through several drafts before the director, Tom Hooper (whose first feature film this was), got involved:

> The thing about BBC Films is that they go through an enormous amount of drafts. I didn't believe when Ruth Caleb said 'Well we're comfortable when we get to the tenth draft' and I do think it's counter-productive ... there were three or four people who were involved, including David Thompson and a couple of script editors/producers on it and other people and they just toss things around. I enjoyed it because it was fun, but in the end when the director, who was quite new, came on board, he had his own take on it and I expected them to really pull him and say 'Look we've been through this and we've been through that and this is what's been decided', but no they just let him carry on so the whole three or four months of doing the rewrites were completely wasted. [22]

In the end Kennedy Martin felt that Hooper did a reasonably good job on the film, despite his reservations about some of the director's decisions. What the production of *Red Dust* illustrates, however, is how even a very experienced writer like Troy Kennedy Martin has to fight battles with producers, script editors and the director over his screenplay. As he admits, this can be a productive process, and in addition to the many drafts that the script went through Kennedy Martin has pages and pages of notes on all stages of the process, from the background to the story, changes that needed to be made to the novel, notes on the characters and on individual scenes, notes on the script editors' notes and notes on the different edits of the film, illustrating the degree of preparation, discussion and debate that took place.[23]

Clearly, the days when the scripts of a writer such as David Mercer or Dennis Potter might have been treated with reverence are long gone in British television. The creation of television drama has always been a collaborative process, but the institutional procedures operating in the twenty-first century mean the writer's work is 'policed' now perhaps more than ever before. This goes some way towards explaining why it can take years for a project to reach the screen and why highly original, innovative or radical scripts rarely reach the screen in the form the writer originally intended, if they get made at all.

Twenty years after *Edge of Darkness*, and nearly fifty years after making his television debut, Troy Kennedy Martin is still working, trying to get projects off the ground without having to compromise unduly in the engagement with contemporary social and political issues. Most of his recent commissions have been adaptations, something he has always done, right from his early days at the BBC in the late 1950s, but now the process of getting work produced takes far longer, if it happens at all.[24]

The writer in film and television drama today no longer has the autonomy once enjoyed by writers in the 1960s, when television drama was writer-led. Even producers do not have the authority they once had in British television. In the competitive, ratings-conscious environment of the new broadcasting age it is television executives who call the shots and the writer has become a functionary who is expected to supply product to enable an increasing number of television channels to compete for a diminishing share of the audience. Reluctant to compromise, or to retire, Troy Kennedy Martin continues to write, adding to the pile of unproduced scripts he has accumulated in recent years in the hope he may yet get one more through the barricades and bureaucracy of British television production in the twenty-first century.

Notes

1 Troy Kennedy Martin, interviewed by the author, 25 September 1998.
2 See the section on *The Italian Job* and the 'problem' of endings in Chapter two, where Kennedy Martin argues that *The Warming* 'did not come to a satisfactory conclusion because the end game wasn't apparent until 2005'. At the time of writing (April 2006) Kennedy Martin is working on a project based on a new book by James Lovelock, *The Revenge of Gaia: Why the Earth Is Fighting Back – and How We Can Still Save Humanity* (Allen Lane, 2006), in which Lovelock argues that nuclear energy is the only way to counter climate change. This new project may enable Kennedy Martin to resurrect The Warming and complete a project he began in the late 1980s.
3 Troy Kennedy Martin, conversation with the author, 18 March 2004.
4 Troy Kennedy Martin, interviewed by the author, 25 September 1998.
5 Ibid.
6 Michael Wearing, interviewed by the author, 2 June 2005.
7 Troy Kennedy Martin, interviewed by the author, 3 August 2005.
8 Troy Kennedy Martin, telephone conversation with the author, 6 September 2005.
9 Troy Kennedy Martin, interviewed by the author, 3 August 2005.
10 Troy Kennedy Martin, interviewed by the author, 25 September 1998.
11 Ibid.
12 Tony Garnett, interviewed by the author, 18 March 2004.
13 Note in *Screen International*, 19 March 1993, p. 8.
14 I am grateful to Troy Kennedy Martin for providing me with a copy of his script for *Ferrari*.
15 Troy Kennedy Martin, interviewed by the author, 3 August 2005.
16 Troy Kennedy Martin, interviewed by the author, 25 September 1998.
17 Troy Kennedy Martin, notes on *Red Dust*, 13 February 2003. I am grateful to Troy Kennedy Martin for providing me with his notes and a draft of the script for *Red Dust*.
18 Ibid.
19 Troy Kennedy Martin, interviewed by the author, 3 August 2005.
20 Ibid.
21 Ibid.
22 Ibid.
23 *Red Dust* was nominated for a BAFTA award in the category of single drama in 2006.
24 Kennedy Martin spent all of 2005 working on an adaptation of a novel by James Fergusson, *Kandahar Cockney: A Tale of Two Worlds* (Harper Collins, 2004), about the friendship between a western journalist and an interpreter he meets in Afghanistan, who is forced to flee and seek asylum in Britain. Kennedy Martin wanted to write it as a two-part drama but the BBC wanted a scaled-down single drama, without the Afghanistan scenes. After more than a year's work *Kandahar Cockney* did not get beyond script stage. In addition to a project on climate change (see note 2), Kennedy Martin is currently (April 2006) also developing a 'House of Lords crime drama', provisionally entitled *Black Rod*, for ITV.

Appendix: list of television programmes, feature films, unproduced scripts and screenplays, awards and publications

Television (Dates given are original transmission dates)

Incident at Echo Six (BBC, 9 December 1958)

The Traitor (BBC, 7 August 1959), adapted from a story by Somerset Maugham.

The Price of Freedom (BBC, 3 April 1960), adapted from a play by John Heron and Maureen Quiney.

Element of Doubt (BBC, 17 April 1961), adapted from a story by Bernard Newman.

Storyboard (BBC, 1961)
The Gentleman from Paris (28 July 1961), adapted (with Michael Imison) from a story by John Dickson Carr.
The Magic Barrel (4 August 1961), adapted from a story by Bernard Malamud.
The Middle Men (11 August 1961), an original script by Troy Kennedy Martin.
The Long Spoon (18 August 1961), adapted from a story by John Wyndham.
I'll Be Waiting (25 August 1961), adapted (with Michael Imison) from a story by Raymond Chandler.
Tickets to Trieste (1 September 1961), adapted from a story by Ken Wlaschen.

The Interrogator (BBC, 22 December 1961)

Z Cars (BBC, 1962)
Ep.1: Four of a Kind (2 January 1962)
Ep.2: Limping Rabbit (9 January 1962)
Ep.6: Friday Night (6 February 1962)
Ep.8: Family Feud (20 February 1962)

Ep.11: Jail Break (13 March 1962)
Ep.13: Sudden Death (27 March 1962)
Ep.16: Invisible Enemy (17 April 1962)
Ep.27: Teamwork (3 July 1962)

Diary of a Young Man (BBC 1, 1964), co-written with John McGrath.
Ep.1: Survival (8 August 1964)
Ep.2: Money (15 August 1964)
Ep.3: Marriage (22 August 1964)
Ep.4: Power (29 August 1964)
Ep.5: Life, Or a Girl Called Fred (5 September 1964)
Ep.6: Relationships (12 September 1964)

Redcap (ABC, 1964–5)
Series 1, Ep.5: Corporal McCann's Private War (14 November 1964)
Series 1, Ep.7: Night Watch (28 November 1964)
Series 1, Ep.13: The Patrol (16 January 1965)

The Chase (BBC 2, 19 December 1964), co-written with Michael Elster for the series *Six*, produced by John McGrath.

The Man Without Papers (BBC 1, 9 June 1965), an original script for *The Wednesday Play*.

The Pistol (BBC 1, 16 June 1965), adapted (with Roger Smith) from the novel by James Jones for *The Wednesday Play*.

The Successor (Anglia, 13 September 1965), adapted from a play by Reinhard Raffalt and Steven Vas and networked as a *Play of the Week*.

The Midas Plague (BBC 2, 20 December 1965), adapted from a story by Frederick Pohl for the series *Out of the Unknown*.

Redcap (ABC, 1966)
Series 2, Ep.1: Crime Passionel (2 April 1966)
Series 2, Ep.3: The Killer (16 April 1966)
Series 2, Ep.4: Buckingham Palace (23 April 1966)

The New Men (Anglia, 8 November 1966), adapted from the novel by C. P. Snow and networked as a *Play of the Week*.

If It Moves, File It (LWT, 1970)
Ep.1: Walled In (28 August 1970)
Ep.2: Surveillance (4 September 1970)
Ep.3: Man Eating Plant (11 September 1970)
Ep.4: Lost and Found (18 September 1970)
Ep.5: Grandmothers (25 September 1970)
Ep.6: Current Affairs (2 October 1970)

Colditz (BBC 1, 1972–4)
Series 2, Ep.4: The Guests (28 January 1974)

The Appointment (BBC 1, 3 May 1974), from the series *Fall of Eagles*.

The Sweeney (Thames, 1975–8)
Series 1, Ep.2: Jackpot (9 January 1975), written under the pseudonym of
   Tony Marsh (see below for other scripts by 'Tony Marsh').
Series 1, Ep.3: Thin Ice (16 January 1975)
Series 1, Ep.6: Night Out (6 February 1975)
Series 3, Ep.1: Selected Target (6 September 1976)
Series 3, Ep.3: Visiting Fireman (20 September 1976)
Series 4, Ep.2: Hard Men (14 September 1978)

Z Cars: Pressure (BBC 1, 20 September 1978), final episode.

Fear of God (Thames, 1980), adapted from a novel by Derry Quinn and
   shown in the *Armchair Thriller* series.
Ep.1: A Question of Gravity (26 February 1980)
Ep.2: The Noise (28 February 1980)
Ep.3: The Music Room (4 March 1980)
Ep.4: Bang! (6 March 1980)

Reilly – Ace of Spies (Thames, 1983)
Ep.1: An Affair with a Married Woman (5 September 1983)
Ep.2: Prelude to War (7 September 1983)
Ep.3: The Visiting Fireman (14 September 1983)
Ep.4: Anna (21 September 1983)
Ep.5: Dreadnoughts and Crosses (28 September 1983)
Ep.6: Dreadnoughts and Double Crosses (5 October 1983)
Ep.7: Gambit (12 October 1983)
Ep.8: Endgame (19 October 1983)
Ep.9: After Moscow (26 October 1983)
Ep.10: The Trust (2 November 1983)
Ep.11: The Last Journey (9 November 1983)
Ep.12: Shut Down (16 November 1983)

The Old Men at the Zoo (BBC 2, 1983), adapted from the novel by Angus
   Wilson.
Ep.1: A Tall Story (15 September 1983)
Ep.2: Godmanchester's Plan (22 September 1983)
Ep.3: Exodus (29 September 1983)
Ep.4: Armageddon (6 October 1983)
Ep.5: The Year of the Yeti (13 October 1983)

Edge of Darkness (BBC 2, 1985)
Ep.1: Compassionate Leave (4 November 1985)
Ep.2: Into the Shadows (11 November 1985)
Ep.3: Burden Of Proof (18 November 1985)
Ep.4: Breakthrough (25 November 1985)
Ep.5: Northmoor (2 December 1985)
Ep.6: Fusion (9 December 1985)

Hostile Waters (BBC 1, 26 July 1997), shown in the BBC *Screen One* series.

Bravo Two Zero (BBC 1, 3–4 January 1999), screenplay by Andy McNab and Troy Kennedy Martin, based on the book by Andy McNab.

Red Dust (BBC 2, 9 July 2005), adapted from the novel by Gillian Slovo.

Feature films

The Italian Job (UK, 1969)
Kelly's Heroes (USA/Yugoslavia, 1970)
The Jerusalem File (USA/Israel, 1971)
Sweeney 2 (UK, 1978)
Red Heat (USA, 1988), screenplay by Harry Kleiner, Walter Hill and Troy Kennedy Martin.

Television drama written by Troy Kennedy Martin under the pseudonym of Tony Marsh

Weavers Green (Anglia, April–September 1966)
Ep.33 (28 July 1966)
Ep.34 (31 July 1966)
Ep.35 (4 August 1966)
Ep.36 (7 August 1966)
Ep.39 (18 August 1966)
Ep.40 (21 August 1966)
Ep.41 (25 August 1966)
Ep.42 (28 August 1966)
Ep.48 (18 September 1966)
Ep.49 (22 September 1966)
Ep.50 (25 September 1966)

Parkin's Patch (Yorkshire, September 1969–March 1970)
Ep.7: The Deserter (31 October 1969)

Ep.10: The Birmingham Con (22 November 1969)
Ep.15: Manchester Passenger (3 January 1970)
Ep.18: Vickory (24 January 1970)
Ep.26: Two Gentlemen Standing (20 March 1970)

The Sweeney (Thames, 1975–8)
Series 1, Ep.2: Jackpot (9 January 1975)

Goose With Pepper (Anglia, 12 August 1975), dramatised (with David
Ambrose) from a radio play by Frederick Bradnum.

Contributions to television programmes

Crime Writers: Police Story (BBC 1, 3 December 1978)
Barlow, Regan, Pyall and Fancy (BBC 2, 31 May 1993)
Without Walls: Z Cars (Channel 4, 2 April 1996)
The Making of The Italian Job (Channel 4, 27 December 1998)
The John Thaw Story (ITV 1, 5 September 2002)
Political Thrillers: Plays of State (BBC 4, 22 June 2003) – on *Edge of Dark-
ness*
Happy Birthday BBC 2 (BBC 2, 20 April 2004) – on *Edge of Darkness*
TV Dramas That Changed The World (Five, 21 November 2005) – on *Edge
of Darkness*

Contributions to DVDs

The Sweeney: Thin Ice (FremantleMedia, 2003) – commentary (with Ted
Childs and Tom Clegg)
The Sweeney: Night Out (FremantleMedia, 2003) – commentary (with
Ted Childs)
Magnox: The Secrets of the Edge of Darkness (BBC Worldwide, 2003)

BBC television training – untransmitted production exercises

Mac (27 September 1960)
Catch 22 – An Extract (28 December 1965)

Unproduced work for television

Inner Circle – Farringdon Street (1959–60), episode for untransmitted
BBC series.

The Little Goat (1959–61), adapted from a play by Gabriel Hahn (Eric Maschwitz).

The Triangle (1960–1), an original script by Troy Kennedy Martin.

Memento Mori (1962), adapted by Troy Kennedy Martin and Roger Smith from the novel by Muriel Spark.

Macheath – Masterspy (1963–4)
Ep.1: The Smithfield Market Mystery
Ep.2: Macheath and the Law
Ep.3: The Man of the Moment
Ep.4: The Great Train Robbery
Ep.5: Macheath and His Memoirs
Ep.6: Macheath In Charge

Great Scott, It's Matilda! (1965–6), written for BBC's *Thirty-Minute Theatre*.

The Inquisitors – The Binney Effect (1968), episode 6 of untransmitted LWT series.

If It Moves, File It (1970), two unproduced scripts written for LWT series: 'Dubcek' and 'The Workmen'.

The Warming (late 1980s), unfinished four-part serial for Australian Television.

The Other Side (early 1990s), unfinished six-part serial for the BBC.

Pizza (late 1990s), unfinished six-part series for Channel Four.

The Angel Tapes (late 1990s), two-part serial, adapted from a novel by David M. Kiely.

The Cruise of the Breadwinner (2001), adaptation of H. E. Bates short story for Carlton Television.

Kandahar Cockney (2005–6), adaptation of the novel by James Fergusson for the BBC.

Unproduced screenplays

One More Time (early 1970s)
Johnstone in Exile (early 1970s)
Crazy Joe (early 1970s)
Open Cut (mid–late 1980s)
Troppo (late 1980s)
Broken Light (late 1980s–early 1990s)
Blinder (late 1980s–early 1990s)

Ferrari (early–mid 1990s)
Watson's Chalk (late 1990s)
The Truth Game (2003–4)

Awards

British Academy of Television Arts Scriptwriter's Award for ***The Interrogator***, 1962.
Writer's Guild of Great Britain Screenwriter's Award for ***Z Cars***, 1962.

Novels

Beat on a Damask Drum, London: Panther, 1959.
Z Cars, London: Trust Books, 1962.

Published scripts

Edge of Darkness, London: Faber & Faber, 1990.

Articles by Troy Kennedy Martin

'Nats Go Home: First Statement of a New Drama for Television', *Encore* 48, March–April 1964.
'*Up the Junction* and After', *Contrast*, Vol. 4, No. 5/6, Winter/Spring, 1965/66.
'Four of a Kind?', in H. R. F. Keating (ed.), *Crimewriters*, London: BBC, 1978.
'From *War Game* to *Law and Order*', *Vision*, Vol. 4, No. 1, April 1979.
'Sharpening the edge of TV drama', *The Listener*, 28 August 1986.
'The James MacTaggart Memorial Lecture 1986: "Opening up the Fourth Front": Micro Drama and the Rejection of Naturalism', in Bob Franklin, *Television Policy: The MacTaggart Lectures*, Edinburgh: Edinburgh University Press, 2005.
'Working with John', in David Bradby and Susanna Capon (eds.), *Freedom's Pioneer: John McGrath's Work in Theatre, Film and Television*, Exeter: University of Exeter Press, 2005.

Articles about Troy Kennedy Martin and his work

Bull, J. (2000), 'Mapping the Terrain: Troy Kennedy Martin's *Edge of Darkness*', in Jonathan Bignell, Stephen Lacey and Madeleine Macmurraugh-Kavanagh (eds.), *British Television Drama: Past, Present and Future*, Basingstoke: Palgrave.

Cooke, L. (1989), 'Interview with Troy Kennedy Martin', *Movie*, 33, Winter.

Cooke, L. (1989), '*Edge of Darkness*', *Movie*, 33, Winter.

Cooke, L. (2001), 'Troy Kennedy Martin: Forty Years of Writing for the Screen', *Television and New Media*, 2:2, May.

Lavender, A. (1993), '*Edge of Darkness* (Troy Kennedy Martin)', in George Brandt (ed.), *British Television Drama in the 1980s*, Cambridge: Cambridge University Press.

References

Alvarado, M. and Stewart, J. (1985), *Made For Television: Euston Films Limited*, London: British Film Institute.

Anon (1964), 'Vicar Raps the BBC's "Filthy Young Man"', *Daily Herald*, 8 September.

Anon (1965a), 'Anarchic Fugitive on the Run', *Daily Telegraph*, 10 June.

Anon (1965b), 'A Ruthless Outlaw', *The Times*, 10 June.

Anon (1965c), 'The Man Without Papers', *Radio Times*, 3 June.

Anon (1966), 'Introducing Weavers Green', *TV World*, 31 March.

Anon (2005). 'The 50 Most Influential People in TV History', *Broadcast*, 26 August.

Ayres, R. (1958), 'Incident at Echo Six', *Radio Times*, 5 December.

Banks-Smith, N. (1976), 'The Sweeney', *The Guardian*, 7 September.

Barnes, C. (1965), 'Gun Turns Private into Man of Power', *Daily Express*, 17 June.

Bell, J. (1964), 'This Redcap is a Hero!', *TV World*, 17–23 October.

Billington, M. (1984), 'A Spy Story Even James Bond Might Envy', *New York Times*, 15 January.

Brunsdon, C. (1990), 'Problems with Quality', *Screen*, 31:1, Spring.

Caughie, J. (2000), *Television Drama: Realism, Modernism and British Culture*, Oxford: Oxford University Press.

Chibnall, S. (2005), '*The Italian Job*' in McFarlane, B. (ed.), *The Cinema of Britain and Ireland*, London: Wallflower.

Clarke, S. (1997), 'Red Alert', *Radio Times*, 26 July–1 August.

Cook, J. R. (1995), *Dennis Potter: A Life on Screen*, Manchester: Manchester University Press.

Cooke, L. (2003), *British Television Drama: A History*, London: British Film Institute.

Cornell, P., Day, M. and Topping, K. (1996), *The Guinness Book of Classic British TV*, 2nd edition, London: Guinness.

Corner, J. (ed.) (1991), *Popular Television in Britain: Studies in Cultural History*, London: British Film Institute.

Craig, S. (1983), 'Fallout at the Zoo', *The Listener*, 8 September.

Creeber, G. (1998), *Dennis Potter: Between Two Worlds*, Basingstoke: Macmillan.

Davidson, J. (1983), Untitled Review, *Glasgow Herald*, 8 October.

Day-Lewis, S. (1970), 'A Miracle in New Comedy Series', *Daily Telegraph*, 29 August.

Day-Lewis, S. (1998), *Talk of Drama: Views of the Dramatist Now and Then*, Luton: University of Luton Press.

Dunkley, C. (1975), Untitled Review, *The Financial Times*, 12 February.

Eastaugh, K. (1965), 'A Battle of Wits in a "Game" of War', *Daily Mirror*, 17 June.

Eeden, J. van (2005), 'The Mysterious Process of Writing: An Interview with Gillian Slovo', *Scriptwriter* 23, July.

Fairclough, R. and Kenwood, M. (2002), *Sweeney: The Official Companion*, London: Reynolds and Hearn.

Field, M. (2001), *The Making of The Italian Job*, London: Batsford.

Fuller, G. (ed.) (1998), *Loach on Loach*, London: Faber and Faber.

Gardner, C. and Wyver, J. (1980), 'The Single Play: From Reithian Reverence to Cost-accounting and Censorship', *Edinburgh International Television Festival – Official programme*.

Garnett, T. (1964), 'Reaction: Replies to Troy Kennedy Martin's attack on Naturalistic Television Drama', *Encore*, 49, May–June, 39–48.

Gilbert, W. S. (1983), 'Interview with Philip Donnellan' in M. Thomas (ed.), *Stories and Songs: the Films of Philip Donnellan*, London: British Film Institute.

Green, J. (1965), 'TV Tonight', *Evening News*, 16 June.

Henry, G. (1985), 'Political Thrills from the BBC', *Televisual*, November.

Holmwood, L. (2003), 'C4 Orders Film Version of Dr Kelly scandal', *Broadcast*, 22 August.

Hudson, C. (1972), Untitled Review, *Spectator*, 27 May.

Jackson, M. (1970), 'Bird is Back on Comedy Perch', *Daily Express*, 29 August.

Jones, E. (1961), 'Storyboard', *Radio Times*, 20 July.

Keating, H. R. F. (ed.) (1978), *Crimewriters*, London: BBC.

Kennedy Martin, T. (1959), *Beat On A Damask Drum*, London: Panther.

Kennedy Martin, T. (1960), 'A Play For World Refugee Year – *The Price of Freedom*', *Radio Times*, 2 April.

Kennedy Martin, T. (1961), 'Red Chick in Trieste', *Radio Times*, 24 August.

Kennedy Martin, T. (1964), 'Nats Go Home: First Statement of a New Drama for Television', *Encore*, 48, March–April, 21–33.

Kennedy Martin, T. (1965/66), '*Up the Junction* and After', *Contrast*, Vol. 4, No. 5/6, Winter/Spring, 137–41.

Kennedy Martin, T. (1978), 'Four of a Kind?' in H. R. F. Keating (ed.), *Crimewriters*, London: BBC, 122–33.

Kennedy Martin, T. (1979), 'From *War Game* to *Law and Order*', *Vision*, Vol. 4, No. 1, April, 5–7.

Kennedy Martin, T. (1986), 'Sharpening the Edge of TV Drama', the *Listener*, 28 August, 9–12.

Kennedy Martin, T. (1990), *Edge of Darkness*, London: Faber and Faber.

Knight, P. (1966), 'Novelty of a Redcap as Detective', *Daily Telegraph*, 2 April.

Laing, S. (1986), *Representations of Working-Class Life 1957–1964*, London: Macmillan.

Laing, S. (1991), 'Banging in Some Reality: The Original "Z Cars"', in J. Corner (ed.), *Popular Television in Britain*, London: British Film Institute.

Lane, S. (1985), 'A Depressing Nuclear Chiller', *Morning Star*, 4 November.

Last, R. (1983), 'Old Men in the Zoo', *Daily Telegraph*, 14 October.

Lewis, P. (1962), 'Z Cars', *Contrast*, Vol. 1, No. 4, Summer.

Lovelock, J. (1979), *Gaia: A New Look at Life on Earth*, Oxford: Oxford University Press.

Lovelock, J. (2006), *The Revenge of Gaia: Why the Earth Is Fighting Back – and How We Can Still Save Humanity*, London: Allen Lane.

Mackie, P. (1964), 'Reaction: Replies to Troy Kennedy Martin's Attack on Naturalistic Television Drama', *Encore*, 49, May–June, 41–4.

McFarlane, B. (ed.) (2005), *The Cinema of Britain and Ireland*, London: Wallflower.

McGrath, J. (1977), 'TV Drama: The Case Against Naturalism', *Sight & Sound*, Spring, 100–5.

McGrath, J. (2002), *Naked Thoughts That Roam About: Reflections on Theatre 1958–2001*, London: Nick Hern Books.

Mitchell, A. (1965a), Untitled Review, *The Sun*, 21 May.

Mitchell, A. (1965b), '75 Minute Rampage – Oh What a Character!', *The Sun*, 10 June.

Murray, J. (1976), 'These Cops are Tops', *Daily Express*, 7 September.

Paget, D. (1998), *No Other Way to Tell it: Dramadoc/docudrama on Television*, Manchester: Manchester University Press.

Patterson, W. (1985), 'A Dramatic Change in Attitudes', *The Guardian*, 13 December.

Potter, D. (1964), 'Reaction: Replies to Troy Kennedy Martin's Attack on Naturalistic Television Drama', *Encore*, 49, May–June, 39–48.

Prior, A. (1964), 'If only they'd film it!', *Screenwriter*, No. 15, Spring, 25–6.

Robinson, D. (1965), 'Nursing the Avant-Garde', *Contrast*, Vol. 4, No. 2, Spring.

Schuman, H. (1996), 'The Last Picture Show', *The Guardian*, 6 December.

Sexton, J. (2003), '"Televerite" Hits Britain: Documentary, Drama and the Growth of 16mm Filmmaking in British Television', *Screen* 44:4, Winter, 429–44.

Smith, R. (1965), 'The Pistol', *Radio Times*, 10 June.

Snow, S. (1966), 'Playbill', *TV Times*, 5–11 November.

Stephens, R. (1966), *Cyprus: A Place of Arms*, London: Pall Mall Press.

Stoddart, P. (1983), 'Of Megabuck Pop Promos Nostalgia and History', *Broadcast*, 16 September.

Summers, S. (1985), 'Ending the Siege of Troy', *Sunday Times*, 3 November.

Thomas, M. (ed.) (1983), *Stories and Songs: the Films of Philip Donnellan*, London: British Film Institute.

Usher, S. (1965), 'Surprising, this *was* Brilliant', *Daily Sketch*, 17 June.

Wheen, F. (1982), *The Sixties*, London: Century.

Wiggin, M. (1965), 'Z Cars with Bells On', *Sunday Times*, 13 June.

Index

EU authorised representative for GPSR:
Easy Access System Europe, Mustamäe tee 50,
10621 Tallinn, Estonia
gpsr.requests@easproject.com